CLASSICAL RHETORICAL THEORY

CLASSICAL RHETORICAL THEORY

JOHN POULAKOS

University of Pittsburgh

TAKIS POULAKOS

University of Iowa

HOUGHTON MIFFLIN COMPANY   Boston   New York

Senior Sponsoring Editor: George Hoffman
Assistant Editor: Jennifer Wall
Senior Project Editor: Fred Burns
Senior Production/Design Coordinator: Sarah Ambrose
Senior Manufacturing Coordinator: Marie Barnes
Marketing Associate: Jean Zielinski DeMayo

Cover design: Dynamo Design
Cover Images: *School of Athens,* Raphael. Vatican Museums & Galleries, Rome. Fratelli Alinari©Superstock.

CONTENTS

ROMAN RHETORICAL THEORY

PREFACE

The textual materials of ancient rhetoric have recently been made more widely available to modern scholars by the expansion and proliferation of on-line archives. Readers interested in accessing the primary works of authors discussed in this book may find it expedient, convenient, and economical to make use of these developing resources.

To access English translations of most works by Plato, visit the Virginia Tech Philosophy Texts page at gopher://gopher.vt.edu: 10010/11/131. This site also carries an extensive collection of Aristotle's writings at gopher://gopher.vt.edu:10010/11/39. The Perseus Project at Tufts University provides access to many of Isocrates' works and offers the additional benefit of providing the reader with Greek and English versions of documents, as well as versions suitable for downloading. Connect at http://www.perseus.tufts.edu/Texts/ chunk_TOC.grk.html#Isocrates. Many other works by Greek playwrights, philosophers, and historians are available at this site by substituting the author's name for "Isocrates" in the aforementioned address. The speeches of Cicero are accessible at the Massachusetts Institute of Technology archive at http://classics.mit.edu/Browse/ index-Cicero.html.

As this book went to press, the works of several authors discussed here were unavailable on the Internet. Because web pages are updated frequently, this may no longer be the case at the time of publication. To find a comprehensive array of links to archives of Greek and Latin texts, see the Library of Congress website at http://lcweb.loc. gov/global/classics/clastexts.html.

ACKNOWLEDGMENTS

We wish to thank the following reviewers for their helpful suggestions: Stephen H. Browne, Pennsylvania State University; Arthur E. Walzer, University of Minnesota; George Pullman, Georgia State University; David Henry, California Polytechnic State University; Barry Brummett, University of Wisconsin-Milwaukee; Dana Cloud, University of Texas at Austin; Ferald J. Bryan, Northern Illinois University.

INTRODUCTION

Although rhetoric has existed for as long as language, most scholars agree that its self-conscious practice and study began in classical Greece in the fifth century B.C.E. Its emergence coincided with the advent of the democratic *polis* (city-state), which it helped establish and strengthen. Soon thereafter, rhetoric came to be regarded as a force that holds human societies together, shaping their social and political sensibilities and determining their direction and destiny. Further, it came to be held in high esteem as the art of public deliberation and to represent the crowning achievement of the well-educated citizen. These views were largely a function of considerable reflection on rhetorical events, in which many citizens rose to prominence by virtue of their capacity to use language in interesting and ultimately persuasive ways. Be it in the domain of politics, law, or other forms of civic life, individual citizens distinguished themselves from the general population by means of their orations and the influence they had on the public's view of the world. Their words, now a permanent entry in the record of history, still attract our ears and invite our studied reflection.

Since its inception in Greek antiquity, rhetoric has had its ups and downs as a field of study, but it has always been at the heart of humanistic thought. As such, it has always concerned itself with the human capacities to reason, to create, to imagine, to move and be moved by means of language. More specifically, rhetoric has always been at the center of public affairs, shaping people's perceptions, addressing their collective needs, and articulating their aspirations. Similarly, rhetoric has always been a catalyst in issues requiring conscious deliberation and demanding sound decisions, appropriate choices, and wise judgments. Likewise, rhetoric has always been the instrumental force behind persuasive efforts to establish human beliefs and values, and to suggest concrete forms of concerted action. Finally, rhetoric has always lent itself to creative expression, the kind that offers people better versions of the world and of themselves. In short, it is difficult to imagine human civilization as we know it without rhetoric.

During the last three decades, several academic disciplines (i.e., economics, history, political science, philosophy, anthropology, philosophy, literature), once indifferent or hostile to rhetoric, have come to the realization that their scholarly activities are not unrelated to the rhetorical enterprise. In particular, they have acknowledged that much of what they do is addressed to both internal and external audiences whose attention and approval they seek to secure. And while it may be too early to tell the degree to which these disciplines have benefited from this realization, it is quite apparent that rhetoric is undergoing a veritable renaissance and is commanding, once again, considerable attention among contemporary scholars.

One of the more interesting phenomena of the current renaissance of rhetoric has been the reconsideration of its earliest past in classical Greece and Rome. This reconsideration has come about as a result of the need to come to terms with rhetoric's present predicament—that is, its various conceptualizations and uses, its modes and manifestations, as well as its scope and function in contemporary society. This book attempts to satisfy part of this need by outlining the rhetorical theories that emerged from the classical Greek and Roman experiences. In doing so, it offers students of rhetoric a glimpse of the intellectual character of the Golden Age of the history of rhetoric. More importantly, it provides them with a theoretical compass meant to ground and guide their efforts to practice their own rhetoric and understand the rhetoric of others.

This book is based on the following set of interrelated ideas. First, rhetoric's present predicament, in and of itself, makes little or no sense; it is meaningless. Understanding it requires something else, something from which we can distinguish it or with which we can compare it. That "something else" is afforded by rhetoric's past. However, rhetoric's past in itself, no matter how interesting, is ultimately useless. But when considered in the light of its present, rhetoric's past can help us understand why the present is the way it is.

Much of the present is not a mass of random, unrelated phenomena and activities. Rather, it is a set of effects causally connected to, and determined by, previous phenomena and activities, which historical study helps identify and illuminate. Accordingly, today's rhetorical practices and understandings are largely a function of many prior ones, the sum of which constitutes our rhetorical heritage. Understanding that heritage can tell us how we have arrived at the moment in history we now occupy. Conversely, not understanding our heritage condemns us to a certain blindness that denies us access to a rich source of insight and strength about ourselves as beings capable of and subject to rhetorical persuasion.

Although the rhetorical tradition includes a wide range of rhetorical practices from a plurality of cultures and historical periods, most of the principles of rhetoric have remained fairly stable. That today's rhetorical practices may be different from those in ancient Greece or Rome does not change the fact that rhetoric still concerns itself with creating appropriate messages for particular audiences and with specific purposes in mind; nor does it change the fact that, like our distant predecessors, we still attempt to persuade one another linguistically; and, finally, it does not change the fact that we are still trying to explain to ourselves and others why rhetoric sometimes fails and other times succeeds. If, then, the principles of rhetoric have remained stable over time, an awareness of the ways in which they were formulated and used in the past can help us to cultivate our own perspectives for addressing today's issues and applying rhetorical principles to our own modernity. To put it differently, a proper understanding of contemporary rhetorical theory and practice demands, indeed requires, a large measure of familiarity with its classical counterpart.

Yet another reason why classical rhetorical theory is important today is that it provides a conceptual apparatus that most subsequent theories have found both necessary and useful when addressing postclassical rhetorical practice. Such concepts as persuasion, *ethos, pathos,* appropriateness, timeliness, belief, probability, possibility, certainty, truth, deception, ambiguity, deliberation, and action are at the heart of both classical and modern theories. At the same time, classical rhetoric offers us a working vocabulary that specifies boundaries of rhetorical discussion and scholarship. Terms like *rhetoric, logic, dialectic, sophistic, theory, praxis, idea, topic, politics, ethics, aesthetics, psychology, epistemology,* and *anthropology* have been adopted from the Greek language and are used in virtually all discussions of rhetoric. The same applies to such terms as *language, rationality, decorum, style, text, civility, forum, ingenuity, justice, republicanism, compromise, value,* and *fact,* all of which are derived from Latin. Finally, classical rhetorical theory designates lines of inquiry still followed by contemporary scholars and practitioners. The analysis of audiences, the consideration of common cultural values, the translation of complex arguments into understandable lay language, the evocation of human emotions, and the evaluation of the prospects of change in the public's attitude and behavior are all items entertained not only by Greek and Roman rhetoricians, but also by their modern-day equivalents.

In effect, what has made classical rhetorical theory classical is not only its historical specificity, but also the fact that it posed enduring questions, questions we still ask when we reflect on and try to explain the rhetorical practices of our day. What makes voters endorse one candidate over all others? How can I best shape my message when addressing a specific audience? What kind of language is appropriate when promoting one point of view over another? What sorts of appeals would help persuade my audience that a given course of action is better than the one advocated by my opponents? How can I speak/write so as to minimize or avoid inattention, misunderstanding, or dismissal from my listeners/readers? What forms of speaking/writing can I produce that will inspire and delight my audience? These and a host of related questions were as important in Greek and Roman antiquity as they are today.

Over time, rhetorical theories of various kinds have come and gone, but classical theories remain; and because they have passed the test of time, classical theories have achieved the status of standards against which subsequent and more recent theories can be judged. Many centuries after their initial articulation, classical concepts are still useful to contemporary study and practice, still relevant to the current uses of language. Even so, the point is not to study classical rhetoric for its own sake—doing so would commit us to an uncritical acceptance of a tradition without regard to the specific character and demands of our own times. Rather, the point is to put our knowledge and appreciation of classical rhetoric in the service of our own lives. If, then, there is benefit in the study of classical rhetoric, that benefit consists of appropriate adaptations of the rhetorics of the Greeks and the Romans, not their wholesale adoption. In sum, there is little profit in espousing entirely the preserved theories of Graeco-Roman antiquity or in ignoring them totally. In the first instance, we would be neglecting the demands of our present, while in the second we would be missing significant connections to our past. The point, then, of studying classical rhetoric is to ground and enrich our own.

Rhetorical practice in classical Greece was plentiful. Predominately an oral culture, the Greek culture offered common citizens many opportunities to address one another in formal ways. Citizens, for example, were expected to help administer the affairs of their city-state and contribute to its social and political vitality. More specifically, they were expected to serve in the assembly as legislators of law and public policy, in the courts as judges or jurors of legal disputes, and at various state functions (public funerals, festivals, athletic events) as featured speakers. All these political and civic functions required that citizens be able to speak competently before an audience of their peers, to deliberate with fellow citizens on matters of common interest, to weigh the arguments of the different sides of an issue, and to inquire or entertain their listeners. Beyond the rhetorical know-how needed to carry out their civic obligations, the Greeks conducted much of their informal public "talk" by way of discussing, disputing, arguing, and debating in the open spaces of two central locations in every city: the *agora* (marketplace) and the *gymnasterion* (gymnasium). The informal talk in these two locations eventually found its way to the more formal sites of the assembly, the court, and the festival.

The many opportunities available for the practice of rhetoric went hand in hand with the rise of rhetorical education and rhetorical theory. Teachers of rhetoric (Sophists) turned rhetoric into a subject of instruction, thus preparing their students for public life. Logographers (speech writers) made a living by writing speeches for their clients. And various intellectuals (playwrights, historians, and philosophers) employed rhetoric as a form of expression and treated it as an object of theoretical reflection and practical criticism.

The Greek rhetorical scene was re-created in Rome. By the time rhetoric arrived in Rome, it had already achieved a high degree of finish and sophistication. As such, the Romans were less compelled to rediscover the art itself than to find out ways in which it could best fit their realities. Accordingly, they generally followed the theoretical tracks of their Greek predecessors, but at the same time, they adapted the practical aspects of the art of persuasion to the needs of their own culture. Specifically, the formal practice of rhetoric was not expected of the common citizens but was reserved mainly for people of privilege and wealth, those who generally managed the affairs of the state and pleaded legal cases in the courts. Demands for rhetorical know-how were placed not on the ordinary citizen, but on the senator, the public administrator, the general, and the advocate.

Today, our rhetorical heritage from classical Greece and Rome includes many speeches, some of which were actually delivered, and others that were used as examples of rhetorical composition, samples for study and analysis, or models for imitation. The same heritage also includes theoretical as well as critical works about rhetoric. When studied patiently and carefully, all these materials tell us a great deal about the ways in which the Greeks and the Romans practiced rhetoric and theorized about it. More important, they provide us with a point of reference from which we can judge and understand the merits of subsequent theories and practices of rhetoric.

The Significance of Theory

The term *theory* comes from the Greek word *theoria*, which means "seeing," "viewing," "observing," "contemplating." Theory seeks to explain why things are the way they are or why events happen the way they do. It offers a conceptual orientation by means of which people approach, and try to make sense out of, the contents of their experience. Using a wide variety of particular materials, a theory attempts to abstract from them common characteristics and to establish general principles.

Theory is necessary. Insofar as human experience is enormously varied and immensely complex, theory affords us ways in which we can connect, classify, and simplify our experiences and, in so doing, order them and render them both manageable and meaningful. At the same time, theory affords us ways in which we can predict what is likely to happen in the future. While theory recognizes the uniqueness of individual experience, it focuses on those aspects of experience that are common. And while it acknowledges the singularity of any one event, it concentrates on typical events, events that tend to happen again and again. In both cases, theory banks on the repeatability and predictability of experience, phenomena, and events.

Theories are rhetorical. Insofar as they emphasize certain things and deemphasize others, theories are necessarily partial. For example, one economic theory may emphasize the accumulation of monetary wealth, while another may accentuate the distribution of wealth among the people of a single country. Likewise, one political theory may concentrate on the regulative powers of the state within its own borders, while another may pay more attention to one country's relations with other countries. Regardless of which things they highlight or shade, theories attempt to shape our perception and understanding in specific ways. To subscribe to a given theory means to approach and view the world in one way rather than another.

A theory is only as good as its explanatory and predictive powers. As long as we can use a theory to explain and predict our experiences

in the world, and as long as our explanations and predictions are satisfactory to ourselves and others, we continue to employ it. When a theory ceases to be useful, it is abandoned or revised. Alternatively, it is
replaced by another with higher or better powers of explanation and
prediction.

Insofar as a rhetorical theory describes the way people interact with
linguistic messages, it can be said to be descriptive. Insofar as it tells us
how we should approach a set of rhetorical practices, it can be said to
be prescriptive. Most theories contain both descriptive and prescriptive
elements.

Rhetorical theory differs from rhetorical practice. Rhetorical theory concerns itself with general principles, while rhetorical practice
concerns itself with particular cases. When practicing rhetoric, we are
acting through language to influence our audience's thoughts or actions. When theorizing about rhetoric, we are trying to explain why
and to predict how language works so as to influence thought and action. Rhetorical theory is also similar to rhetorical practice. When advancing a theoretical position, we are engaging in the practice of
persuading an audience that our theoretical position merits adoption.
Rhetorical practice and rhetorical theory are reciprocal. Practice is
based on certain theoretical assumptions, which are often unstated or
implicit, while theory is profitably derived from an examination of representative samples of practice.

A given rhetorical theory is always situated within the larger intellectual milieu of a particular culture and period. This means that theory draws materials from the resources of that milieu for both its
construction and its approval. At the same time, a given rhetorical theory seeks to transcend its cultural and temporal specificity and inform
rhetorical practice in other cultures and periods.

The Materials of Rhetoric

Although one can bring a variety of materials to bear on the articulation of rhetorical theory, the speech or the oration constitutes the most
typical unit of classical rhetoric. In Greek and Roman antiquity, the speech
or the rhetorical composition was the finished product of the orator's
art. It was what public audiences listened to, and was the form of language dramatists, historians, and philosophers often used to accomplish
their purposes. As one might expect, speeches also constituted the material that rhetorical theorists examined in their theoretical commen-
taries. Today, the materials of rhetorical theory still center on, but are not

limited to, the speech; rather, they include everything from a public demonstration to a statue, from a set of televisual images to a literary work, from a scientific report to graffiti—in short, everything that comes to our attention and, as such, has some impact on our consciousness. This change is largely due to the modern notion that everything we become aware of "tells" us something, "speaks" to us in some way.

A speech does not exist in a vacuum. Rather, it exists within a larger horizon of linguistic practices and understandings, which it helps support or challenge. At the moment of its initial creation, a given speech is designed to address one or more specific issues and be addressed to a particular audience. Later on, one may read the same speech in order to extract from it historical information and insight, to inquire into its formal characteristics and argumentative structure, or to determine its possible effects then or now. One may also read a speech out of intellectual curiosity, for pleasure, or in order to discern its relevance to one's own predicament.

Generally, a speech does not make the speaker's theoretical views explicit. These views can be discerned by raising a host of questions whose main purpose is to uncover the unstated assumptions and values of the speech and to discover what ideas made its words possible. When read for its theoretical value, a speech is examined in the light of a set of interrelated principles that specify the relationships between speaker, language, and audience. The degree to which one may generalize from a single speech is limited. Generalizations in rhetorical theory are more encompassing and more persuasive if they are derived from a wide range of speeches. The more speeches one considers, the stronger the generalizations one can make.

Some speeches have transhistorical qualities. This is so because they rise above the particularities of their audience, time, occasion, and topic and can address audiences generation after generation. If a speech is heard/read again and again, if it continues to attract attention and elicit discussion among people, and if it continues to provide inspiration, it assumes the status of a masterpiece in the rhetorical tradition. Consider, for example, such speeches as Pericles' *Funeral Oration,* Cicero's *Catilinarian Orations,* Lincoln's *Gettysburg Address,* or Martin Luther King Jr.'s *I Have a Dream.* All of them are qualitatively so superior to others of the same kind that, long after they were first delivered, they still speak to audiences across cultures and epochs.

The materials for this book come from fragments, speeches, rhetorical compositions, dialogues, and treatises as they have been preserved from antiquity. We hope that students will find our discussion of these materials interesting. More important, we hope that they will not be content with what we have to say, but will turn to the study of these materials themselves, as well as to the discovery of materials we have not used.

The Organization of This Book

This book is organized along a set of differences and commonalities. The differences are provided by those practical concerns of rhetoric that depend on the social, political, and cultural scenes of a historical epoch. On the other hand, the commonalities are furnished by those theoretical concerns of rhetoric that depend on certain conceptual creations of human thought. Accordingly, the first three chapters act as reminders that rhetoric assumes a different character when situated in such specific settings as the court, the political forum, or the festival. The next two chapters point to the fact that rhetoric is always subject to the conceptual treatments of such objects as language and knowledge. The last chapter contains within itself the differences that inform the first three chapters and the commonality of language. At the same time, it projects the concerns of the first four chapters onto another historical period. In so doing, it sets in motion the argument that rhetorical theory is a function of differences and commonalities obtained as we move from one culture to another and from one historical period to the next.

The organization of this book makes an additional argument. Rhetorical theory is not simply a function of individual mental activity; rather, it is a unique response to a configuration of political events, social conditions, and cultural practices. But if this is so, rhetorical theory can be better understood as a history of rhetorical practices conceived in a particular way rather than as a sequence of self-contained insights divorced from the sources of their inspiration. That is why we begin each chapter by alluding to rhetoric's location within a milieu of conditions, practices, and institutions. In effect, such an arrangement posits that the study of rhetorical theory yields a richer harvest if it is historically informed.

At the end of the book we raise a set of questions meant to generate discussion and prompt further explorations of the material discussed. We have also provided a list of selected readings meant to direct students to additional sources of information and insight. Finally, we have provided an appendix of speeches, which includes several representative texts from most of the authors we discuss.

GREEK
RHETORICAL
THEORY

᪥

CHAPTER 1

RHETORIC
AND
LAW

&

According to several accounts, rhetoric originated in the fifth century B.C.E. in Syracuse, Sicily, following the overthrow of the Syracusan tyrants. Under a new form of democratic government and a new legal system, many citizens filed claims for property that had been confiscated by the tyrants. Of course, the claimants had to prove to a court rightful ownership of the property in question. But how to prove one's case successfully? On what grounds? Unaccustomed to the demands of rhetorical persuasion in a court setting, the citizens sought help with their cases from Corax and Tisias, two men claiming expertise in legal rhetoric.

Corax and Tisias met the demand for legal assistance and eventually wrote what are considered to be the earliest handbooks on rhetoric. The handbooks do not survive, but the ingenuity of the two rhetoricians does in the following anecdote. Corax taught Tisias rhetoric, but Tisias refused to pay his teacher at the end of the course, claiming that he had learned nothing. Corax sued the student and advanced this argument: "I have taught my student well; therefore, he owes me the amount we agreed upon. If I win this case, he obviously must pay me. But even if I lose it, he still must pay me because my loss would demonstrate that I have taught him how to use rhetoric effectively." Tisias responded with the following counterargument: "Corax has taught me nothing about rhetoric; therefore, I should not have to pay him. If I win this case, I obviously do not have to pay. But even if I lose it, I still would not have to pay because my loss would demonstrate that he has not taught me how to use rhetoric effectively." According to one account, the judges were perplexed. Even though they saw merit in both arguments, they ultimately sided with Corax, telling Tisias that he should have known that from a bad crow comes a bad egg (*corax* in Greek means "crow").

Whether this story is true is not the point. The point lies rather in what the story suggests about rhetoric in general, and about legal rhetoric in particular. To begin with, the story asserts that part of the experience of humans living with one another involves conflicts. A conflict has at least two opposing sides to it and can be resolved either violently, through physical force, or linguistically, by means of words. Ancient Greek intellectuals often point out that one of the most significant signs of human progress was the conquest of *bia* (violence) with *logos* (language). Second, the story suggests that societies set up formal institutions (the courts) in which people with conflicts can go to seek their fair resolution. Although conceptions of justice and law vary from society to society, all societies have laws regulating human behavior. Under a single-man rule (king, tyrant, emperor, dictator), laws are made and applied by the individual in power; but in a democracy they are made and applied by the people themselves. Third, the story intimates that the parties to a legal dispute agree to argue their case within the procedural parameters of the court and to abide by the verdict of the judge(s). Finally, it hints that a legal verdict is largely a function of the way a particular case is argued.

In this chapter, we first examine the ways rhetoric was practiced in the courts of classical Greece, especially Athens. Next, we explore how legal rhetoric was conceptualized by the Sophists, Plato, Isocrates, and Aristotle in the context of Greek society and thought. As we will see, there are considerable differences among the four conceptualizations. Even so, they all explore the relationship between rhetoric and law.

The result of these explorations is a provocative body of thought that goes to the heart of the issue of justice in a democratic society.

The main cause of the early development of legal rhetoric was not the ingenuity of a handful of people like Corax and Tisias; rather, it was the structural changes the Athenian courts underwent during the city's political transformation from an aristocratic to a democratic form of government. Before the first part of the fifth century B.C.E., legal cases were heard by appointed magistrates. The disputing parties appeared before the magistrate, answered his questions, and presented the evidence he requested. Some cases were tried in the Areopagus, a court consisting of a panel of former magistrates. Under this system, the role of the litigants during legal proceedings was insignificant.

All this changed sometime during the second quarter of the fifth century B.C.E., when all jurisdiction was handed over to juries. Each year 6,000 citizens formed a designated pool, from which panels of 201 were chosen by lot and assigned to specific cases, mostly private trials. Typical public trials were heard by 501 jurors. Especially grave cases required even larger juries. Under the new system, the role of the magistrates became a mere formality; they still presided over some trials but had no power over their outcome. A jury's decision was reached by a simple majority, and its verdict was final. The jurors voted through secret ballot without consulting formally among themselves. Before a jury of their peers, litigants had one chance to present their case in the form of a speech and one chance for rebuttal. Both parties were given equal time. Time was kept by a waterclock. Insofar as the law made no provisions for a public prosecutor, any citizen could bring charges against another. And since there were no lawyers, citizens accused of a crime had to represent themselves in court and conduct their own defense. For their service, jurors received some payment.

The new structural changes in the courts created the need for rhetorical training on how to compose and deliver a speech to persuade a jury of one's case. This need was an extension of the need for rhetorical education in the domain of politics. Citizens wishing to participate in the governance of their city went to the assembly, where they could listen to political debates and cast their votes on a proposed piece of legislation. But they did not have to speak. Only those who wanted to play a major role in the affairs of the city had incentive to learn the techniques of political oratory. Law, however, was an altogether different matter. As litigation abounded in Athens, anyone could become entangled in a lawsuit; and legal entanglements required rhetorical adeptness.

This situation gave rise to two professional groups: teachers of rhetoric and logographers (speech writers). Teachers of rhetoric generally taught methods of proof and refutation, argumentative strategies based on rational as well as emotional appeals, lessons in human motivation and psychology, and techniques of effective oral presentation before a jury. They also published rhetorical handbooks mainly devoted to instruction on, and illustration of, the generation and employment of arguments in a wide range of legal cases. The sophist Antiphon, for example, published speeches for the prosecution and the defense in his *Tetralogies,* speeches for hypothetical but typical cases involving various crimes. The rhetorician Gorgias turned to mythology for his materials and wrote one speech defending Helen of Troy and another defending Palamedes. The second professional group, the logographers, offered short-term legal assistance. A person involved in a lawsuit could hire an expert logographer to compose a speech to be delivered by the client in court. To advertise their craft, logographers published their winning speeches. The more famous the trial, the more prestige for the logographer behind the trial; and, of course, the more famous the speech writer, the higher his fees.

The practice of rhetoric in the courts led to the formulation of theoretical principles whose application extended beyond the legal forum to all rhetorical settings. In this section, we discuss three such principles: *dissoi logoi* (twofold arguments), *to prepon* (the appropriate), and *kairos* (the opportune moment).

Dissoi Logoi

The notion of *dissoi logoi* posits that on every issue there are at least two arguments opposing one another. Attributed to the sophist Protagoras, this notion posits that the world of discourse is informed by fundamental differences and divisions in perception, language, and understanding. More specifically, it asserts that universal agreement on any one subject is impossible. This means that people do not all perceive and understand the world in the exact same way. In a perfect world with ideal conditions for communication, every utterance would have a single meaning, every subject would have its unquestionable truth, and all the people would see things as they are. In such a world there would be no conflicts or disagreements and, therefore, no need for debate and deliberation. But in the world as we know it, the status of any one thing, any one view or position, is questionable—hence the need to resolve questions of truth, understanding, and interpretation by declaring one view superior to others.

The principle of *dissoi logoi* becomes most apparent in the legal setting, where the two parties in dispute represent diametrically opposing views of justice, responsibility, and truth. On the stage of the court, the claims of guilt and innocence collide. Each side tries to secure a favorable verdict by bolstering its own case and discrediting that of the other. If the truth of a given case were one, both sides as well as the jury would eventually arrive at it. But each side claims its own truth, and both truths cannot exist simultaneously—ultimately, the one must yield to the other. This state of affairs issued a great challenge to rhetoricians and logographers. The challenge was how to discover and articulate for the jury the more persuasive account, the account that would prevail in the end. Some teachers of rhetoric professed to be able to make the weaker of two opposing accounts the stronger.

To Prepon

Clearly, the notion of *dissoi logoi* involves a choice between two or more competing arguments. But choices are not automatic—they are subject to influence. And one way to influence a choice is by reference to considerations of what is appropriate, fitting, or proper. The principle of *to prepon* governs linguistic choices in the arguments, organization, and style of an oration. In turn, these choices are meant to influence the choice of those charged with the task of adjudicating a legal dispute. What is appropriate to say depends on the occasion, the subject, the speaker's purpose, and the audience. This is another way of saying that what is appropriate in one situation may not be so in another. Even so, linguistic choices within particular contexts tend to become normative over time. Thus the court calls for a certain kind of rhetorical discourse, the assembly for another, and the festival for another still. In other words, orators can find what is appropriate by following earlier rhetorical practices in similar situations.

In the legal setting, the notion of the appropriate assumes a specific form, a form meant to fulfill a set of specific expectations in the audience. The jurors, for example, expect that each party will defend its own case and attack the case of the other. They also expect that both sides will address the jury respectfully, and will try not to offend the judges or show disrespect for the institution of the court. Further, they expect that each side will focus on different facts of the case and advance contrary interpretations of the law. Finally, they expect to hear appeals to common sense, decency, fairness, and goodness. These expectations have been shaped over time by repeated encounters with courtroom orations. This, however, is not to say that all legal discourses are based on a formula; rather, it is to point out that, despite their uniqueness, legal discourses share common features, features dictated by a culturally determined definition of what constitutes appropriateness in a specific context.

Kairos

While the notion of the appropriate offers guidance on what to say, that of *kairos* offers guidance on when to say it. The principle of the opportune moment stipulates that there is a right and a wrong time to say something. As such it reminds orators that the same thing said at different times may have different effects. It also reminds them that a situation, no matter how typical or similar to others, has unique traits that require a unique treatment. Springing from one's sense of timing, *kairos* alludes to the realization that speech takes place in time and that speaking either responds to or creates opportunities. But if this is so, the principle of the opportune moment counsels speakers to approach a rhetorical situation not in terms of preexisting categories but in terms of immediate realizations formulated at the moment of speaking. To do so means to improvise and speak on the spur of the moment.

In legal as well as in other contexts the notion of *kairos* manifests itself in unexpected utterances, the kind that, because they exceed typical expectations, audiences find surprising. These utterances are generally rare, and it is mainly accomplished orators who, trusting on the inspiration of the moment, depart from their script and speak freely and spontaneously. Insofar as today's legal setting in the courts is highly controlled, improvisation and ad-libbing are not encouraged. But in the classical Greek culture, speakers had more freedom to speak on the spur of the moment.

THE SOPHISTS: GORGIAS

The Sophists were a prominent part of the two professional classes that emerged in response to the demand for political and judicial rhetorical know-how. They traveled from city to city teaching young men aspiring to a career in public life how to speak effectively in the assembly or the courts. Some of them also worked as logographers, writing political or legal speeches for their clients. A number of these speeches are preserved to this day. Also preserved are legalistic speeches written for instructional purposes. We have already alluded to some of the extant orations of two of the better known Sophists, Gorgias and Antiphon. Along with other materials, these orations constitute important sources of information about the classical Greek understanding and practice of rhetoric in the legal setting.

In the light of the structural changes in the court system, the Sophists taught a practical rhetoric, a rhetoric measured by success, not by theoretical integrity. Even so, the thinking underlying their teaching methods consists of several theoretical constructs that give us a good sense of their conception of judicial rhetoric. Essentially, the Sophists took the legal system at face value. This means that they accepted unquestionably the conditions and rules of the process of adjudication. Working within the system, they saw their task as providing their students or clients with the best means possible to emerge victorious from a legal affair. Since the adjudication of legal disputes rested with a jury, victory in the court was reserved for those who presented the more compelling arguments, those who persuaded the jurors to see the issue from their point of view rather than from the view of the opposition.

According to the Sophists' perspective, the court was an arena of symbolic competition. Like the competitors of a wrestling match, the contestants in the court fought against one another before their peers, the judges. At the end of the contest, the accused was pronounced either innocent or guilty. A verdict of innocence counted as a loss for the prosecutor but as a victory for the defendant. By contrast, a verdict of guilt counted as a victory for the prosecutor but as a loss for the defendant. In the light of this perspective, the Sophists construed judicial rhetoric as an instrument that could be used either for attack or for defense. In either mode, however, the idea was to anticipate and neutralize the opponent's maneuvers. Thus every charge could be challenged as groundless or as the result of base motives (i.e., vendetta, envy, malice, jealousy), and every explanation could be dismissed as unsatisfactory. The invocation of any principle could be counterbalanced by the weight of particular circumstances; certainty could be tempered by the claims of probability; and the assignment of responsibility for an action could be offset by proofs pointing in the direction of an accident. In short, every argument could be opposed by a counterargument.

Part of the Sophists' thinking on legal rhetoric can be discerned through an examination of their extant speeches. In this section, we take a close look at one such speech, Gorgias' *Encomium of Helen*. Another one of his speeches is his *Defense of Palamedes*. Both works take their material from mythology but situate the traditional myths in a new context, the context of the public court. The first defends Helen against the charge of adultery, and the second defends Palamedes against the charge of treason. According to Greek mythology, Helen was the queen of Sparta and the most beautiful woman in the world. When Prince Paris of Troy was visiting Sparta, she fell in love with him, and the two eloped to Troy. The incident caused an uproar among all the Greeks, who launched a military expedition against the Trojans known as the Trojan War. The purpose of this expedition was to reclaim Helen and return her to Sparta. In the popular imagination and the works of poets, Helen was the target of blame for having committed adultery. The myth of Palamedes says that he collaborated with the enemy for money, and in so doing betrayed the Greeks. For his treasonous act, he was condemned to death.

In both speeches Gorgias employs the apagogic method of proof, a method that considers all the possibilities of a case and shows that each is untenable. In the *Encomium of Helen,* Gorgias identifies four possible causes for Helen's action:

> For either by will of Fate and decision of the gods and vote of necessity did she do what she did, or by force reduced, or by words seduced, or by love possessed. (6)

The first possibility, then, is that the gods had ordained her action. If so, Helen should not be held responsible because human will is always subordinate to divine will. As Gorgias puts it:

> God's predetermination cannot be hindered by human premeditation. For it is the nature of things, not for the strong to be hindered by the weak, but for the weaker to be ruled and drawn by the stronger, and for the stronger to lead and the weaker to follow. God is a stronger force than man in might and in wit and in other ways. If then one must place blame on Fate and on a god, one must free Helen from disgrace. (6)

The second possibility Gorgias considers is that Helen was forcefully subjugated and abducted by Paris. If so, she should not be blamed because women do not have the physical strength to resist men's physical violence. In Gorgias' words:

> If she was raped by violence and illegally assaulted and unjustly insulted, it is clear that the raper, as the insulter, did the wronging, and the raped, as the in-

sulted, did the suffering. It is right then for the barbarian who undertook a barbaric undertaking in word and law and deed to meet with blame in word, exclusion in law, and punishment in deed. And surely it is proper for a woman raped and robbed of her country and deprived of her friends to be pitied rather than pilloried. He did the dread deeds; she suffered them. It is just therefore to pity her but to hate him. (7)

The third possibility is that Helen was seduced by Paris' words. If so, she should not be charged because people cannot resist the persuasive power of language. Gorgias' explanation here is especially interesting because it provides a remarkably contemporary theory of persuasion. According to this theory, persuasion is a function of the vulnerability of human beings to language. As we will see in Chapter 4, Gorgias observes that language is a powerful entity that affects people psychologically and intellectually, leading them to understand or do certain things but not others. Asserting that humans are creatures of passion and reason, Gorgias suggests that their emotional and cognitive makeup is shaped by language. This means that what and how they think is largely the result of the interaction between their biological nature and linguistic learning; it also means that their actions issue directly from their thought. Thought and understanding, however, cannot remain fixed; they are subject to change because people constantly encounter new forms of language. That this is so, Gorgias notes, is evident from the fact that scientific explanations, ordinary opinions, attitudes, beliefs, and values do change. As he puts it:

> To understand that persuasion . . . is wont . . . to impress the soul as it wishes, one must study: first, the words of astronomers who, substituting, opinion for opinion, taking away one but creating another, make what is incredible and unclear seem true to the eyes of opinion; then second, logically necessary debates in which a single speech, written with art but not spoken with truth, bends a great crowd and persuades; and third, the verbal disputes of philosophers in which the swiftness of thought is also shown making the belief in an opinion subject to easy change. (13)

Clearly, Gorgias suggests, experience tells us that people change their minds, they adopt new perspectives, and are prepared to replace older scientific explanations with newer ones. In all three cases, the cause of change is language.

Concluding his discussion of the power of linguistic persuasion on people, Gorgias returns to Helen's case, and suggests that she is not culpable because she was persuaded by Paris' words. Thus if there is culpability, it is Paris who must bear its burden. As Gorgias puts it:

What cause then prevents the conclusion that Helen similarly, against her will, might have come under the influence of speech, just as if ravished by the force of the mighty? For it was possible to see how the force of persuasion prevails; persuasion has the form of necessity, but it does not have the same power. For speech constrained the soul, persuading it which it persuaded, both to believe the things said and to approve the things done. The persuader, like the constrainer, does the wrong and the persuaded, like the constrained, in speech is wrongly charged. (12)

Evidently, Gorgias' point is that Helen's will, however strong, was overpowered by Paris' language. As in the case of his physical force, she could not resist his linguistic advances.

The last possibility Gorgias entertains is that Helen fell in love with Paris. If so, she should not be held in contempt because people do not fall in love deliberately; and when they are struck by love, they lose their minds. Gorgias' explanation here extends his theory of persuasion to include images as persuasive stimuli. People, he observes, are susceptible to images of things. Whether they issue from language or sight, images affect people in various ways, creating in them emotional responses ranging from fright to pleasure to desire to madness. Essentially, images impact people's minds the way words do. But if this is so, certain sights are clearly persuasive and thus can account for people's actions. With this explanation in place, Gorgias reasons:

If, therefore, the eye of Helen, pleased by the figure of Paris, presented to her soul eager desire and contest of love, what wonder? If being a god, love has the divine power of the gods, how could a lesser being reject and refuse it? But if it is a disease of human origin and a fault of the soul, it should not be blamed as a sin, but regarded as an affliction. For she came, as she did come, caught in the net of Fate, not by the plans of the mind, and by constraints of love, not by the devices of art. (19)

Applied to the legal context, Gorgias' theory of persuasion posits that the guilt or innocence of a person charged with a crime is a function of the kinds of language and visual imagery the defendant uses and the ways in which those words and images affect the members of the jury. One set of arguments and images from the defendant or the accuser coupled with a correspondingly favorable set of understandings from the jurors spells innocence or guilt. In either case, however, the point remains the same: guilt and innocence in a legal system of trial by jury are not predetermined truths; rather, they are relative and situational determinations that depend largely on the many variables of the speaker-audience interaction. Naturally, both prosecutor and defendant will try to put forth the best case they can in order to persuade the jury. But ultimately the jury will have to compare the two cases and decide which one is the stronger.

Whether Gorgias' speech was successful in persuading his readers to change their minds and see Helen in a positive light is not the point. However compelling his arguments might have sounded, his audience continued to be exposed to the poets' opposing arguments: Helen was responsible because she did what she did deliberately and of her own free will; she allowed herself to be persuaded; she offered no demonstrable resistance, and so on. Moreover, his speech was not meant to alter people's view of a mythical figure. Rather, it was designed to offer his students an example of a legal defense, a way of arguing in court to fight against a specific set of accusations. It may also be that, along with the *Defense of Palamedes,* the *Encomium of Helen* acted as an advertisement of Gorgias' ingenuity as a legal logographer. The purposes or effects of the speech aside, it is important to note that for Gorgias it is the speaker who must formulate a message of words and images, sounds and sights so as to influence the jury's decision in the desired direction. Such formulation requires extensive experience with language and supporting images, considerable knowledge of the jury's ways of thinking, and a sharp nose for anticipating and deflating the arguments of the opposition.

Regardless of how impressive or practical the Sophists' program for legal rhetoric may have been, it left many issues—most noticeably, the issues of truthfulness and justice—unaddressed. As we noted above, the Sophists took the judicial system at face value. However, both the judicial system and the Sophists' willingness to work within it became objects of severe criticism by subsequent intellectuals. To see what this criticism entailed, we first turn to Plato, the harshest critic of legal rhetoric.

PLATO

In several of his works, Plato is critical of rhetoric in general, and of legal rhetoric in particular. Much of his criticism of rhetoric in general revolves around the distinction between instruction and persuasion. Instruction, he maintains, is preferable to persuasion because it aims at knowledge of the truth, whereas persuasion aims at the adoption of opinions. His particular criticism of legal rhetoric is based on his observations of the shortcomings of the judicial system in classical Athens and on his conception of justice. Essentially, Plato condemns rhetorical practice in the courts because it is interested in winning legal disputes by any means whatsoever, not in seeing justice prevail. For him, however, securing an unjust verdict is an abomination, not a victory. Conviction or acquittal, he maintains, should in all cases be consistent with the dictates of justice. The convicted, in other words, must be truly guilty and the acquitted truly innocent. In any society, the conviction of an innocent person is tragic, while the acquittal of a criminal is abhorrent.

Saddened by the prosecution, condemnation, and death of Socrates, his beloved teacher, Plato observes that legal rhetoric is mostly employed to pervert truth and justice by seeking either to help wrongdoers escape the punishment due to them or to impose legal penalties on the innocent. Judicial rhetoric accomplishes these goals by advancing clever interpretations of the law, impressing the audience with refined words and phrases, and manipulating the emotions of the jury. For their part, jurors do not listen to the disputants with an eye to the truth of the case; nor do they care about the justice of their own verdict. Rather, they listen for their entertainment and pleasure. They are more interested in the rhetorical artistry of the speakers—that is, their clever arguments and the elegance of their language—and less in the truth of the case at hand. Worse, they allow themselves to be swayed by the emotional pleas of the contestants. But in so doing, they neglect the dictates of reason and the demands of the truth. Consequently, their verdicts lack both responsibility and judicial integrity.

Plato's critique of the rhetoric employed in the Athenian courts is consistent with his conception of justice, which stipulates that justice is a cosmic principle of balance and harmony in both the state and the individual person. Justice, for Plato, is an inborn sense, a sense that cannot be taught explicitly. Further, it is a good thing both in itself and for its consequences. The greatest consequence of justice is that all people eventually get what is due to them. Accordingly, the just achieve wholeness and self-consistency. In and through this achievement, they preserve the natural condition of their souls and maintain order and peace in their states. By contrast, the unjust allow the worse parts of themselves (the pursuit of pleasure, the satisfaction of the appetites) to enslave their better parts (the pursuit of the good, the exercise of reason). The consequences of injustice include a diseased soul in the person of the wrongdoer, pain and suffering in the person of the victim, a disorderly state, and the displeasure of the gods.

Beyond these stipulations, Plato's conception of justice finds specific elaboration in the *Gorgias* and the *Republic* (especially Books I–IV), two works in which he undertakes to refute four interrelated propositions supposedly held by some of his contemporaries: (1) that justice is nothing but the interest of the stronger; (2) that it is preferable to commit than to suffer injustice; (3) that the unjust live happier lives than the just; and (4) that avoiding legal punishment through rhetorical eloquence is a prized ability. Plato's detailed refutations aside, it is important to realize that one of his many philosophical projects was to replace the authority of power with that of justice. In the *Gorgias,* Callicles, the sophistical character who represents the authority of power, tells Socrates that conventional justice is really the creation of weak-minded people. By contrast, natural justice, which cannot be eliminated by human designs, favors the survival and dominance of the stronger:

> Those who framed the laws are the weaker folk, the majority. And accordingly they frame the laws for themselves and their own advantage, and so too with their approval and censure, and to prevent the stronger who are able to overreach them from gaining the advantage over them, they frighten them by saying that to overreach others is shameful and evil, and injustice consists in seeking the advantage over others. For they are satisfied, I suppose, if being inferior they enjoy equality of status. That is the reason why seeking an advantage over the many is by convention said to be wrong and shameful, and they call it injustice. But in my view nature herself makes it plain that it is right for the better to have the advantage over the worse, the more able over the less. And both among all animals and in entire states and races of mankind it is plain that this is the case—that right is recognized to be the sovereignty and advantage of the stronger over the weaker. (483b–d)

Plato has Socrates challenge Callicles' view by pointing out that justice is a question of cosmic order, not power. Justice is a state of perfection, a state whose preservation requires discipline. Undisciplined people disturb justice by transgressing its rules. The return to it requires punishment. In the following statement we get a glimpse of the substance of Socrates' response to Callicles, which represents Plato's thinking on the centrality of justice in human happiness:

> The man who wishes to be happy must, it seems, pursue and practice temperance, and each of us must flee from indiscipline with all the speed in his power and contrive, preferably to have no need of being disciplined, but if he or any of his friends, whether individual or city, has need of it, then he must suffer punishment and be disciplined, if he is to be happy. This I consider to be the mark to which a man should look throughout his life, and all his own en-

deavors and those of his city he should devote to the single purpose of so acting that justice and temperance shall dwell in him who is to be truly blessed.
He should not suffer his appetites to be undisciplined and endeavor to satisfy
them by leading the life of a brigand—a mischief without end. For such a man
could be dear neither to any other man nor to God, since he is incapable of
fellowship, and where there is no fellowship, friendship cannot be. Wise men,
Callicles, say that the heavens and the earth, gods and men, are bound together by fellowship and friendship, and order and temperance and justice,
and for this reason they call the sum of things the "ordered" universe, my
friend, not the world of disorder and riot. (507c–508a)

A great deal of Plato's critique of legal rhetoric finds a particularly
interesting manifestation in his *Apology*. Written a few years after
Socrates' death, this work purports to represent the actual speech
Socrates delivered in defense of himself in his trial in 399 B.C.E.
Whether the *Apology* reports faithfully what Socrates did say, whether
it is Plato's own composition, and how much of the speech is Socrates'
and how much Plato's are interesting questions, but ones that fall outside the scope of this section. Our purpose here is to inquire into
Plato's view of legal rhetoric; one way we can do this is by examining
how he himself would handle a legal defense and how such a defense
might differ from its sophistical counterpart.

Before doing so, it is important to keep in mind that Plato's *Apology* was not written for delivery in an actual court—Socrates was already dead. Rather, it was meant as a statement in defense of the
principled life of the philosopher and as an indictment of normative legal practices that lack intellectual foundation. Socrates was accused of
impiety (preaching deities not sanctioned by the state) and of corrupt-
ing the youth. Obviously, he failed to persuade the majority of the jury
that he was innocent, for he was convicted and sentenced to die. However, Plato turned his teacher's death into an occasion for making a
most compelling case for the uncompromising nature of the truth. At
the same time, he turned the event of Socrates' trial and conviction
into a cause for exposing the conceptual flaws of rhetorical persuasion
in the courts.

The Socrates of the *Apology* looks nothing like a defendant whose
life is on the line. As Plato portrays him, he is sometimes rude, other
times testy, arrogant, ironic, funny, sarcastic, even defiant. Much of
what he says violates normal expectations. Yet he is also a sympathetic
character who makes a great deal of sense. Socrates opens his speech by
telling the jury that all they will get from him is the truth in plain
language:

> From me you shall hear the whole truth—not . . . in flowery language like theirs [the accusers'], decked out with fine words and phrases. No, what you will hear will be a straightforward speech in the first words that occur to me . . . and I do not want any of you to expect anything different. (17b–c)

Aware that rhetoric relies on the effects of stylistic elegance and that audiences tend to treat language as an object of beauty rather than a vehicle for truth, Socrates asks the jurors to disregard his unadorned speech and ask themselves only whether his claims are just: "This is the first duty of the juryman, just as it is the pleader's duty to speak the truth" (18a).

The next part of his speech is devoted to an account of his life of seventy years as a philosopher pursuing the truth and combating ignorance in all its forms. Doing the work of philosophy, he explains, is like answering a higher call, a call he attributes to the gods. As such, he notes, he has never had any time or desire for participation in political affairs or such vain pursuits as wealth, reputation, and public honors. His singlemost preoccupation has been to urge his interlocutors to care more about their intellectual and spiritual development and less about earthly trivialities. This, he reasons, has caused envy and hostility in many people who have encountered him in the open spaces of Athens. When these sentiments are combined with people's love of slander, he concludes, they translate into the charges he is facing. But, he adds, he is not willing to change his ways, even if he is offered a plea bargain (to go free on the condition that he stop philosophizing):

> Supposing . . . that you should offer to acquit me on these terms, I should reply, Gentlemen, I am your very grateful and devoted servant, but I owe a greater obedience to God than to you, and so long as I draw breath and have my faculties, I shall never stop practicing philosophy and exhorting you and elucidating the truth for everyone that I meet. (29d)

Toward the end of his defense, Socrates once again frustrates the expectations of the jury by telling them that he deliberately will not resort to another typical practice in the courts, the use of witnesses supporting his case. The logic of this choice is the same one he employs in the passages cited above: the truth can stand on its own and, therefore, needs nothing beyond itself. This is how he puts the matter:

> It may be that someone of you, remembering his own case, will be annoyed that whereas he, in standing his trial upon a less serious charge than this, made pitiful appeals to the jury with floods of tears, and had his infant children produced in court to excite the maximum of sympathy, and many of his relatives

and friends as well, I on the contrary intend to do nothing of the sort, and that, although I am facing, as it might appear, the utmost danger. It may be that one of you, reflecting on these facts, will be prejudiced against me, and being irritated by his reflections, will give his vote in anger. . . . I do not think it is right for me to use any of these methods. (34b–e)

After the verdict of death is announced, Socrates reflects on his defense and asserts that he was convicted because he did not "play the game" of the typical defendant. Confident of the truthfulness of his case, he tells the jury that he followed the course he did because he is a man of integrity, unconcerned with the consequences of his stance. He would rather suffer death than resort to methods unbecoming to a man of principled commitments:

No doubt you think, gentlemen, that I have been condemned for lack of the arguments which I could have used if I had thought it right to leave nothing unsaid or undone to secure my acquittal. But that is far from the truth. It is not a lack of arguments that has caused my condemnation, but a lack of effrontery and impudence, and the fact that I have refused to address you in the way which would give you most pleasure. You would have liked to hear me weep and wail, doing and saying all sorts of things which I regard as unworthy of myself, but which you are used to hearing from other people. But I did not think then that I ought to stoop to servility because I was in danger, and I do not regret now the way in which I pleaded my case. I would much rather die as a result of this defense than live as the result of the other sort. (38d–e)

Clearly, Plato does not hold the rhetoric practiced in the courts in high esteem. Although quite aware of the power of rhetoric to influence legal decisions and actions, he is critical of the direction of that influence. Plato understands the capacity of language to falsify and deceive. He knows that falsification and deception can and often do persuade because they dazzle and flatter an uncritical audience. He realizes that juries, like most public audiences, are pleasure-seeking spectators indifferent to what is being said. He acknowledges that they are vulnerable to emotional manipulation. And he sees that in many cases their judgments lack wisdom. In short, he is unwilling to accept instances of aborted justice as the consequence of those realities, which he explains as examples of human weaknesses. Accordingly, he tries to raise the critical consciousness of his readers and help them resist the temptations in the court. As illustrated by the *Apology,* his conception of justice points to the uncompromising character of the truth and the priority of principle over circumstances.

ISOCRATES

Isocrates started out his career as a court logographer, but after ten years he abandoned that profession and became a teacher of rhetoric. Around 390 B.C.E., he opened a school in Athens for the study of rhetoric. Along with his new occupation came a shift in his focus from the narrower scope of legal rhetoric to the wider one of political rhetoric, which he regarded as significantly more crucial to the welfare of a city. Under his new focus, rhetoric was to be put to better uses by concerning itself mainly with "questions of public welfare" (*Antidosis* 80) and promoting public awareness of "affairs of the state" (40). Isocrates understood the necessity of judicial rhetoric; however, he also thought that the rhetoric of the courts was receiving more attention than it should. As legal rhetoric came under the kinds of attacks we saw in the last section, Isocrates grew increasingly embarrassed about his earlier profession—so much so that he eventually denied having ever been a legal logographer.

By virtue of his work as a court logographer and a teacher of rhetoric, Isocrates belongs to the same class as some of the Sophists who preceded him. But by virtue of his views of judicial rhetoric, he comes closer to his contemporary Plato. Like the Sophists, he held rhetoric in high esteem and considered a rhetorical education the quintessential mark of the ideal citizen. Like Plato, however, he thought that the pressure to win at all costs was forcing the practitioners of judicial rhetoric to put the art of persuasion into such unethical uses as misleading, lying, deceiving, using false witnesses, and so on. Because these practices were giving rhetoric a bad name, Isocrates thought he could restore its reputation as an art by shifting its focus to the political domain, thus giving it a wider area of application, and more opportunities to prove beneficial to a greater number of people. His rationale was that whereas legal rhetoric is limited to private disputes and aims at personal advantage, political rhetoric concerns itself with issues affecting the general population of a whole community and the collective advantage of all its citizens.

Isocrates' views on judicial rhetoric are reflected in his practical understanding of justice. Essentially agreeing with Plato that it is better to suffer than to commit wrongdoing, he places justice in opposition to the pursuit of wealth. Although he does not define justice abstractly, he asserts that people seek wealth out of greed, and that greed leads to many forms of injustice and wickedness; by contrast, he notes, justice constitutes a source of many blessings, most notably honor. But if this is so, he reasons that it is better to be poor and just than wealthy and unjust. As he admonishes the young Demonicus, one should aspire to be a just person:

> Put yourself in a position in which you have the power to take advantage, but refrain when you have your fair share, so that men may think that you strive for justice, not from weakness, but from a sense of equity. Prefer honest poverty to unjust wealth; for justice is better than riches in that riches profit us only while we live, while justice provides us glory even after we are dead, and while riches are shared by bad men, justice is a thing in which the wicked can have no part. Never emulate those who seek to gain by injustice, but cleave rather to those who have suffered loss in the cause of justice; for if the just have no other advantage over the unjust, at any rate they surpass them in their high hopes. (*To Demonicus* 38–39)

In the previous section, we saw in Socrates' response to Callicles the claim that justice and temperance require discipline and account for friendship and public order. Isocrates echoes these sentiments when he suggests that human relations characterized by these two virtues are beneficial both to the people involved and the society at large. By contrast, relations characterized by injustice and intemperance are the source of personal and societal troubles:

> The most sovereign of the virtues are temperance and justice, since not only do they benefit us in themselves, but, if we should be minded to look into the natures, powers, and uses of human relations, we should find that those which do not partake of these qualities are the causes of great evils, whereas those which are attended by temperance and justice are greatly beneficial to the life of man. (*Nicocles* 29–30)

Isocrates also reflects Plato's view that an unjust state is no state at all when he observes that justice "constitutes the chief concern of all well-regulated states" (*Archidamus* 35). Finally, Isocrates agrees with Plato that justice is not a subject that can be taught explicitly. Speaking from a practical orientation, he asserts that "just living cannot be taught" and that "there does not exist an art of the kind which can implant sobriety and justice in depraved natures" (*Against the Sophists* 21). Even so, Isocrates claims, these two virtues can be cultivated in students indirectly, through the study of political rhetoric: "I do think that the study of political discourse can help more than any other thing to stimulate and form such qualities of character" (21). How and why this is so we will explain in Chapter 4.

In one sense, Isocrates' remarks on justice in the above passages are to be expected—one can hardly praise injustice openly. In another sense, his remarks lack the kind of precision needed for a better understanding of what he means. Does the pursuit of wealth necessarily lead to injustice? Is it possible to seek riches and still be a just person? If material greed is the cause of many forms of injustice, what is the cause of greed? Can greed be eradicated from human nature? If so, how so? If not, what is the use of talking about it? Can people be taught fairness? What would lessons in fairness consist of? Who would teach them? What is a depraved nature? What do human relations characterized by injustice look like? Can they be reformed? What do all these remarks have to do with judicial rhetoric? These and related questions require a higher level of specificity, the type for which Isocrates is not especially famous. Even so, an examination of his *Antidosis,* one of his better-known rhetorical compositions, helps answer some of these questions, if only indirectly.

The *Antidosis* received its title from an Athenian legal procedure. Every year a list of the wealthiest Athenians was published for the purpose of taxation. Those listed were required by law to bear the expenses of public projects or services (financing a warship for the fleet, subsidizing a theatrical performance, etc.). If a citizen on the list thought that another, unlisted citizen was wealthier than himself, he could challenge him to an *antidosis*. The challenge took this form: "Either agree that you are wealthier than me, in which case you have to pay for the project at hand, or you and I exchange all our assets, in which case I agree to pay." Apparently, Isocrates was challenged to such an *antidosis* and lost his case in court. Although the specifics of the trial are not known, it is clear that Isocrates thought that his challenger prejudiced the jury by misrepresenting his wealth, disparaging his profession, and attacking his moral character. Written after the trial, the *Antidosis* was designed to clear Isocrates' name.

Like Plato's *Apology,* the *Antidosis* is a defense of a way of life spent teaching and an elaborate explanation of an educational philosophy. Similarly, it criticizes commonly held notions and societally permitted practices, especially those that obtained in the court setting. But unlike Plato, who speaks in uncompromising terms, Isocrates tries hard to secure a sympathetic hearing from his readers. At stake for him is not only his reputation but also his version of rhetoric.

Isocrates attributes rhetorical persuasion to three objects of desire, which function as powerful motivating forces: "Everyone does everything which he does for the sake of pleasure or gain or honor . . . no desire springs up in men save for these objects" (*Antidosis* 217). As one might expect, he associates the rhetoric of the courts to pleasure and gain, but links the kind of rhetoric he teaches to honor. For Isocrates, honor obtains when one serves dutifully an idea (i.e., justice) or one's fellow citizens and does so at his own expense. But, he notes, many teachers of judicial rhetoric ignore honor and teach their students "the kind of eloquence which enables people to gain their own advantage contrary to justice" (89). Worse, he tells his Athenian readers, litigation-minded people with a knack for court oratory neither "keep their hands off citizens who live soberly" nor "bring before you only those who do evil"; rather, they shamelessly "advertise their powers in their attacks upon men who are entirely innocent, and so get more money from those who are clearly guilty" (24). These unscrupulous people spend their lives practically living in the courthouse (38), and daily "lay information, hale people into court, and covet the property of others" (99). Not only are these people indecent folks, they also give rhetoric a bad name.

Unlike Gorgias, who approaches the workings of rhetorical persuasion from the individual defendant's view, Isocrates approaches it from the corrupt accuser's perspective. Of course, the difference in approach and purpose leads to different remarks. Accordingly, Gorgias shows how Helen was practically victimized by Paris' persuasive force. Isocrates, on the other hand, attempts to explain how and why the court sycophants, despite widespread condemnation, are successful in swaying juries to rule in favor of their wicked ways. His answer is that it is the condition of poverty that makes people vulnerable to injustice—Isocrates knew that most juries consisted of poor people, many of whom counted on the nominal fee they received for their service. More than any other fact, Isocrates believes, it is the jurors' poverty that accounts for the sycophants' success. Again and again, they manipulate their poor audiences by appealing to their desire for gain. Suggesting that the rich are the main cause of every poor person's condition, the sycophants seek to cultivate envy and resentment against a whole class of people. In practical terms, their manipulation leads to the conviction of innocents who happen to be well-to-do and the acquittal of criminals who happen to be poor. In effect, then, the sycophants are prospering financially by preying on the wealthy and spreading corruption and depravity among their fellow citizens: "And who more than these sycophants would like to see many of our citizens corrupted and depraved, since they know that when they live among such characters they wield great power" (241).

The effects of the sycophants' questionable tactics in the courts are disastrous in several ways. For one thing, they mislead their listeners by

creating in them false hopes. Their arguments to the poor take the following form: "If you penalize monetarily this rich defendant, you will
help this poor accuser overthrow the oppression of the wealthy. If you
award damages to this poor accuser today, juries like the one you sit in
will do the same for you tomorrow." For another, this kind of rhetoric
undermines human relations throughout the community. Over time,
people begin to look at each other not as potential friends or allies existing within the same space but as targets of hostility and potential
sources of gain. For yet another, the system of justice suffers as more
and more people use the courts to improve their own lot rather than to
maintain a lawful and orderly society.

In an interesting move, Isocrates transfers his critique of legal
rhetoric to the domain of politics via this analogy: what the sycophants
are to judicial rhetoric, demagogues are to political rhetoric. What
unites these two groups is their disregard of honor and their use of appeals to pleasure and gain. Like the sycophants, the demagogues exploit weak people's greed for acquisition and thirst for power. And like
the sycophants, the demagogues have proved to be a bane to Athens.
While the sycophants' rhetorical practices are undermining the moral
health of the society, those of the demagogues have undermined the
political strength of the city. In an argument that informs several of his
works, Isocrates shows that what had begun as a legitimate alliance between Athens and other city-states eventually degenerated into a devi-
talizing quarrel among several city-states. The primary cause for this
sad turn of affairs is the demagogues. They are the ones who fueled the
Athenian desire for gain to the point where its legitimate quest for
leadership turned into an illegitimate and self-destructive search for total domination. By making false promises, the demagogues managed
to persuade Athens to overextend itself; when it did so, it brought
about its own downfall. Isocrates suggests that Athens' political troubles began "when men of this character took over the supremacy of the
rostrum" (*On the Peace* 121). Their mode of operation is always the
same: they "speak for the gratification of the audience but plunge
those who are persuaded by them into many distresses and hardships"
(*Panathenaicus* 140).

Isocrates contrasts the rhetorics of pleasure and gain with the
rhetoric he teaches and endorses: the rhetoric of honor. In the legal
setting, this rhetoric aims at justice; in the political domain, it aims at
goodness. Those who practice this rhetoric are seeking to discover how
best to serve their city and fellow citizens, not themselves. The reward
for this rhetoric may not be materially tangible, but it is noble and eth-

ically satisfying. Isocrates claims in the *Antidosis* that the kind of rhetoric he teaches prepares students to become unselfish public servants, conscientious citizens, and honorable human beings. As evidence of his success as a teacher, he boasts that many of his students have been "crowned by Athens with chaplets of gold" (94) "in recognition of their worth" (144).

Clearly, Isocrates has a distinct perspective on judicial rhetoric. Unlike the Sophists, who discussed the rhetoric of the courts in terms of its power to persuade a jury of one's case, Isocrates discusses it along the lines of its motives, goals, and consequences. Although he agrees with the Sophists that the court is a forum of competition, he argues that legal victories should be secured by fighting fairly, not by resorting to questionable tactics, shady practices, and unethical means. On this issue, he sides with Plato. But whereas Plato posits that the only obligation of judicial rhetoric should be the truth, Isocrates goes one step further and includes honor. In so doing, he makes more allowances for rhetoric and societal understandings of honor. At the same time, he anticipates Aristotle's view that a legal issue should be resolved by reference to the facts of the case.

ARISTOTLE

Unlike his predecessors, Aristotle did not write legal speeches. Instead he articulated his conception of judicial discourse in his treatise on rhetoric. Aristotle begins his *Rhetoric* by criticizing the authors of handbooks on legal rhetoric. His criticism is that they mostly instruct readers how to arouse the audience's emotions and how to talk about things irrelevant to the case tried. Although Aristotle understands the crucial role the emotions play in rhetorical persuasion (he devotes ten chapters of his *Rhetoric* to discussing them), he still holds that reasoning should play a greater role. Aristotle also understands why people stray from the issue at hand—they are trying to curry favor with the jurors, who are judging a matter that does not affect themselves directly. Even so, he maintains that litigants should focus on the facts of the case and try to prove whether something did or did not happen, whether the alleged facts are or are not so.

Beyond his critical remarks on the rhetorical handbooks, Aristotle offers a more systematic treatment of legal rhetoric. He starts out by observing the four structural features of forensic rhetoric: audience, divisions, time, and goal. Its audience, he notes, consists of judges deciding whether the alleged events have happened. Its divisions are either the accusation or the defense of someone. Its time is always the past, actions already done. And its goal is to establish the justice or injustice of some action. With this framework in place, Aristotle next discusses the motives for wrongdoing, the kinds of thoughts criminals entertain, and the kinds of people that typically are victimized. His discussion provides a general prospectus of human motivation as well as a set of insights that help one understand the nature of legal disputes. His assumption throughout is that the practice of rhetoric in the courts must change by grounding itself on the kinds of understandings his discussion purports to furnish.

After defining wrongdoing as "injury voluntarily inflicted contrary to law" (I, x, 3), Aristotle differentiates between special and general laws. Special laws, he claims, are the written or unwritten laws that regulate the life of a community. General laws are principles acknowledged by all people everywhere. By "general laws" Aristotle means the invariable principles of nature. The most pertinent principle in the study of legal rhetoric is the principle of natural justice, which is binding on all people. Aristotle continues his preliminary remarks by observing that to do something voluntarily or intentionally means to do it consciously, deliberately, and without constraint. The causes of doing deliberate injury to others are vice and lack of self-control. In other words, wrongdoing is a function of a faulty character. People's character, for Aristotle, consists of a cluster of dispositions, and their actions are the result of those dispositions. Thus, Aristotle notes, the mean-spirited person will harm others in matters involving money, the profligate in matters of physical pleasure, the effeminate in matters of comfort, and the coward in matters of danger.

The next part of Aristotle's discussion addresses the causes of human action. When people do wrong, he points out, they are trying to get or to avoid something. Every action of every person is either due to the person or to some other cause. Actions caused by a person are due either to habit or to craving. There are two kinds of craving. Rational craving is craving for something good (i.e., a wish); people do not wish for something unless they think it good. Irrational craving is craving whose source is either anger or desire. Actions not due to the person are due either to chance, or compulsion or nature. Of the causes of human action, forensic rhetoric is interested in habit, reasoning, anger, and desire. This is so because accusation and defense always revolve around the issue of responsibility—that is, whether the alleged deeds were done voluntarily, intentionally. An action is due to habit when it can be determined that it has been done often before. Actions are due to reasoning when they are done because they appear useful either as ends in themselves or as means to an end. Anger is the cause of acts of revenge, while desire is the cause of all actions that appear pleasant. In short, all voluntary actions are done because they are, or they appear to be, good or pleasant.

The next step for Aristotle is to consider those things that are good and those that are pleasant. His discussion of the good things includes things that are useful. Both classes are relevant to legal rhetoric as they provide insight into the causes of human action. Because Aristotle understands the multifaceted character of goodness, his definition of a good thing encompasses a wide range of interrelated classes of good things. He defines a good thing as whatever is desirable for its own sake, or for the sake of which we choose something else; or that which is desired by all things, especially those that have reason; or that whose presence makes a person fit and independent; or that which produces or preserves such things. Among the things that fall within this definition are the virtues (i.e., justice, courage, temperance, magnanimity, magnificence) because they tend to produce good works and good deeds. Also included are pleasure and beauty—pleasure because it is the nature of all animals (including humans) to pursue it, and beauty because it is either desirable in itself or productive of pleasure. Health is also a good thing because it is a state of bodily excellence and productive of numerous other good things (i.e., life, pleasure). The same is true of wealth, friendships, honor and reputation, the faculties of speech and action, and all the sciences and arts. Aristotle concludes his list of things commonly taken to be good with reference to life, something desirable in itself, and justice, the cause of good to the community.

Aristotle next considers things that are pleasant. He begins by defining pleasure as a movement that brings the soul into its natural state of being. From this it follows that whatever leads the soul to its natural state is pleasant. Habit, for example, is pleasant because it is virtually natural. Habit resembles nature in the same way that things that happen often resemble things that happen always—hence our reference to habit as "second nature." Things that are not compulsory are also pleasant. Among the things that belong to this class, Aristotle considers ease, freedom from toil, relaxation, amusement, rest, and sleep. By contrast, what is forced on us is painful because force is unnatural. If this is so, acts that require much concentration, strong effort, and strain are painful unless they have become habitual, which would make them pleasant.

Other pleasant things include those that we desire, since desire is a craving for pleasure. Aristotle discriminates between irrational and rational desires. Irrational desires are those that originate in the body (rather than the mind) and are understood as natural; they include hunger, thirst, sex, touch, taste, smell, hearing, and vision. Rational desires are those that we are induced to have. Aristotle posits that there are many things we desire because we have been told about them and believe them to be good. Things imagined are also pleasant. This is so because imagination is a feeble form of sensation. People who remember or anticipate something always imagine what they remember or anticipate. And because they imagine, they also feel some kind of sensation. But if this is so, Aristotle reasons, things that are pleasant are either present and perceived, past and remembered, or future and anticipated. Aristotle's analysis of pleasure includes a longer list of pleasant things. However, the point of his discussion remains the same throughout: the pursuit of pleasure constitutes one of the main causes of illegal action.

Having established the motives for wrongdoing, Aristotle embarks on a discussion of the thinking of people who intentionally do injury to others contrary to law. These people, he observes, think that they can commit a crime without being detected; or that if they are detected, they can escape punishment; or that if they are punished, the pain will be less than the gain. Generally, people think they can escape punishment if they possess eloquence, practical ability, considerable legal experience, many influential friends, or a great deal of money. They also think they are safe if they are on good terms with their victims or with the judges—they reason that they will make some arrangement with their victims and avoid prosecution; and they believe that the judges will either let them off altogether or impose a light sentence. Further, they think they can avoid detection if their appearance is inconsistent with the charges that might be brought against them. For instance, Aristotle notes, "a weakling is unlikely to be charged with violent assault, or a poor and ugly man with adultery" (I, xii, 5).

Wrongdoers tend to commit crimes in areas in which people, unable to imagine the possibility of crime, take no precautions. They also feel safe if they have no enemies, which means that nobody is watching them closely. If they do have enemies, they still might venture doing wrong because they believe they can maintain their innocence by arguing that nobody would have taken such a risk. Another line of criminal thinking is that if one is found out, one can avoid a trial, postpone it, or bribe the judges. Alternatively, convicted criminals think they can postpone paying damages indefinitely or avoid doing so altogether, or that they are so badly off that they have nothing to lose. Criminals may be encouraged to commit crimes if they have done them in the past without getting caught, or if they have tried before but failed. They often think that their pleasure or gain will be immediate, while their pain or loss will not come until much later. Conversely, they may believe that their pain and loss will be immediate and short-lived, whereas their pleasure and gain will come later and last longer. Some criminals think that they will be able to make their crime appear due to chance or necessity or natural causes, that in fact they failed to do the right thing rather than committed a wrong. Others believe that they will be judged leniently. If they have a good reputation, they believe that people will not suspect them of wrongdoing; if they have an especially bad one, they believe nothing they can do will make it worse. Aristotle's analysis of the thinking of wrongdoers is lengthier than the above discussion. In its entirety, however, it provides the prosecution and the defense with a set of arguments revolving around the issue of intention. The prosecution will always try to prove that the accused did the alleged deed and did it in a calculating and deliberate manner. For its part, the defense will try to prove either that the defendant did not do what the prosecution contends or that the defendant did do the alleged deed but did not intend harm.

Having identified the thought processes of a criminal, Aristotle next discusses the kinds of people wrongdoers victimize. Specifically he notes that we consider people to have been victimized if they have suffered actual harm and have suffered it against their will. Victims include those who have what the criminals want and those who are generally trusting of others instead of being cautious. They also include those who are too easygoing or too inept to prosecute an offender, or too sensitive to fight over issues of money. Another category of victims includes those who have been wronged often but have not prosecuted the perpetrators. Then there are those who take no precautions: of these, some believe that they will not be victimized because nothing of the sort has ever happened to them before; others, who *have* been victimized, think that it surely cannot happen to them again. Another likely class of victims consists of one's friends or one's enemies—it is easy to injure the former and pleasant to injure the latter. Those who cannot wait for a trial or damages are also a target of wrongdoing. The same is true of those who would be too ashamed to talk publicly about the wrongs done to them. Finally, those who have often wronged others are almost asking to be harmed themselves—

harming them is like carrying out the dictates of justice. Aristotle's discussion of victims is lengthier and more detailed. But in its entirety it aims at the same twofold purpose: to issue a general understanding of people likely to suffer wrongdoing, and provide the prosecution and the defense with a set of arguments revolving around the issue of suffering. The prosecution will always try to prove that the victim(s) suffered unnecessarily and unjustly. For its part, the defense will try to prove that the victim either did not suffer or did, but not as much as the prosecution contends.

Aristotle next undertakes a classification of just and unjust actions with reference to two kinds of laws (particular and general) and two classes of people (specific individuals and the community). In a court setting, the justice or injustice of an action is always contested. A defendant will often admit to having done the alleged action but not to the label placed on it by the prosecution. Aristotle furnishes several examples. A man, he notes, "will admit that he took a thing but not that he 'stole' it; that he struck someone first, but not that he committed 'outrage'; that he had intercourse with a woman, but not that he committed 'adultery'" (I, xiii, 9). But if this is so, it is important to determine what is and what is not theft, outrage, or adultery. Aristotle observes here that the justice or injustice of an action, and by extension the guilt or innocence of the accused, hinges on this determination. In turn, this determination depends on the establishment of intention. As Aristotle explains:

> It is deliberate purpose that constitutes wickedness and criminal guilt, and such names as "outrage" or "theft" imply deliberate purpose as well as the mere action. A blow does not always amount to "outrage," but only if it is struck with some such purpose as to insult the man struck or gratify the striker himself. Nor does taking a thing without the owner's knowledge always amount to "theft," but only if it is taken with the intention of keeping it and injuring the owner. And as with these charges, so with all the others. (I, xiii, 10)

Aristotle acknowledges that in addition to written laws, humans regulate their conduct by reference to unwritten laws. According to him, there are two kinds of unwritten laws: those that arise from acts exceeding the legal standard of virtuous or viceful conduct and those supplementing written laws. Naturally, the responses to the first kind include praise, honor, and decoration, or censure and dishonor, respectively. The second kind is what Aristotle calls "equity." Equity, according to him, supplements laws that are defective or serves in the place of laws that have not been legislated. It applies to forgivable actions, and it makes us discriminate between criminal acts and errors of judgment or misfortunes. Equity bids us to be merciful to the weaknesses of human nature; to pay more attention to the spirit than to the letter of the law; to spend more time considering one's intentions and less one's actions; to ask not what a man is now but what he has generally been throughout his life. To be equitable means to take into account not details but the whole story; to remember benefits rather than injuries; to be patient when wronged; and to prefer arbitration over litigation.

Clearly, Aristotle's conception of forensic rhetoric provides a systematic and theoretical approach to the study of human conflicts and their rhetorical resolution. Insofar as his conception is based on human motivation as the cause of wrongdoing, it is psychological in character; and inasmuch as it considers social understandings of the good, the pleasant, and the desirable, it is sociological in nature. His analysis of the dispositions of criminals and their victims and his discussion of just and unjust actions in the light of both written and unwritten laws furnishes an overview of the many considerations litigants and juries have to take into account. At the same time, it provides a detailed blueprint of arguments for both the prosecution and the defense.

SUMMARY

In this chapter we have seen how judicial rhetoric evolved and developed in classical Greece. We have noted that its birth and growth were a function of specific structural changes in the legal system during the fifth century B.C.E. We have also observed that these changes created the need for legal education and professional advice. The practice of rhetoric in the legal setting, we have pointed out, led to the development of such theoretical notions as twofold arguments, appropriateness, and the opportune moment.

Against this background, we have examined four conceptions of judicial rhetoric as formulated by the Sophists, Plato, Isocrates, and Aristotle. We have discussed the Sophists' practical conception, which was formed by the demands of the newly established legal system and the dictates of rhetorical persuasion. Using Gorgias' *Encomium of Helen* as an illustration of a legal defense, we have suggested that this work shows a method of proof at work and advances a theory of persuasion. In contrast to this sophistical view, we have presented Plato's criticisms of legal rhetoric on the grounds that it is predicated on the principle of power. We have highlighted Plato's conception of justice as a principle of balance and order that leads to happiness for those who obey it. Using the *Apology* as an illustration of Plato's version of a legal defense, we have shown that he critiques normative court practices and underscores the superiority of the truth over persuasion. Our discussion of Isocrates has shown that he appropriates elements of the Sophists' practical and Plato's critical conceptions of judicial rhetoric. Using his *Antidosis* as a paradigmatic work, we have noted that he disapproves of rhetorical practices aiming at pleasure and gain, and praises those seeking honor. Finally, we have shown that Aristotle's conception of forensic rhetoric is founded on the structural elements of a legal dispute adjudicated in a court of law. Following his discussion in the *Rhetoric,* we have identified his stipulations about wrongdoing, its causes vis-à-vis popular notions of good and pleasant things, and the dispositions of criminals and their victims. After discussing his distinction between just and unjust actions, we have observed that Aristotle's conception of forensic rhetoric offers both an understanding of legal disputes and an elaborate set of arguments for both sides of a legal issue.

CHAPTER 2

RHETORIC AND POLITICS

❧

In the last chapter, we saw how rhetoric can affect judgments about past actions by reference to the criterion of law. The domain of law, we noted, concerns itself with actions already done and evaluates whether they were deliberate (the result of deliberation) or due to chance, compulsion, or necessity. In this chapter, we discuss some of the ways in which rhetoric influences future actions in the absence of preexisting criteria. The domain of politics, we will see, concerns itself with yet-to-be-done actions and considers whether they are feasible and desirable. Like judicial rhetoric, the political kind (also called deliberative rhetoric) is not interested in accidental, compulsory, or necessary actions, but in deliberate ones. However, unlike its judicial counterpart, which judges what has been done, political rhetoric deliberates on what can and should be done. To deliberate means to exchange views and ideas, to entertain possibilities, and to discuss alternatives.

Whether it refers to an individual dilemma, a communal problem, or a national issue, deliberation is the process of making decisions in the face of uncertainty and in the absence of established criteria. While the motives of deliberation are ambiguity and doubt, its goals are decision and action.

Just as the Athenian courts provided a space where rhetoric could affect the adjudication of human conflicts, the Athenian assembly offered a forum where rhetoric could direct public deliberation and political action. The assembly discussed legislative issues, debated proposals, entertained solutions, and reached decisions. Unlike today's Congress, where only the representatives of the people have a direct voice in the making of decisions, the assembly was open to any Athenian citizen wishing to play a role on the political stage. The assembly was large enough to accommodate several thousand participants, and on a day when a weighty issue was to be considered, an attendance of five thousand citizens (approximately one-sixth of the citizenry) was not unusual. The right of every citizen to contribute to the decision-making process was underscored by the ritualistic words of the council, which opened every session with the following question: "Who wishes to speak?" These words not only announced the start of the day's proceedings but, more importantly, invited the attendees to involve themselves directly with the political affairs of their city. Like verdicts in the court, decisions reached in the assembly were final. At the end of the day, the city was obligated to carry out the expressed wishes of its citizens.

The very existence of the assembly attested to a form of democracy that was prepared to accept the outcome of people's deliberations as official law or policy. The establishment of the assembly had marked an end to other forms of political governance (i.e., kingship, aristocracy) and the beginning of democracy. In fifth-century Athens, political power rested ultimately with the citizens, who gathered to speak and listen, to persuade and be persuaded, to evaluate speeches, and to arrive at conclusions. It is not surprising, therefore, that rhetoric should flourish at a time when political decision making rested on open participation. Under a kingship, there had been no need for public rhetoric—the word of the king commanded absolute authority, leaving no room for debating the efficacy of his orders or suggesting alternative policies. Nor had there been any need for public rhetoric under aristocratic rule, a system in which power was in the hands of a small, closed circle of wealthy individuals—their words carried the considerable weight of wealth and family name. But under democratic arrangements, the opportunities for rhetoric increased dramatically as ordinary people were allowed, indeed expected, to address public issues, evaluate suggestions, and approve or disapprove each other's proposals. Under these arrangements, approval was neither ritualistic nor reluctant; it was voluntary. It went neither to the most powerful figure nor to the most affluent group but to the one whose idea promised to serve his peers' interests best.

Theoretically, access to the assembly was equal. In practice, however, deliberations were dominated by the better orators. Even though anyone could contribute, a typical session took the form of a debate between two principal speakers arguing different sides on an issue before the gathered audience. As one might expect, those speakers who time and again addressed issues intelligently and commanded the attention of their listeners unquestionably rose above the rest of the members in power and reputation. In the personalities of the dominant speakers, politics and rhetoric became indistinguishable—in fact, the Greek word for orator and politician was the same *(rhetor)*. Before too long, it became apparent that anyone wishing to play a major role in Athenian politics had to be a formidable orator. Importantly, being a formidable orator did not necessarily require wealth or aristocratic roots—in principle, any one could meet the challenges of political rhetoric. Clearly, the value of polished skills in public oratory confirmed the Athenian commitment to political equality and freedom of expression. At the same time, it set into motion the search for an aristocracy of ideas (the Greek word for "best" is *aristos*). And even though this search did not always materialize, the ideas that came out of the assembly did have the support of the majority.

The main issues discussed in the assembly were war and peace. War was a constant condition for the Greek city-states, which fought one another to preserve or extend their borders, ravage each other's land, or teach each other a lesson. War generated the need for making alliances, while breaking an alliance served as a cause for further war. While the Greeks looked to war as a way of settling their irreconcilable differences, they also celebrated their commonalities as Greeks in regularly held athletic and religious festivals. To participate in these events, the warring parties declared a period of truce, came together to celebrate the festivities, parted peacefully and, in due time, resumed hostilities. While the consequences of war varied widely, it was common for the victor to bring members of the conquered population home as slaves. Thus the issue of war was inseparable from issues of liberty and autonomy; what was often at stake in the Athenian assembly was nothing less than the possibility of the city's utter annihilation.

Issues of war and peace called for responses to situations marked by urgency and uncertainty. What would be the best way to deal with a former ally that had just rebelled against Athens and had sworn allegiance to Sparta? Destroy the rebels, so as to deter other allies from following a similar course? Ignore them so as to demonstrate that the Athenian alliance was held together by mutual benefit rather than fear of force? Strike and make Sparta witness a show of strength? Hold back and avoid repercussions from Sparta? Wait until Sparta committed its forces to too many fronts? Considerations such as these presented Athenian citizens in the assembly with difficult decisions. Each situation was unique, with its own set of complexities and range of potential benefits and risks. Each situation was part of a larger system of relations; a quick remedy for one problem could create bigger problems; a good solution at one point in time could prove detrimental at another. Finally, each situation often encompassed conflicting and competing values. For example, Athens' decision to help a potential ally, and thus increase her power, often entailed an act of war; but such a decision also risked jeopardizing the security and safety of other allies, something that could weaken the foundation of Athenian power.

Theorists studying the rhetoric that emerged out of typical situations in the Athenian assembly developed a set of theoretical principles meant to guide speakers to address recurring issues more methodically. While each theorist made unique contributions to the art of rhetoric and placed different emphasis on different principles, they all made the following principles an integral part of deliberative rhetoric.

1. *Deliberation provides responses to urgent situations.* Deliberation concerns itself with urgent situations requiring prompt responses. It asks participants to consider alternative courses of action and choose the best option available under the circumstances. Because urgent situations call for swift decisions, deliberation takes place within finite time-constraints. Urgency allows no room for endless deliberation and infinitely deferred action. The best decision and the best plan for action under the circumstances are all that deliberation can produce.

2. *Deliberation takes place at the limits of knowledge.* Deliberation begins with some form of doubt and uncertainty. It takes place because humans have only partial and incomplete knowledge. If they possessed perfect knowledge, there would be no need to deliberate—decisions would be self-evident or automatic, and the consequences of actions

would be known in advance. Deliberation takes into account available knowledge, acknowledging all along the limits of what is known at the time.

3. *Deliberation aims at provisional consensus.* Given the limits of available knowledge, political deliberation looks to consensus as the next best thing; in other words, it seeks the kinds of decisions that most citizens will find most satisfactory under the circumstances. Since decisions are made on the basis of limited knowledge, consensus is never final, but always provisional. As new knowledge emerges, new deliberations can lead to a new consensus. Thus deliberation seeks consensus but understands its temporary character.

THE SOPHISTS: PROTAGORAS

As noncitizens, the Sophists could not participate in Athenian politics. Therefore, their contributions to political rhetoric are the result of their observations of political life in Athens, not of their own experience inside the arena of Athenian politics. Of the Sophists, it was Protagoras who theorized most explicitly about the role of rhetoric in public deliberation. His thinking on this matter is informed by three propositions attributed to him: (1) man is the measure of all things; (2) for every issue there are two sides opposing one another; and (3) the weaker argument can be made the stronger. As we will see in this section, these three propositions are at the heart of political deliberation in a democratic society.

Protagoras posits that a democratic society (i.e., Athens) acknowledges that insights on collective problems can come not only from the experts but from any one individual, regardless of profession, privilege, or social status. As he remarks in Plato's *Protagoras,* when the Athenians come "to deliberate on something connected with the administration of the State, the man who rises to advise them on this may equally well be a smith, a shoemaker, a merchant, a sea-captain, a rich man, a poor man, of good family or of none" (319d). This is so because the principle of political equality makes no distinctions among different people. Within a society that affirms equality and individual worth, a single person has several opportunities to affect the entire community.

But how can an individual's words affect an entire community if each individual sees things differently? How can there be agreement in a community in which each person is the "measure" of things? How is consensus possible given the relativity of opinion suggested by the "man measure" principle? According to Protagoras, individual views may be equally valued but are not equally persuasive. The moment the expression of an individual view captures the views of the audience, it stops functioning as a statement of a private perspective and becomes a statement representing the views of the entire group. This is possible because any forum for deliberation provides a space for the give-and-take of ideas, opinions, and arguments and counterarguments. In this kind of atmosphere, the participants speak and listen to one another, trying to persuade the majority. Views regarded as too narrow and too limited always yield to those seen as more spacious and representative of the collective will. Thus political deliberation may begin with many individual views, but it generally ends with that vision which incorporates most views.

If this is so, the "man measure" principle can be interpreted not as an endorsement of extreme individualism but as a proclamation of the idea of self-determination. In the domain of politics, self-determination requires the articulation of ideas from within the "body politic." To the extent that these ideas affect all the members of the community, responsibility for their articulation rests with each member of the collective. By extension, responsibility for political action rests on those who make the decisions. And when everyone participates in decision making, everyone is equally responsible for the consequences of communal action. But if this is so, Protagoras' "man measure" principle constitutes a call inviting citizens to understand themselves as the arbiters of individual and communal well-being, and to regard their beliefs and decisions as the forces that lead to concerted forms of action.

For Protagoras, then, deliberation is crucial to the creation of a social order from within the community, a social order that the majority of citizens would be willing to uphold, defend, and reform. But how can a society ruled by the majority ever change? How can people consider anything other than the established views or the dominant beliefs of a society? Protagoras maintains that as long as the commitment to public deliberation remains intact, the views of the minority have many opportunities to be voiced and to persuade the majority to rethink its position. Those holding minoritarian opinions or oppositional values can always reshape their arguments, refine their language, and reformulate their ideas with an eye to persuasion. Of course, the success of their efforts depends on their ability to demonstrate to their audience that their position is more advantageous and more desirable than the position already in place. This line of thought explains Protagoras' proposition that the weaker argument can be made the stronger.

Deliberation not only creates a democratic social order; it also can contribute to the betterment of society. In Plato's *Protagoras,* Protagoras claims that his teaching can improve the moral character of his students by making them politically more sensitive. His instruction, he claims, can "make men good citizens" (319a). Socrates contests this claim vehemently by arguing that there is no connection between the results of political deliberation and virtue—just because a proposal receives the endorsement of the majority of citizens, it does not necessarily follow that the proposal is a virtuous one. There are too many instances in which the position of the majority has proved wrong and immoral. Therefore, Socrates argues, there is no essential link between consensus and goodness.

In response to Socrates' argument, Protagoras recounts a myth on the origin of civilized life—what has come to be known as his "Great Speech." The myth says that when the gods first created living creatures on the earth, they charged Prometheus and Epimetheus with the task of giving each living creature abilities appropriate to its survival. Epimetheus persuaded Prometheus that he could do this task alone and that Prometheus could do the inspection after all the abilities had been distributed. Epimetheus went on to distribute speed, strength, and other abilities to the animals, making sure that each received what it needed for survival. But he squandered all abilities too freely, and when it came to human beings he had none left to give. Upon inspection, Prometheus found that the animals were sufficiently endowed but humans were "naked, unshod, unbedded, unarmed" (321c). Feeling sorry and responsible for them, Prometheus stole from the gods fire and the arts of daily life and gave them to humans. While Prometheus received a severe punishment from the gods, human beings were able to survive on account of the stolen gifts. They used fire to keep themselves warm, and the arts of daily life, including speech, to communicate, come together in numbers, create cities, and invent daily necessities. But because they did not possess the civic arts, humans fought against each other and headed down the path of destruction.

Seeing all this, Zeus felt sorry for humans and ordered Hermes to go down to earth and give them the two elements of the civic arts: justice and respect for one another. According to the myth, Hermes asked Zeus how he was to distribute these gifts: give justice to some and respect to others, or both justice and respect equally to all? "To all," replied Zeus. "Let all have their share; for cities cannot be formed if only a few have a share of these as of other arts. And make thereto a law of my ordaining, that he who cannot partake of respect and [justice] shall die the death of a public pest" (322d). This is why, Protagoras explains, when the Athenians "meet for a consultation on civic art, where they should be guided throughout by justice and good sense, they naturally allow advice from everybody, since it is held that everyone should partake of this excellence, or else that states cannot be" (323a). For Protagoras, then, deliberation is more than the art of advocating a specific course of action for the city. It is a human excellence inextricably tied to the virtues of justice and respect—the two most important constituents of social coherence. When people deliberate, then, they do so in accordance with the laws of their city and the ethical norms of their community. When they articulate their interests, they speak not as individuals driven solely by their own personal desires, but as citizens concerned with the common good. If, during their deliberations, people speak as citizens, their speeches act as reminders that to deliberate means to uphold those virtues that hold the community together and strengthen its bonds. It is in this way, then, that deliberation can be said to contribute to the moral betterment of society. It is also in this way that Protagoras' claim, that his instruction in rhetoric helps make people virtuous citizens, becomes intelligible.

Past the myth, Socrates challenges Protagoras once again. If deliberation is an innate faculty leading to virtue, why is it that the sons of some of Athens' prominent political leaders are neither virtuous nor knowledgeable of their fathers' art? On the other hand, if deliberation can indeed be passed on from father to son, where is the need for teachers of the art? What is there for people like Protagoras to do? Protagoras replies by reference to the imaginary city of flute players. Suppose there were a city, Protagoras says, in which flute playing was considered essential to the existence of the city. In that city, flute playing would be valued so much that it would be promoted daily. Those capable of playing the flute would teach others less capable, and the art would be passed on from father to son and from friend to neighbor. Through constant encouragement and criticism, everyone would eventually become a proficient flute player. But there would still be a marked difference between proficient and exceptionally talented flute players—some people would take to the art better than others. Those with natural talent would excel and become the leaders and the best teachers in the city. On the other hand, those without talent would rely on their friends, neighbors, and professional teachers to become as good as they could. Thus even though everyone would be capable of teaching the art of flute playing, there would still be a need for professional teachers—the only ones able to turn a citizen's basic capacity into an actual and noticeable practice. Nevertheless, not everyone would attain excellence, since not everyone would start out with natural talent. This implies that the sons of professional teachers would be no more prone to excellence than anyone else. Without some talent, even the best instruction can only do so much. This line of thought explains why the art of flute playing would be both transmittable (from neighbor to friend) and not transmittable (from professional teacher to son).

For Protagoras, then, political deliberation is an excellence inextricably tied to justice and respect, two virtues that bind a community of citizens together. Because political deliberation is highly valued in Athens, Protagoras suggests, its citizens aspire to political excellence by seeking to refine their ways of giving advice to their city. In this search, they rely not only on their own untutored skills but also on the judgments of their fellow citizens. But if this is so, the most compelling case is something that emerges out of a plethora of presentations and judgments. In turn, the most compelling case serves as a model of aspiration.

In this section, we have shown that Protagoras' conception of political deliberation urged Athenians to understand themselves and their relation to their city in the light of the limitations and possibilities of political deliberation. More specifically, it called into existence a notion of citizenship that could be played out in the Athenian assembly. However, the link between this notion of citizenship and its fulfillment in the polis did not last. Not long after Protagoras' teachings, the conduct of the Athenian empire toward its allies advanced another model of political decision making, the model of sheer force. Athens' growth into a naval power dominating the Mediterranean Sea showed the Athenians that alliances with other city-states stood in the way of her further growth and ambition. In the context of these new developments, the notions of community and citizenship advocated by Protagoras were bound to become obsolete. Equality and compromise, once the requisites for the city's self-determination, became burdens the weak imposed on the strong. Justice and respect, once the essential conditions for communal coexistence, became obstacles to Athens' pursuit of power. In this new climate, political deliberation stopped concerning itself with the problem of collective representation. Now the problem was how to subjugate the will of the many to the will of the few.

By the time Plato and Isocrates surfaced on the intellectual scene, Athens had suffered a devastating blow in the hands of Sparta in a war that lasted nearly twenty-five years and precipitated the fall of Athens. With Athens no longer enjoying the status of the premier city of Greece, intellectuals revisited the issue of political deliberation with two attitudes: the critical (as articulated by Plato) and the optimistic (as expressed by Isocrates). The next two sections are devoted to these two attitudes.

PLATO

In many of his works, Plato has Socrates critique the Sophists and their ideas. In the *Protagoras,* his specific purpose is to discredit the two Protagorean claims we examined in the previous section: that political deliberation can be taught, and that instruction in political deliberation can improve the moral character of the student. Early in the dialogue, Socrates asks Protagoras to define his profession and explain exactly what he can teach to his prospective students, which include the young Hippocrates. What will Hippocrates learn should he decide to become one of his students? Were Hippocrates to take up the profession of a painter or a sculptor, everyone would know the nature of the art he was pursuing and the type of skills he was trying to master. What should people expect him to master by studying under Protagoras? Protagoras answers that Hippocrates would excel in the affairs of the state as he learns the art of deliberation. Socrates probes further, demanding a precise definition of Protagoras' profession, the nature of its subject matter, and the special knowledge it requires.

Socrates' strategy from the start is to treat political deliberation as a *techne* (art) similar to painting or sculpture, and, once he establishes this association, to demand a precise statement on the kind of technical know-how political deliberation requires. Thus, when Protagoras gives his lecture on the origin of civilization, Socrates is quick to point out that the kind of deliberation represented in the myth requires no technical expertise. If all citizens are equally given by Zeus the capacity to deliberate, then, how can political deliberation amount to a distinct, technical profession? If everyone knows how to practice it, what is technical about it? A doctor, Socrates argues, has the expert knowledge required to diagnose the symptoms of a disease and prescribe a cure. But when the city is faced with a problematic situation and must follow a remedial course of action, how will those trained in political deliberation know what course of action to prescribe for the city? What will guide them to choose the correct path? Socrates' questions push Protagoras to accept the need for, and superiority of, technical knowledge and the scientific certainty that goes with it. Obviously, Socrates does not accept the sophistic premise that deliberation is a practical art, something between total ignorance and total certainty, something all citizens are capable of in varying degrees.

Nor does Socrates accept Protagoras' assertion that deliberation, grounded as it is on the virtues of justice and respect, can improve the moral character of those deliberating on political matters. In a lengthy section of the dialogue that resembles an interrogation, Socrates presses Protagoras to provide answers to questions pertaining to the virtues he purports to teach. Through the method of dialectic, the posing of precise questions that demand precise answers, Socrates engages Protagoras in a philosophical discussion that exposes contradictions between the answers Protagoras gives and his earlier claims. If Protagoras claims to teach some virtues, does he know how they are related to each other and to the whole? Are justice and respect parts of the virtuous life? If so, are they different from the whole in the same way that a mouth and a nose are parts of the human face yet qualitatively different from it? Or, are they parts only quantitatively but qualitatively identical to the whole—as pieces of gold are parts of a stick of gold but also identical in substance with it? Through these questions, Socrates compels a reluctant Protagoras to admit, first, that particular virtues are identical parts of the idea of virtue, and second, that virtue amounts to one thing only: knowing that which is good and acting according to it. Only when people truly know the nature of the good, Socrates concludes, can they make the right choice in a situation that demands such. Only knowledge of the good can guide people to choose the right course of action.

Having shown that virtue amounts to knowledge of the good, Socrates goes on to demonstrate that unless political deliberations are founded on this knowledge, any action that results from them will be wrong. When people say, Socrates argues, that they "give way to pleasure," they mean that they opt for something pleasurable knowing that it will cause them harm later on. They choose to eat sweet things knowing that they are not good for their health. But this predicament, Socrates notes, demonstrates not a weakness in moral character but a weakness in reasoning. They choose the smaller pleasure (eating something tasty) over the larger pleasure (having good health) because the smaller pleasure is closer at hand. But if people relied on their reason, they would make their claims only after determining what brings the greatest pleasure to them. Reasoning, for Socrates, acts like a pair of scales weighing pleasure with pleasure (or pain against pain, or pleasure against pain) and showing accurately the relative weight of each. This is why, Socrates concludes, people do not err willingly—that is to say, they do not choose knowingly the lesser good.

Socrates offers two hypothetical instances in which choice rests on the knowledge of right standards. If our lives depended on choosing length and avoiding shortness, we would have to discover a *techne* of measurement to keep us from mistaking short for long distances. Such a *techne* would keep us from relying on our senses and making choices on the basis of misleading appearances. Once mastered, this art would eliminate the cause of our errors and save our lives. Similarly, if our lives depended on choosing correctly odd from even, we would have to devise a *techne* that would teach us to discriminate the one from the other and enable us to choose the right one every time. Through these examples, Socrates articulates four requirements for a true *techne:* (1) it must be universal—that is, it must hold true not only with familiar cases but also with new cases; (2) it must be reliable—that is, it must yield the same results every time and in every case; (3) it must be teachable—that is, it must be such that it can be communicated to someone else; and (4) it must have explanatory power—that is, it must give answers to "why so" questions.

By the end of the dialogue, Socrates has shown that in comparison to a true *techne,* Protagoras' view of political deliberation is too unsystematic. Socrates concedes that political deliberation is part of common sense and practical reasoning. At the same time, he insists that the Protagorean version of the art of deliberation fails to provide the right guidance to people wishing to make the right decisions. Without a rational standard or a reliable method of measurement, deliberation falls repeatedly in the traps of error and deception. In a word, Protagoras' instruction fails to produce the very results he claims it can. Only knowledge of the good, Socrates insists, can guide people to make ethically correct decisions. Clearly, Socrates has turned all civic problems into moral problems, and all political deliberations into ethical deliberations. At the same time, he has turned the wish for education in political leadership into the need for instruction in philosophy. Thus, what started out as a critique of Protagoras' pedagogy ends as a total rejection of the art of political deliberation and a complete renunciation of the world of politics. The *Protagoras* closes with the implicit hope that the young Hippocrates will abandon his plans to pursue a career in politics and instead dedicate himself to the study of philosophy.

*　　*　　*

Why was Plato so critical of the process of political deliberation? Why did he reject altogether, rather than try to improve, the political process in the Athenian assembly? Why did he oppose so vehemently the notion that politics might be able to offer ways to better the condition of the polis? In answering these questions, we must take into account not only Plato's expressed attitudes but also the historical context within which he lived and taught philosophy.

Plato grew up during the Peloponnesian War and witnessed first-hand the gradual decline of Athens. He saw corrupt and greedy politicians rise to power by manipulating the masses and advocating decisions that advanced their own personal interests at the expense of the city. He saw a city becoming increasingly divided, weakened, and misled. In other words, he saw a glorious city being destroyed from within. During the leadership of the great general and statesman Pericles, Athens had prospered, had expanded her domain, and had enjoyed the respect and admiration of other city-states. Following the death of Pericles, a series of poor military and political decisions weakened gravely the strength of the Athenian empire, squandered the city's surplus wealth, and made Athens vulnerable to Sparta. The loss of the city's prosperity was followed by a scramble in which everyone was out for private gain. Poor citizens cried for war so that they could be employed as rowers by the navy, and politicians rose to positions of leadership by advocating popular military expeditions that led to further disaster. The welfare of the polis as a whole had ceased being the common preoccupation of leaders and citizens alike.

A witness to this state of affairs, Plato saw political rhetoric as a capacity for disguising one's own selfish interests in order to pursue them without detection. In his mind, rhetoric made it possible for politicians incapable of leading to obtain positions of leadership. It helped the ignorant defend eloquently their ignorance and thus appear knowledgeable, the unskilled to present themselves as skillful, and the untrained to convince others of their training. It enabled the greedy to mask their greed under the veil of selfless devotion to the public good, and the power-hungry to hide their personal ambition under the pretext of representing the wishes of the people.

This explains why Plato sets the dramatic date of the *Protagoras* in 433 B.C.E., before the outbreak of the Peloponnesian War. By inviting his readers to imagine a conversation between Socrates and Protagoras at a time when Athens was still at the zenith of its glory, Plato heightens the significance of the drama between the two characters. Had Socrates' view prevailed over Protagoras', had the Athenians really understood Socrates' critique of political deliberation—Plato seems to be saying—some of the ensuing disasters might have been avoided. In this way, Plato makes the fall of Athens appear as the natural consequence of ill-conceived deliberations that took place without true knowledge of the good. Had the Athenians opted for Socrates' way, had they followed his teachings and listened to his advice, history would have unfolded differently. What real plan Socrates' philosophical teachings would have presented to the Athenians the *Protagoras* does not say. Plato had little faith in the collective wisdom of the populace and never saw philosophy as part of the education of the masses. Rather, his hope was for a single leader educated philosophically. The real alternative suggested by the *Protagoras,* therefore, may be the following: had the Athenians seen the first signs of demise in their ethical horizon, had they understood the implications of this demise and the potentially devastating results, they would have known that only a philosopher could have guided them in the right direction and that only a strong leader, a ruler or a king, would have been able to take them down the path illuminated by the philosopher's vision. As Plato puts it elsewhere:

> Unless, said I, either philosophers become kings in our states or those whom we now call our kings and rulers take to the pursuit of philosophy seriously and adequately, and there is a conjunction of these two things, political power and philosophical intelligence . . . there can be no cessation of troubles, dear Glaucon, for our states, nor, I fancy, for the human race either. (*Republic* 473d)

More than offering a critique of Protagoras' view of political deliberation, the *Protagoras* also conveys one of Plato's favorite themes: when a society chooses the path of rhetoric and democracy over the path of philosophy and aristocracy, the result is always tragic.

ISOCRATES

A contemporary of Plato, Isocrates also grew up during the Peloponnesian War, which devastated Athens and reduced the once most glorious and powerful city into just one more Greek city-state. Unlike Plato's tragic outlook, however, Isocrates' viewpoint partook of the general optimism of the times—the widespread feeling during the early part of the fourth century that Athens had entered an era of reconstruction and was already making steady progress in the direction of rebuilding her strength. It is this optimism that informs Isocrates' theory of political deliberation. Sharing with Plato the view that Athens' fall was brought on by irresponsible leaders, greedy politicians, and manipulative orators, Isocrates nevertheless saw that Athens' future depended on sound political decisions and responsible moral choices. His dream was simple: if future leaders were educated in the art of deliberation, if they learned to make sound choices and defend these choices to the public, then Athens could regain its past greatness. The belief that the art of deliberation was essential to the betterment of the polis had its source in Protagoras' theory. But, as we will see, Isocrates brought to the Protagorean vision a pragmatic outlook.

Less interested in theorizing about the relationship between deliberating practices and the social order, Isocrates dedicated his efforts to the more pragmatic task of training students interested in entering the political life of Athens how to deliberate wisely and how to approach tough decisions and difficult choices as wise leaders. Less concerned than Protagoras with the link between deliberation and morality, Isocrates kept his eye on the outcomes of specific rhetorical deliberations and their beneficial or harmful effects on the polis. "I have singled out as the highest kind of oratory," he remarked, "that which deals with the greatest affairs and, while best displaying the ability of those who speak, brings most profit to those who hear" (*Panegyricus* 4–5). Of all forms of oratory, Isocrates regards as the most important that which deals with issues affecting the entire city. At the same time, he posits that good oratory is that which confers to the polis the highest benefits. Accordingly, a proposal in favor of a certain course of action should be judged not on the basis of its eloquence or cleverness but on the basis of its beneficial outcome for the community. At the heart of the Isocratean theory of political deliberation, then, lies the orator's ability to translate the good of the polis into specific action.

Isocrates' pragmatic outlook has little room for Plato's idealism. The philosopher's dream, that knowledge of the good is the only way to ensure correct decisions, has no grip on Isocrates. He, instead, puts his faith in the prospect of educating students to make the best choices possible under the circumstances, and to advance the welfare of the city one step at a time, as each situation presents itself. Plato's dream was out of touch with the world as Isocrates saw it. For Isocrates, the world is ruled by partial knowledge, limited options, and imperfect choices. In this world, the only certainty is that "it is not in the nature of man to attain a science by the possession of which we can know

positively what we should do or what we should say" (*Antidosis* 271).
Given the nature of the human condition, a wise person is not one
who knows (in the philosophical sense of the word) but one "who is
able by his powers of conjecture to arrive generally at the best course"
(271). For Isocrates, the goal of deliberation is not absolute certainty
but wise judgment. Accordingly, the task of the teacher of rhetoric
is the cultivation of his students' judgment. As he puts it in the *Antidosis,* "Men who have been gifted with eloquence by nature and by
fortune, are governed in what they say by chance, and not by any standard of what is best." Yet those trained under him, he goes on, "never
speak without weighing their words, and so are less often in error as to
a course of action" (292). Unlike Plato, Isocrates was preoccupied
with the world of human opinion. As such, he saw training in deliberative rhetoric as aiming to turn opinion and chance into mature
judgment.

   "I know," Isocrates remarks, "that in times when your city deliberates on matters of the greatest import those who are reputed to be
the wisest sometimes miss the expedient course of action, whereas now
and then some chance person from the ranks of men who are deemed
of no account and are regarded with contempt hits upon the right
course and is thought to give the best advice" (*Panathenaicus* 248).
Because political deliberation revolves around considerations of future
outcomes and unforeseen consequences, it is implicated with chance; a
lucky guess can oftentimes outdo the most wisely calculated prediction. The recognition that luck plays an important role in human affairs, however, does not mean that things should be left up to chance.
As we saw with Protagoras' account of the origin of human progress,
people were able to transcend their primitive condition precisely because they did not let chance determine everything for them. Instead,
they turned their efforts against the world of chance: in anticipation of
bad weather they built shelters, in anticipation of danger they came together in numbers, and so on. Just as civilized living requires the im-
position of human intelligence over the world of chance, so does
political deliberation depend on anticipation and foresight in the
struggle against a chaotic existence. For Isocrates, the ability to deliberate cannot eliminate chance altogether, but it can reduce substan-
tially the hold chance has over humans.

   But how can humans impose their will on chance when they dwell
in a world of opinion and uncertainty rather than in a world of knowledge and certitude? How can one person's opinion provide a more reliable prediction about the future than someone else's opinion? How

can one opinion be better than another? These questions are at the core of Isocrates' view of political deliberation, which banks on the possibility of turning opinion into practical wisdom. We can best address these questions by considering the following passage from the *Antidosis,* a work devoted to Isocrates' rhetorical education. In this passage, Isocrates outlines the steps rhetoricians must follow when instructing their students in the art of political deliberation:

> When they have made them familiar and thoroughly conversant with these lessons [about oratory], they set them at exercises, habituate them to work, and require them to combine in practice the particular things which they have learned, in order that they may grasp them more firmly and bring their theories into closer touch with the occasions for applying them—I say "theories," for no system of knowledge can possibly cover these occasions, since in all cases they elude our science. (184)

The first part of this passage presents deliberation in terms of theory and application: students must first learn rhetorical theory and then apply it to individual cases. Of these two steps, the application of theory is the more important. Learning rhetorical theory is relatively easy because it does not require much thinking on the part of the student. Learning how to apply rhetorical theory to individual cases, however, is infinitely more difficult because every individual case has its own unique aspects and idiosyncratic demands. Isocrates reiterates this point elsewhere:

> I hold that to obtain a knowledge of the elements out of which we make and compose all discourses is not so very difficult. . . . But to choose from these elements those which should be employed for each subject, to join them together, to arrange them properly, and also, not to miss what the occasion demands . . . these things, I hold, require much study and are the task of a vigorous and imaginative mind: for this, the student must not only have the requisite aptitude but he must learn the different kinds of discourse and practice himself in their use. (*Against the Sophists* 16–17)

Learning how to apply theory can only come with constant practice.

The second part of the passage from the *Antidosis* explains why the application of theory is difficult. We have already mentioned the gap between theory and its application: the uniqueness of each situation often escapes the theoretical orientation of the one approaching it. Knowledge of theory is not the same thing as knowledge of how to use theory to read a new situation. In Isocrates' words, a theoretical framework cannot tell us how to bring theory "into closer touch" with a given occasion. The number of contingencies that may characterize every occasion is so great that it is impossible to construct a theoretical framework that can account for all eventualities. As Isocrates remarks, "No system of knowledge can possibly cover these occasions, since in all cases they elude our science." The application of theory is difficult, therefore, because it does not constitute a subject matter that we can master. Learning how to apply rhetorical theory to particular situations requires imagination and experience; it is the kind of learning that can be acquired only through practice. The kind of learning Isocrates attaches to the art of political deliberation, then, relies on the ability to make seasoned judgments in those affairs that are ambiguous and, as such, defy what is already known.

The passage from the *Antidosis* offers us a way of understanding Isocrates' claim that his instruction in rhetoric can help students interested in politics turn their opinions into practical wisdom. That people are surrounded by a multitude of opinions does not mean that everyone's opinion is equally valid: some people have the ability to read a certain situation, perceive what is unique about it, and understand its peculiar meaning better than others. This ability can be cultivated. The starting point, for Isocrates, is conventional wisdom. Students interested in political deliberation must first become acquainted with the conventional wisdom of society, the normative beliefs of the community, and the prevailing opinions in the city. Such an acquaintance facilitates judgment in deliberation much like a roadmap facilitates the identification of new paths. It offers the interpreter ways of reading and understanding new situations, and of deciphering the individual case as an example of some general category. In effect, it helps the interpreter say: "This is the type of situation we have here." The first step, in other words, entails the task of replacing personal opinion with educated opinion. Moreover, the political orator must be prepared to recognize the limits of conventional wisdom: some situations do not fit the categories of conventional wisdom. In the face of a truly unique situation, the orator must be prepared to proceed imaginatively rather than cognitively. In such cases, customary knowledge yields to improvisation, and the new situation revises the standards of conventional wisdom.

For Isocrates, then, practical wisdom is the result of an interplay between the ideas gained from conventional wisdom and the perceptions generated by a new situation. Each part shapes the other: conventional wisdom tells us how to read a new situation, and a new situation tells us how to revise the norms of our conventional wisdom.

In the next section, we will examine this same relationship as Aristotle understands it. For now, we turn to the *Panegyricus* to see how Isocrates puts to practice the theory of deliberation he articulates in the *Antidosis*.

Pretending to be addressing a Panhellenic festival and to having Greeks from several city-states as his audience, Isocrates opens the *Panegyricus* by stating directly the course of action he is advocating: "I have come before you to give my counsels on the war against the barbarians and on concord among ourselves" (3). The proposal for a united Hellenic expedition against the Persians was not new. Other orators before him had also expressed the view that the Greek city-states should stop fighting amongst themselves and instead should attack Asia, avail themselves of its riches, and put an end to the threat of a future Persian invasion of Greece. By revisiting an old theme through this imaginary address, Isocrates attempts to show the Athenians what he can do as a rhetorician, and that he can translate familiar themes into specific proposals for collective action:

> For the deeds of the past are, indeed, an inheritance common to us all; but the ability to make proper use of them at the appropriate time, to conceive the right sentiments about them in each instance, and to set them forth in finished phrase, is the peculiar gift of the wise. (9)

The claim that his proposal is the result of practical wisdom makes the *Panegyricus* especially important, for we know that Isocrates used his orations as required texts for his students' instruction. The *Panegyricus* may very well have been the principal text Isocrates used while training politicians-to-be, the textbook on how to deliberate wisely.

The crux of Isocrates' proposal is that Athens, rather than Sparta, should be the leader of the Greek expedition against the Persians. To demonstrate that Athens deserves the position of leadership, Isocrates makes a long detour to the past. The *Panegyricus* is filled with fictional and factual narratives recounting the various roles of leadership Athens had played throughout the passage of time. From the earliest, mythical origins of the city, to the recent actual battles Athenians had fought to defend against the Persian invasion, the narratives of the mythical and historical past make the same point: Athenian leadership in the present is warranted on the basis of its past leadership. In this way, Isocrates demonstrates his ability to read the present situation from the perspective of the past and to perceive the uniqueness of the present situation from the categories of conventional wisdom. The issue of Athenian leadership is an issue about demonstrated ability and resources. But if this is so, the case for Athenian leadership can be made easily, through myth as well as through history. Conventional wisdom dictates that if you have already done something well in the past, you will probably be able to do it again in the future. Yet, as we noted earlier, reading the present from within the accepted categories of conventional wisdom is only one part of deliberation. The other part, we observed, entails the task of reading the present situation in its uniqueness—that is, apart from the familiar or the known.

What is unique about the situation Isocrates faces is the following problem. Advocating in favor of Athenian leadership was likely to be perceived by other Greek city-states as a call for Athenian tyranny. If they accepted Athenian leadership, what would prevent Athens from turning into the ruthless empire it once was? If power was granted to the Athenians, what would prevent them from treating their allies, once again, as subjects to Athens' rule rather than as true friends? The problem facing Isocrates was one of perception. How could he make other city-states perceive Athens as the competent leader it once was but not as the ruthless ruler it eventually became? How could he use the past in order to assert Athens' capacity to lead without also invoking memories of a leadership turned into tyranny? How could he make the case that Athens was at once capable of repeating the past (in terms of leadership) and breaking away from it (in terms of abusing her leadership)?

The prolonged attention Isocrates devotes to Athens' conduct toward her allies following the Persian Wars shows his awareness of the unique problem he is facing. The narratives he recounts not only invoke the authority of past precedent; they also redefine Athens' imperial conduct in the past in ways that would hopefully eradicate all connotations of imperialism and tyranny. Accentuating similarities between Athens and Sparta and minimizing their differences, Isocrates' narrative works to forge unity out of division. Because they face the same foreign enemy, the Athenians and the Spartans are portrayed as eagerly running to the defense of all other city-states; at the same time, they are depicted as competitors for the honor of the Greeks' gratitude. In view of the common threat posed by the Persians, the relationship between Athens and Sparta is redefined from animosity to rivalry and from hostility to competition:

Now while our forefathers and the Lacedaemonians [Spartans] were always emulous of each other, yet during that time their rivalry was for the noblest ends; they did not look upon each other as enemies but as competitors . . . and their rivalry with each other was solely to see which of them should bring [the safety of Greece] about. (85)

The point Isocrates makes is quite clear: even though Athens had mistreated her allies in the past, the threat of a foreign enemy has always made her treat other Greek city-states as true friends by putting her differences with them aside and cooperating with them for the good of Greece. This is an interesting point because it makes the case for the future by means of a narrative about the past. In effect, Isocrates redefines the meaning of "we" and "they" for his audience. "We" no longer means "we Athenians" but "we Greeks"; and "they" no longer means "they the Spartans or other Greeks" but "they the Persians." Thus Isocrates resolves the dilemma he confronts by creating the perception that Athens has been and will continue to be on the side of Greece every time an enemy threatens Greek sovereignty.

This, then, is how Isocrates demonstrates his practical wisdom in the *Panegyricus*. From what we have seen, wise deliberation means using the past to influence the audience's perception of a present situation, and letting the present situation contribute to the reevaluation of the past. Moreover, wise deliberation means using conventional wisdom to interpret the situation at hand, and redefining conventional wisdom by means of the novelty of the present situation. By initiating an interaction between familiar theory and new circumstances, deliberation leads audiences to make the wisest decision possible. Indeed, even though the proposed expedition never took place, Athens continued on the path to reconstruction only insofar as she was able to persuade her allies that she was genuinely interested in forging alliances with them and not repeating her past imperialistic policies. Not long after the *Panegyricus* was published, a new naval league was established among the prominent city-states of Greece under the leadership of Athens.

ARISTOTLE

In his discussion of political rhetoric, Aristotle observes that "political speaking urges us either to do or not to do something" (*Rhetoric* 1358b 8). He further notes that the goal of all political oratory is expediency, which can be established by reference to the usefulness or harmfulness of a proposed course of action. Like his predecessors, Aristotle locates the concerns of political rhetoric in the future and in the effort to offer advice on how things might turn out. Of course, advice cannot be about necessary, inevitable, or accidental things; it can only be about things in our control. As he puts it:

> [Advice] can only be given on matters about which people deliberate; matters, namely, that ultimately depend on ourselves, and which we have it in our power to set going. For we turn a thing over in our mind until we have reached the point of seeing whether we can do it or not. (*Rhetoric* 1359a 27–30)

As in the case of forensic rhetoric, Aristotle's view of political rhetoric includes a lengthy analysis of various factors relevant to the issue of deliberation. These include the meaning of, and arguments for, utility; popular conceptions of happiness and their constituents; views of the idea of the good; and the particular features of four forms of government (democracy, oligarchy, aristocracy, and monarchy). Yet the analysis of all these factors revolves around the process of decision making, or deliberation. As we will see in this section, Aristotle's theory of political deliberation integrates the views of his predecessors in an interesting way. At the same time, it takes their thinking into a new area of investigation, an area in which political and ethical deliberation overlap.

Aristotle agrees with Plato that wise choices and sound decisions require a criterion of judgment. But unlike Plato, who located the criterion in knowledge of the good, Aristotle locates it in the person who embodies prudence, or practical wisdom. As he points out in his *Nicomachean Ethics (EN),* deliberation entails the act of "determining the choice of actions and emotions, consisting essentially in the observance of the mean relative to us, this being determined by principle, that is, as the prudent man would determine it" (1106b36–1107a2).

Aristotle approaches deliberation as a practical matter, a rhetorical enterprise involving human beings trying to decide what to do without having a perfectly reliable guide. "The function of Rhetoric," he points out in the *Rhetoric,* "is to deal with things about which we deliberate, but for which we have no systematic rules" (I. ii. 12). It was this lack of systematic rules that set into motion Plato's search for a universal standard. But according to Aristotle, Plato's standard of the ideal good concerns another world, the world of permanent forms and divine beings. Plato's ideal good, Aristotle points out, is not "any more good because it is eternal, seeing that a white thing that lasts a long time is no whiter than one that lasts only a day" (*EN* 1096b3–4). For Aristotle, when we speak about the good in relation to deliberation, we must speak about what is good for us humans, not about the divine good; for the divine good is the subject of another discourse and another inquiry. In Aristotle's mind, the human good is always tied to human values, and human values are always context-relative. This means that values such as justice and respect cannot be subsumed by the idea of the good itself. Friendship cannot, as Plato wished, be put into the same scale, weighed together, and judged on the basis of a common notion of the good. Each value is different from the rest, and therefore not interchangeable. Depending on the context, each value can be intrinsically good, and pursued for its own sake. To choose one value over another may be troublesome; but to try to avoid troublesome choices by reducing them all to a single standard is to lose sight of what it means to be human.

Even though a practical enterprise, deliberation does seek appropriate standards for making ethical and political choices. And these standards generally come, as we have mentioned, from persons of practical wisdom. According to Aristotle, these kinds of persons approach an issue requiring deliberation by relying on general rules. But because the practical sphere contains so many particularities, people who have practical wisdom guide themselves by a general understanding of particulars. To the extent that a new situation exhibits some general features, it can be understood in terms of an established cognitive or moral conception—say, as an example of efficiency or justice. With regard to the most common topics in political deliberation, Aristotle remarks that "it is not only possible to acquire a general view from individual experience, but in view of advising concerning them it is further necessary to be well informed about what has been discovered" (*Rhetoric* I. iv. 8). Unlike Plato, Aristotle treats individual experiences and discoveries only as guides that help us to identify the recognizable features of every new situation. Given that all the features of a new situation cannot be known, these guides provide us with summary decisions and prevent us from making gross errors. But these guides do not constitute invariable universals. Deliberation concerns itself with the practical grasp of particulars, not the scientific understanding of universals. In Aristotle's words, "Although universal principles have a wider application, those covering a particular part of the field possess a higher degree of truth; because conduct deals with particular facts, and our theories are bound to accord with these" (*EN* 1107a30–33).

Unlike Plato, who would approach a new situation looking for its universal features, Aristotle scrutinizes the new case with an eye to its particular traits, and evaluates it as a prudent person would. People who make every decision on the basis of antecedent rules, Aristotle remarks, are like architects who measure curves with straight rulers (*EN* 1137b30–32). Such decision making shows poor judgment. Good judgment, for Aristotle, adapts itself to what it finds; it is flexible and responsive to the concreteness of the situation it judges. Good judgment respects the fact that the world of practical affairs is characterized by change, indeterminacy, and particularity. The person of practical wisdom is prepared to meet the new with flexibility, with attention to its particularity and responsiveness to its uniqueness. Aristotle compares the situation facing the person of practical wisdom to the situation facing a person in the fields of medicine or navigation. Neither the physician nor the navigator proceeds only on the basis of what they know and regardless of what they encounter in the individual patient or the individual journey. So, too, in deliberation, "the agents themselves have to consider what is suited to the circumstances on each occasion" (*EN* 1104a8–10).

In political and ethical deliberation, then, the particular features of the case at hand have a higher authority than fixed principles. As a result, judgment in deliberation rests not on the understanding of universal principles but on the apprehension of particulars. Particulars are best apprehended through perception, and perception is more appropriate than intelligence when dealing with particular matters: "Prudence then stands opposite to Intelligence; for Intelligence apprehends definitions, which cannot be proved by reasoning, while Prudence deals with the ultimate particular thing, which cannot be apprehended by Scientific Knowledge, but only by perception" (*EN* 1142a24–28). Through perception, then, the person of practical wisdom can respond to the salient features and nuances of a situation in a way and to a degree that abiding principles cannot: "Such questions of degree depend on particular circumstances, and the decision lies with perception" (*EN* 1109b23–24). The emphasis on insights attained through perception explains why Aristotle puts a premium on experience. Experience gradually shapes the ability to grasp accurately the unique features of the particular case. When we refer to people of practical wisdom, we say, Aristotle remarks, that "experience has given them an eye for things, and so they see correctly" (*EN* 1143b12–14). Conversely, people without experience in life cannot understand the practical meaning of particulars and, as a result, cannot be said to possess practical wisdom. As he puts it, "We do not consider that a young man can have Prudence. The reason is that Prudence includes a knowledge of particular facts, and this is derived from experience, which a young man does not possess; for experience is the fruit of years" (*EN* 1142a12–17).

Like Isocrates, Aristotle considers sound deliberation to be the result of the practical wisdom that issues from the understanding of the general rule and the perception of the particular case. People of practical wisdom bring to deliberation not only their knowledge of general principles but also their perceptual abilities and experience. By means of their knowledge of general principles they can read a situation as an example of a general principle; by means of their perceptual abilities and experience they can read the particularities of a situation as elements that exceed or question an antecedent principle. The person of practical wisdom resembles the navigator who, having charted out in advance the best course possible, goes to sea prepared to deviate from the planned course in the face of an unexpected storm.

Aristotle does not only consider the ways in which the general and the particular affect political and ethical deliberation. He also takes into account the impact of the passions on the process of making decisions. Plato had thought that the passions constitute obstacles against sound reasoning and had sought to subordinate them to the intellect. By contrast, Aristotle regards the passions as playing a key motivational role in deliberation and action. For him, the passions guide our actions by informing us of what is and is not desirable and telling us what we should pursue and avoid. For Aristotle, we do not discern intellectually that a situation calls for an emotional response; rather, we allow our emotions to guide our response to it. Because deliberation is a function of one's character, and because character issues from a disposition toward appropriate emotional and intellectual responses to situations, judgment in deliberation issues both from the intellect and the emotions. For Aristotle, character combines intellect and passions in such a way that the intellect informs the passions and the passions drive the intellect. Accordingly, even if it were possible to eliminate the passions from deliberation, it would not be wise.

Aristotle does not restrict the role the passions play in deliberation to motivation but assigns them an intrinsic value. A virtuous choice requires a passionate response: a person cannot choose to be generous, for instance, without enjoying or taking pleasure in generosity. In Aristotle's words:

> [M]en erring on the side of deficiency as regards pleasures, and taking less than a proper amount of enjoyment in them, scarcely occur; such insensibility is not human. Indeed, even the lower animals discriminate in food, and like some kinds and not others; and if there be a creature that finds nothing pleasant, and sees no difference between one thing and another, it must be very far removed from humanity. (*EN* 1119a6–10)

Even the bodily appetites, which Plato relegated to the realm of automatic reflexes, are given here an intrinsic value. Appropriate eating, drinking, and sexual activities are intrinsically good for they fulfill human needs; without these needs and the pleasure in their fulfillment, one would not be human.

Sound deliberation, then, issues from the interplay between the general and the particular case on the one hand, and that between the intellect and the emotions on the other. Exclusive priority of the general over the particular case precludes the possibility of responding to the specificity and richness of political and ethical matters. Likewise, a singular preference for the intellect over the emotions closes off the opportunity to experience the world with the kind of emotional feeling that characterizes our humanity. While making political and ethical choices, the person of practical wisdom relies on the knowledge of antecedent principles and general rules as much as on the perception of the salient features of the particular case, on planning and forethought as much as on surprise and improvisation. Likewise, the person of practical wisdom relies on the power of the intellect as much as on the power of desire, and brings to the new situation both intellectual commitments and emotional attachments, calculation and passion alike.

Clearly, Aristotle's understanding of political and ethical deliberation responds to Plato's view by reiterating Protagoras' claim that deliberation is a practical yet teachable enterprise, and by reinforcing Isocrates' idea that deliberation is a function of practical wisdom. As we have seen, Plato had tried to make deliberation follow the example of scientific inquiry. But as Aristotle warns, such a project, if successful, would take deliberation outside the domain of practical affairs. This is a warning Aristotle issues explicitly in the *Rhetoric* in reference to the arts of rhetoric and dialectic:

> But in proportion as anyone endeavours to make of Dialectic or Rhetoric, not what they are, faculties, but sciences, to that extent he will, without knowing it, destroy their real nature, in thus altering their character, by crossing over into the domain of sciences, whose subjects are certain definite things, not merely words. (I. iv. 6–7)

SUMMARY

In this chapter we have seen how deliberative rhetoric was practiced and understood in classical Greece. We have noted that its emergence and development were functions of the democratic form of government and the institution of the assembly. We have also observed that the practice of rhetoric in the political setting led to the understanding that deliberation operates with limited knowledge and seeks consensus in order to provide responses to urgent situations.

With these stipulations in mind, we have examined four conceptualizations of deliberative rhetoric: the Sophistical, the Platonic, the Isocratean, and the Aristotelian. We have discussed the Sophists' conception as represented by Protagoras. Using three propositions attributed to him, as well as his "Great Speech," we have suggested that he regards deliberation as a practical and teachable skill, a skill encouraged and refined in a political culture committed to democratic politics. In contrast to this conception, we have discussed Plato's critical view of deliberative practices. Relying on his *Protagoras,* we have shown that his conception of political deliberation insists on a standard of certainty, a standard afforded only by knowledge of the good. Our discussion of Isocrates' view has shown that he integrates Protagorean as well as Platonic elements in his theory. Using his *Antidosis* and *Panegyricus,* we have suggested that he grounds his conception of political deliberation on practical wisdom and the pragmatic criterion of political benefit. Finally, we have shown that Aristotle's conception is predicated on the standard of the prudent person. We have observed that prudence is a function of practical experience and sense perception. Moreover, we have suggested that for Aristotle political and ethical deliberation relies on two things: the interaction between the general and the particular, and the interaction between intelligence and the passions.

CHAPTER 3

RHETORIC
AND
DISPLAY

☙

Rhetoric is more than persuasion and deliberation; it is also a matter of display. Whether it encourages action or promotes agreement, rhetoric moves audiences not only through sound arguments and valid reasoning but also through eloquence, the beauty of discourse, the charm of words. Eloquence grants language the appearance of beauty. Elegant phrases turn a piece of discourse into an art object, thereby inviting audiences to experience language aesthetically. As with the logical and pragmatic dimensions of rhetoric, the aesthetic dimension received much attention from classical orators and theorists.

While eloquence is a goal of all rhetoric, it is most pronounced in the epideictic genre, the genre concerned with praising or blaming people, objects, deeds, or ideals. Accordingly, an examination of epideictic rhetoric in the classical period can help us understand how rhetoric's preoccupation with effectiveness steered public discourse in an aesthetic direction. As we examine the Sophistical, Platonic, Isocratean, and Aristotelian orientations in this chapter, we will first consider how each approached and discussed the artistic resources of language. Second, we will observe how each orientation used the art of display to inform its own conception of rhetoric. Third, we will see how each orientation dealt with rhetoric's capacity to move not only by means of logical arguments but also through beautiful images and pleasing sounds. Before turning to these issues, it is important to take a brief look at the way some cultural practices formulated rhetoric's epideictic genre. This look will give us a better sense of the parameters within which each orientation conceptualized rhetoric as an art of linguistic display.

While the forensic and deliberative genres grew out of rhetoric's association with the city's institutions—the court and the assembly, respectively—the epideictic genre developed through its connection to a number of civic occasions and societal functions. In religious and athletic festivals, for example, rhetoric played an official role and served a public purpose. Attached to the cultural traditions and communal customs celebrated in these festivals, rhetoric displayed the ideals of the community and invited audiences to acknowledge and reaffirm the greatness of these ideals. Display, in these instances, meant revealing ideals and values in all their magnificence, laying bare intangible notions that held the community together and propelled it to greatness.

Funeral orations were an integral part of religious festivals. They generally marked the beginning of the ceremonies by commemorating the dead. At the same time, they exalted the community's greatest accomplishments and glorified its commitment to ancestral values. Speakers of funeral orations sought to ease the pain of the survivors by bringing it under the light of the community's traditions, for the sake of which the dead had sacrificed their lives. Speeches in athletic festivals also celebrated the community by displaying the excellence of its grand legacies and core values. These speeches opened the festivities by sanctifying the gods of the city, glorifying the city's customs, and lauding participating athletes. Speakers often connected the physical excellence of the athletes to the spiritual excellence of the community, displaying both in full relief for the pleasure and edification of the spectators.

Sanctioned by the city, the public occasions of religious and athletic festivals provided an institutionalized mechanism that fostered the development of rhetoric as an art of display. Serving its official function of praising the community, epideictic rhetoric evolved into the artistic enterprise of putting on linguistic display great people, deeds, or values. The purpose of speaking about the assumed greatness of the city was to lead its citizens to a deeply felt appreciation of their traditions, legacies, and customs.

In addition to official speeches, epideictic rhetoric included speeches displaying an orator's virtuosity in rhetoric. Beyond athletic contests, many festivals also held competitive events in public speaking, with orators competing for prizes before audiences, which chose the winners. Contests in improvisation, composition, and delivery provided several opportunities for orators to exhibit their art by displaying their impromptu skills, their innovative approaches to traditional themes, or their experimentation with style. Outside the domain of competition, another type of epideictic speeches purported to exhibit an orator's dexterity with language and delight his audience. Of these, the most important showcased the linguistic artistry of a master rhetorician and exhibited his unique pedagogical style and distinct approach to rhetorical education. Throughout the classical period, and especially with the Sophists, some speeches delivered in small public gatherings served as advertisements of a rhetorician's trade. The orator's challenge in these instances was to demonstrate his expertise in rhetoric and thereby interest students to study under him.

Used either to address communal longings or to pursue professional ambitions, rhetoric followed two main paths on its way to becoming an art of display. On the one hand, it tackled the problem of uncovering what lay hidden, of bringing into the open what remained covered and disclosing it to plain view. On the other hand, it confronted the challenge of highlighting some form of excellence, already apparent but overshadowed by mundane preoccupations and daily distractions. Attached either to depth or to surface, the art of display developed along two different aesthetic lines. The one line constituted culture as a set of deep-seated meanings and concealed truths; the other constituted culture as a collection of surfaces, self-evident truths, and manifest meanings.

These two distinct lines figure prominently in all four rhetorical orientations of the classical period. Before looking at each orientation separately, it is important to see how rhetoric was driven by the aesthetics of surface or depth, even as it came in contact with other cultural practices and valuations. The encounter between epideictic rhetoric and Greek culture accentuates in all four orientations the following characteristics of rhetoric: (1) its affinity for competition;

(2) its propensity to become a spectacle; (3) its proclivity to excess and exaggeration; and (4) its susceptibility to the propagation of dominant values.

Competition

Like other human endeavors in Hellas, rhetoric was shaped by the cultural ethic of competition. According to this ethic, the drive for excellence was to be tested through contests, struggles, and battles. While warriors fought for victory, athletes vied for glory, and artists competed for fame, orators engaged in linguistic contests and symbolic battles with a view to triumph over their opponents and rivals. As we have seen, it was the impetus to win that drove the oratory of the courts and the assembly. In these two forums, one speech was pitted against another, and speakers were divided into clear winners and losers. Epideictic oratory was even more susceptible to competition. Orators delivering speeches in funereal or athletic events were competitively selected by city officials, and Athenians attending these civic occasions expected not only to hear ceremonial speeches of display but also to witness some of the best oratorical performances by the city's most prominent speakers. Similarly, unofficial speeches of personal display were not only eloquent demonstrations of rhetorical aptitude or pedagogical expertise, but also competitive gestures vying for prestige, reputation, and a limited pool of prospective students. Displays of communal ideals or individual talent, therefore, were not isolated acts with intrinsic ends but public performances meant to fulfill audience expectations and to receive competitive awards. Whether exhibiting an ideal or a talent, the art of rhetorical display was driven by the pursuit of excellence and shaped by the ethic of competition.

Spectacle

Epideictic rhetoric was also influenced by the culture's fondness of, and delight in, exhibition. Whether in the form of gymnastic games, theatrical performances, or state festivals, spectacles were an important part of everyday life in the Greek culture. This widespread form of cultural activity shaped rhetoric by making public discourse a matter of performance and exhibition. Developed along the lines of a spectacle, epideictic rhetoric helped create the awareness that words do more than call forth the world; they also create and display symbolic worlds of human design and purpose. More than an instrument of communication or a vehicle for meaning, language was also shown to be a form of action performed on stages of its own making for the pleasure of the spectators. Like drama, which provided many opportunities for diversion and entertainment through the representation of human conflicts, epideictic rhetoric sought to please and entertain audiences by representing great deeds, people, and ideals, or by exhibiting a rare talent in public oratory and rhetorical artistry. These representations created virtual experiences that delighted not only by virtue of their content but also by the brilliance of their style and the flamboyance of their delivery. Whether disclosing communal ideals or highlighting personal talents, uncovering hidden meanings or amplifying surface manifestations, rhetorical displays treated audiences to discursive spectacles that exhibited the magnificence of language and the splendor of discourse.

Excess and Exaggeration

As we have noted, epideictic rhetoric does not simply represent the world by reflecting actual events, people, and ideals; its also creates worlds by displaying idealized versions of communal life and exhibiting perfected notions of human coexistence. Indeed, one of the ways in which epideictic rhetoric serves its function is by means of exaggeration and excess. Much like a spotlight that illuminates something and makes it stand out, epideictic rhetoric highlights some features of the world by exaggerating them while minimizing others. Through hyperbolic language, epideictic rhetoric can make the customary appear exceptional and the ordinary extraordinary. In official speeches, the ideals of the community were portrayed as constituting everything good and noble in life and guaranteeing everything sacred and valuable in the community. The dead soldiers were typically depicted as outstanding human beings who had performed deeds of unsurpassed heroism, sacrificing their lives for the preservation and glory of the city. Speeches advertising rhetorical education often made the common appear uncommon and exhibited rhetorical mastery by making insignificant events appear exceptionally significant. Rhetorical ingenuity was thus demonstrated by the orator's ability to endow barely noticeable things with unusual beauty and to infuse the everyday with the greatness of what happens once in a lifetime. The drive toward exaggeration and excess was not hindered by the material limitations of the real. On the contrary, orators found ingenious ways to adorn the monotony of daily reality with the brilliance of fiction and to embellish dry reports of past events with the grandeur of myth.

Dominant Values

Rhetoric reaches audiences by advancing a particular message within the larger framework of beliefs and ideas already in circulation. In other words, it works by tapping into the prevalent system of beliefs and values and by attaching itself to the established ideology of a society. Insofar as epideictic rhetoric concerns itself explicitly with communal values and ideals, it makes an especially interesting case for studying the relation of rhetoric and ideology. True enough, official speeches in athletic and religious festivals, whose institutional purpose was to exalt the ideals of the community, functioned as important carriers of ideology, as discursive practices designed to perpetuate the prevalent system of beliefs and values in classical Athens. In the same spirit, the praise of the dead soldiers, more than an exaltation of heroism and sacrifice, served to legitimize the wars and the imperialistic policies of the city. Finally, the exaltation of the dead as a group rather than as individuals, along with the custom of entombing them side by side regardless of military rank, worked to perpetuate the democratic ideals of Athens by casting it as a city that paid equal tribute to soldiers and generals and gave equal treatment to citizens of ordinary birth and those of aristocratic origin.

Even though epideictic rhetoric functions within a determinate system of values, it recognizes that no system is free of ambiguities or contradictions. Democracy in classical Athens was far from perfect. Its system of values existed side by side with aristocratic notions of self and society despite the fact that aristocratic forms of governance had long lost their popularity. As one might expect, these two contradictory conceptions of being in the world pulled citizens in opposite directions. Rhetoric, seizing on this phenomenon, could side with either set of valuations and advance either more democratic or more aristocratic positions. Thus, the praise of Athenian ideals in Pericles' *Funeral Oration* operates within a democratic framework, whereas Plato's praise of Athenian ideals in the *Menexenus* works from a set of aristocratic values. Similarly, Pericles' oration perpetuates the ideology of imperialism more than Isocrates' *Panegyricus*. These examples demonstrate the complex character of ideology and attest to its capacity to maintain simultaneously competing systems of belief. They also point to epideictic rhetoric's complicated relation to ideology, its ability to weave in and out of opposite systems of thought, and its power to promote dominant as well as alternative values. They finally invite us to examine the ideological function of epideictic rhetoric by analyzing particular cases rather than relying on general claims and assertions.

THE SOPHISTS: PRODICUS

Rhetorical displays by the Sophists often assumed the form of a public lecture, a speech meant to demonstrate the speaker's expertise in rhetoric and to show his unique perspective on rhetorical education. In several of his works, Plato gives us a good sense of what happened when a traveling Sophist came to Athens. The news of a Sophist's arrival was typically met with great anticipation by Athenian intellectuals, who were anxious to meet the famous visitor in person and judge for themselves whether his fame was warranted. A prominent member of the intellectual community usually acted as a host to the visiting Sophist and invited interested people, especially students looking for a teacher, to gather in his house for the formal lecture. The lecture typically addressed a mythical theme and showcased the Sophist's views on language, interpretation, or education. During a question-and-answer session after the lecture, the participants asked the Sophist to clarify, elaborate on, or defend his views. Gorgias, Protagoras, Prodicus, Hippias, and Thrasymachus are all represented by Plato as Sophists who delivered public lectures and displayed their rhetorical virtuosity in order to entertain their audiences and at the same time explain their philosophy of education. In this section, we will examine Prodicus' extant lecture known as *The Choice of Heracles*.

Prodicus' work is a variation of the standard myth of Heracles. When he comes of age, Heracles finds himself at a crossroads where two ways of becoming a man present themselves to him in the form of two women, Vice and Virtue. Prodicus has each woman urge the mythical hero to follow her way of life to happiness. Vice directs Heracles to the path promising carefree living, sensuous pleasures, full satisfaction of bodily appetites, and a life filled with ease, leisure, and unlimited enjoyment of other people's labors. Virtue directs him to the path whose rewards (divine favors, human love, community honors, national admiration, and bodily vigor) require service to the gods, community, country, and friends, hard work, and the subordination of the body to the mind. Unlike the standard story, which recounts events by means of a narrative, Prodicus' version includes a heated exchange between Vice and Virtue. In the exchange, each woman argues for the superiority of her way to happiness as well as the inferiority of the way of her competitor. The story ends with no sign of decision on the part of Heracles. Even so, Prodicus' audiences thought that Heracles decided to follow Virtue's path—to devote himself to a life of hard labors and to earn the reputation of one of Hellas' greatest heroes.

In *The Choice of Heracles,* Prodicus follows a method typical of the Sophists. He uses a myth in order to display expertise in the art of rhetoric and hint at his educational philosophy. However, we cannot be certain what Prodicus himself intended to convey (the story we have was preserved by the historian Xenophon). Even so, we can still make intelligent observations about his thinking by relying on the content of the story, as well as on some information we have from antiquity about the teachings of Prodicus.

To begin with, the story contains all the elements of the standard myth about Heracles at the crossroads. But by having Vice and Virtue speak in their own voices and engage in a debate, Prodicus' rendition puts an emphasis on argument over narration. Part of the story unfolds not through the narrator's voice but through the direct presentation of the two women's arguments, each articulating and defending her own view of happiness and dismissing that of the other. The change from narrative to argument takes the meaning of the story away from the narrator's voice and places it onto the two protagonists. As such, the conclusions audiences reach about Vice and Virtue will be conclusions drawn from what the two protagonists say themselves, not from what the narrator reveals about them. In Prodicus' version, the meaning of the story does not lie hidden behind the events, and as such it does not require the narrator's agency to uncover it for the audience. Rather, the meaning lies on the surface of the story, readily decipherable by the arguments advanced, easily apparent in the very words spoken by the two characters.

Unlike the standard story, Prodicus' rendition ends without a definite conclusion, no hint of a final decision reached by the hero. This feature of open-endedness draws attention away from the process of revealing the truth and places emphasis onto the contest between the two truths displayed. Throughout the exchange between Vice and Virtue, the issue facing the audience is not discerning the truth, or determining who is right and who is wrong; rather, it is deciding whether each side has put forth the most persuasive case it can, and in so doing made itself a viable contender. In this symbolic representation of a contest, the two contenders vie for the audience's approval in the same way that competing orators pursued victory before the audiences of the courtroom or the assembly.

More than a contest, however, Prodicus' story of Heracles is also a display of prevailing values. Had it been told through a narrator's voice and had it ended with a definite conclusion, the story would have simply reflected the closed world of the mythical past, a world in which all action had already been completed, and all value and significance determined. But without a narrator to communicate the truths of past events, without an ending to affirm conclusively the values of past experience, Prodicus' rendition of the myth highlights events and values as they are unfolding in the indeterminate present. Putting part of the story in the form of a debate at the end of which nothing gets settled is a way of representing truths in the process of their formation, a process that is open-ended, inconclusive, and ongoing.

Prodicus' mode of representation resonates with a classical rather than an archaic community, and reflects a democratic rather than an aristocratic society. Through this mode, Prodicus demonstrates his skill of praising the values of Athenian democracy even as he recounts a myth produced during the age of aristocracy. Mirroring the world of classical Athens, Prodicus' story represents a symbolic world in which valuations are not the result of fixed standards already in place, but the outcome of the democratic practices of deliberation and debate. Similarly, Heracles' dilemma announces that the impending decision must be made not by reference to a system of established values but by reference to deliberations about the quality of the arguments advanced and the nature of the positions advocated. In this way, Prodicus' encomium of a mythical hero can be seen as a tribute to democracy's commitment to deliberation and debate, two activities that sustained the vitality of Athenian democratic institutions and values.

The parallels between the mythical story and the contemporary circumstances of the Athenians must have been recognized and appreciated by Prodicus' audiences. For, through the myth of Heracles, Prodicus had found an ingenious way of demonstrating the important role rhetoric plays in people's lives, their collective decisions, and their democratic forms of self-governance. Moreover, Prodicus had discovered a means of displaying his ability to adapt mythical tales to contemporary thought, and showing his capacity to adjust ancient themes to his audience's current preoccupations. Furthermore, Prodicus had found an interesting way of attracting students. Judging from his story, his message to them effectively said: "If you study rhetoric under my instruction, you will learn how to advance your own arguments without neglecting what is already familiar to your audience. You will also learn to employ what your listeners find entertaining as a resource for persuading them. Finally, you will learn to take a standard myth and work it so as to give it contemporary meaning and relevance."

The above comments on Prodicus' lecture are largely supported by ancient commentators. They generally portray Prodicus as an orator of high reputation, a teacher of the art of politics, and a rhetorician notorious for his public displays of eloquence. Ancient sources also depict Prodicus as specializing in fine distinctions of meaning between words commonly regarded as synonyms. In Plato's *Charmides* (163d), Socrates says that he has listened to "innumerable discourses" of Prodicus on the distinction of names. In the *Protagoras* (337a), Plato shows Prodicus to be making distinctions between such synonymous terms as *debate* and *dispute, esteem* and *praise, satisfaction* and *pleasure.* Prodicus' discussion of synonyms was reportedly the most distinctive feature of his lectures, which included the one "On the Correctness of Names." The manner in which he distinguished the meaning of closely related words made a lasting impression on Socrates, who frequently refers to him in Plato's dialogues as his teacher in this skill, his friend or companion. Obviously, Prodicus' insistence on the careful use of words had certain affinities with Socrates' habit of asking his interlocutors to define their terms precisely. Still, while Socrates claims to have learned this skill from Prodicus, it is clear that Prodicus' lessons on linguistic precision aimed at correct speaking and served a rhetorical rather than a philosophical purpose.

Since the lecture on Heracles is not preserved in Prodicus' own words, it is nearly impossible to shed any light on his method of making semantic distinctions between virtually synonymous terms. As preserved, the work offers two sharply contrasting portraits of happiness effectuated through a series of clear oppositions and stark contrasts rather than a set of interconnected meanings and interrelated terms. Judging from *The Choice of Heracles,* it appears that he arranged a cluster of interrelated terms (i.e., satisfaction, pleasure, desire, joy) around a central opposition between two ethical views. But if this is so, the subtle distinctions of meaning emerge from the polar force each term achieves when placed on either side of the opposition. Consider, for instance, the following argument by Vice and Virtue's response to it.

VICE: If you should accept my friendship and follow me, I shall show you the path of greatest enjoyment and ease, and you will not fail to experience every last pleasure, while living quite free from trouble. First of all, you will have no thought for wars or woes, and your only concern will be to decide which delicious food or drink you may look for, what sights and sounds you might enjoy, or what pleasures of smell or touch will please you, what amorous connections will satisfy you most, how you will sleep most contentedly, and—in short—how you will gain all these good things with the least effort.

VIRTUE: Hussy! What good have you to offer? Or what pleasure, you who will do nothing to gain even *that*? You who do not even wait for the urging of desire, before you rush to stuff yourself with enjoyments? You eat before hunger and drink before thirst. You drench your food in sauces to enjoy it the more; you scour the world for expensive wines and ices in the summertime in order to get some pleasure from what you drink. To sleep more comfortably you contrive all manner of luxurious bedding—indeed, you seek sleep not to refresh yourself from labors but just because you have nothing to do.

Both characters employ the same terms (i.e., pleasure, enjoyment, satisfaction) to support different views of happiness. Vice promises effortless pleasure, immediate enjoyment, and instantaneous satisfaction, whereas Virtue challenges the view that anything effortless or instantaneous can be the source of pleasure, enjoyment, or satisfaction. What gives these two views opposite meanings is their differing notions of duration and effort: pleasure, satisfaction, and enjoyment can be either instantaneous or delayed, effortless or the result of labor.

Although, then, we do not know Prodicus' exact method, we can assume that his lecture on Heracles illustrated his view on clear and precise uses of language. Unlike Gorgias' bombastic style, which sought to reflect the ambiguity of language and capture the magical potency of discourse, Prodicus' style seems to have been born out of the effort to confront the ambiguous character of words and to resolve difficulties in their meaning. The uniqueness of his style aside, Prodicus joined Gorgias and the rest of the Sophists in the effort to help shape an awareness about language and a self-consciousness about its use. Far from mere entertaining pieces and self-displays, the Sophists' public lectures on mythical commonplaces became means of casting innovative views on language and rhetoric in the familiar light of the cultural inheritance of myth.

PLATO

Plato objected vehemently to the epideictic practices of rhetoric. He regarded them as exhibitions devoid of any meaningful content, mindless spectacles designed to entertain and please unrefined audiences. For Plato, epideictic orators were paying more attention to the beautiful appearance than to the substantive content of their speeches. In the process, they were doing nothing to develop the aesthetic tastes of their listeners or to cultivate their standards of pleasure and beauty. As a result, audiences were becoming increasingly corrupted: "The lovers of sounds and sights," Plato remarks in the *Republic,* "delight in beautiful tones and colors and shapes and everything that art fashions out of these, but their thought is incapable of apprehending and taking delight in the nature of the beautiful itself" (476b).

Plato's criticism of the orators' efforts to produce beautiful speeches should not be taken as an outright condemnation of epideictic rhetoric. For, even as he spoke against the practices of his contemporaries, he was intrigued by two aspects of the epideictic genre: its educational potential and its aesthetic function. The potential to educate through discourses of praise appealed to Plato's sense of duty as a philosopher committed to his students' moral development. This explains why, despite his exclusion of artists from the ideal state in the *Republic,* he kept two forms of epideictic: hymns to the gods and praises of great men. Further, the potential of the genre to delight through the beauty of discourse appealed to his wish to express his thoughts in the most attractive way possible. Accordingly, in several of his dialogues, especially in the *Symposium,* the argumentative structure of philosophical discourse is frequently punctuated by beautiful speeches. In both cases, Plato exploits epideictic rhetoric as a means of displaying the splendor of the truth and uncovering the correct meaning of ideas. In effect, Plato saw in epideictic rhetoric an instrument that could help him reveal universal principles hidden under the surface of appearances. When properly used, he seems to reason, epideictic discourse can supplement dialectic, whose reliance on the strict rules of logic can appeal only to those few disciples of philosophy endowed with a rigorous mind.

The pedagogical and aesthetic aspects of epideictic rhetoric are fully explored in the *Phaedrus,* a work examining philosophy's relation to the beauty of language as well as philosophy's capacity to employ epideictic discourse for moral education. The possibilities of epideictic for philosophy led Plato to adopt a less critical stance toward rhetoric and to rethink the relationship between philosophy and rhetoric. Accordingly, the *Phaedrus* portrays philosophy as relying on eloquence in order to meet its pedagogical goal, and rhetoric as needing the precision of logical and psychological distinctions in order to persuade audiences of the truth. The dialogue ends on a note of optimism, specifically that rhetoricians like Isocrates will hopefully use their skill of speaking effectively to large audiences in order to spread the message of philosophy.

Much like Prodicus' *The Choices of Heracles,* Plato's *Phaedrus* dramatizes the moment of decision. The young Phaedrus finds himself at a moment in his life when he must choose the future direction of his career and the further development of his character. The choice facing Phaedrus is between two teachers, the sophist Lysias or the philosopher Socrates; between two forms of education, rhetoric or philosophy; and between two pursuits, an active career in Athenian politics or a contemplative one in study and reflection. The magnitude of Phaedrus' choice is dramatized through the speeches of Lysias and Socrates on the nature of love, or *eros*. Phaedrus' decision, therefore, hinges on his ability to choose the better speech. Thus, even though Plato is elsewhere critical of oratorical contests, the way he structures Phaedrus' choice in the *Phaedrus* resembles the form of a contest between two speakers, each displaying his art with eloquence, each trying to outdo the other on the topic of love and thereby win the approval of the audience. The nature of the topic itself reinforces the idea of a contest, for the topic of *eros* was a commonplace that gave orators a chance not only to demonstrate their artistry but also to debate the controversial issue of pederasty, whether the student-teacher relation ought to include sex.

The difference between the contest in the *Phaedrus* and oratorical contests in general lies in the stakes for Phaedrus and, consequently, in the nature of the judgment he must make and the consequences to follow. How Phaedrus answers the question of whether Lysias or Socrates is the better speaker will determine not only the sort of education he will receive but also the kind of life he will live and, consequently, the type of person he will become. The nature of these stakes gives Phaedrus' judgment much greater import than the judgments of spectators at festivals, who must weigh only whether a particular speech is entertaining or pleasurable. By making Phaedrus a judge of speeches, and by investing his judgment with serious consequences, Plato dramatizes the urgency of making accurate distinctions between real teachers and pretenders, true love and false love, genuine praise and affected display.

Representative of a typical self-display, Lysias' speech in the *Phaedrus* addresses the theme of love by taking a new approach, an approach that results in the praise of the nonlover over the lover. Lysias' unusual claim that the nonlover is more praiseworthy than the lover is supported by several clever arguments. The nonlover is a dispassionate person, unaffected by love's burning desire, immune to the fervent whirls of passion. Driven neither by jealousy nor possessiveness, the nonlover treats the beloved more like an associate, eager to promote the beloved's welfare rather than seek to satisfy his own impulses. Unmoved by love's emotion, the nonlover can be trusted to be in control of himself and to act in predictable ways. In truth, the beloved can expect to enjoy the benefits of a disinterested love, most notably the freedom to explore personal advancement and career interests without interference from the nonlover. The totality of Lysias' arguments construes love as a convenient arrangement, a contractual partnership designed to attend to the separate interests and advantages of two people.

Phaedrus is impressed with Lysias' speech. For him, the speech not only demonstrates Lysias' intellectual agility and innovative thinking but also explains why Lysias has earned a prominent place in the Athenian political scene. Phaedrus feels confident that under Lysias' expert rhetorical training and knowledgeable guidance in the political affairs of the city, he will one day launch a successful political career. Prompted by the enthusiastic Phaedrus to match Lysias' oration, Socrates begins delivering a speech praising the evil lover, thereby demonstrating how Lysias' logic can be employed to make a case for a different view of love. The speech favoring the evil lover proceeds in a manner similar to Lysias' oration, and it is equally innovative in the claims it makes, equally clever in the arguments it advances. The stage is set, in other words, for Socrates to demonstrate through his own display that he can beat rhetoricians at their own game. But the speech is cut off abruptly. Socrates explains to Phaedrus that, midway in the speech, he felt a divine sign informing him that he was going about his praise the wrong way and that his comments were debasing Eros, the god of love. Socrates proceeds to recant and then begins a new speech, this time in praise of the noble lover. By means of his premature interruption and sincere recantation, Socrates introduces new considerations in judging speeches, considerations missing in Phaedrus' judgment of Lysias' speech: speakers should be held accountable to what they say, and their words should aim to please not only humans but, more importantly, the gods. The new considerations cast a great deal of doubt on whether rhetoric, with its exclusive attention to beautiful words, clever arguments, and creative designs, can satisfy the requirement of accountability and the demands of divine pleasure. The skills rhetoric teaches may lead to success in politics, but a successful political career may not be valuable after all, especially if it requires that one relinquish one's responsibility to the truth of the subject matter and to the ideal audience of the gods.

Delivered under divine inspiration, Socrates' second speech recounts the nature of the relationship of the lover and the beloved in a way that brings together physical desire and spiritual love. Initially, the lover is shown to be physically attracted to the beloved. But the beauty of the beloved triggers an awakening in the lover's soul, a vivid remembrance of the heavenly beauty he had once witnessed but now can recollect only dimly. The speech explains the lover-beloved relationship in terms of Plato's doctrine of the soul. Proceeding analogically, Plato likens the soul to a charioteer (reason) guiding an earthbound black horse (bodily desire) and a heaven-bound white horse (lofty aspiration). Possessed by *eros,* the soul travels around the heavens following the god most akin to itself until it becomes worthy enough to ascend to the realm of the Forms. There it takes an unmediated look at the perfect ideas of the good, the beautiful, and the true. This analogy accounts for the spiritual attraction the lover feels toward the beloved; at the same time, it depicts the beloved as a catalyst for the lover's recollection. Guided by his recollection of true beauty, the lover involves himself with the beloved in the spirit of true love—that is, attending to the beloved's soul with the utmost care. Socrates' speech ends with a characterization of love as the kind of erotic and spiritual encounter that cultivates the lovers' souls in accordance with the heavenly place from which they originated and to which they will ultimately return.

By means of the beautiful myth of the soul's heavenly journey, Plato demonstrates the central difference between philosophical and rhetorical approaches to epideictic discourse and its educational function. Lysias and Socrates' speeches are shown to exploit the aesthetic resources of epideictic discourse, putting thoughts into beautiful words and directing the splendor of eloquence to an educational end. What divides the two speeches is the question of whether knowledge of the nature of beauty is requisite to the task of educating by means of beautiful discourse. According to Plato, sophistical speeches, like Lysias', attempt to educate through a dispersed display of clever arguments and a diffused array of beautiful words, a disunited spectacle of random eloquence. But dressing up meaningless thoughts with splendid words is hardly an art. Like other dialogues, the *Phaedrus* exposes rhetoric as a knack of manipulating language to influence audiences in an unspecified way; and even though rhetoric occasionally does influence, it has nothing worthwhile to teach.

However, Plato's position that rhetoric cannot claim to be an art unless it founds itself on knowledge of the truth, takes an interesting turn in the *Phaedrus*. Unlike other dialogues, which make it a point to expose rhetoric's inadequacies and criticize its false pretenses, the *Phaedrus* shifts Plato's critical stance in a positive direction. The precise character of this shift is discussed in Chapter 5. Here it suffices to note that the *Phaedrus* goes beyond Plato's philosophical critique of rhetoric by offering Socrates' second speech as an example of a superior form of epideictic rhetoric.

Socrates' second speech takes a first step in the direction of a newly theorized relationship between rhetoric and philosophy. The speech tries to convey a philosophical lesson through the beauty of words. In doing so, it seeks to reach audiences whose souls are open to the truth of ideas and susceptible to the influence of beautiful stories and eloquent language. To these audiences the speech offers a magnificent display of pleasing images and sounds and provides a spectacle of surface beauty that fascinates and intrigues in its own right. More importantly, the speech teaches that the beauty it displays is only an imperfect imitation of the perfect form of beauty, the form that all people once witnessed but have now forgotten. In Socrates' speech, epideictic rhetoric is employed so as to activate in the audience the truth about beauty and love, thereby moving it from the transient world of appearances to the permanent world of ideas.

ISOCRATES

Epideictic rhetoric has a unique place in Isocrates. The praise of people, places, and ideals occurs frequently in his works, but it always takes place within a specific context and as part of a specific end. As used by Isocrates, epideictic rhetoric serves not only an intrinsic, aesthetic purpose but also an extrinsic, political one. The praise of Athens in the *Panegyricus,* for example, is an extended display of the city's values and ideals. At the same time, it is the prelude to a political proposal, a plan to undertake a united Hellenic expedition against the Persians under the leadership of Athens. Thus connected to a political proposal, the linguistic praise of Athens does not simply serve a typically epideictic end—to illuminate the excellence of communal ideals so as to edify the audience. Rather, the praise is an integral part of the proposal. In effect, the *Panegyricus* advances the following propositions: "These are the perennial ideals of Athens. History shows that the Athenians have always upheld them. If the Athenians are granted the leadership of the expedition against the Persians, they can be expected to uphold these ideals once again."

The combination of epideictic and political rhetoric that Isocrates tried to effect modifies both genres. For him, political oratory in the assembly, typically concerned with issues of advocacy and expediency, was incomplete because it did not pay enough attention to the values and ends implicit in a political proposal. To become more complete, political rhetoric had to include considerations of the ideals behind a particular argument and the valuations behind a particular recommendation. Accordingly, the proposal about Athenian leadership in the *Panegyricus,* attached as it is to the display of Athens' excellence, does not limit itself to arguments of expediency but outlines which ideals Athenian leadership would uphold and which values it would maintain. Isocrates also thought that epideictic rhetoric, typically concerned with displays of communal values and cultural ideals, was equally incomplete because it did not translate values into some form of beneficial action. To become more complete, epideictic rhetoric would have to fulfill an important political purpose rather than offer a display for the sake of display. Accordingly, the exaltation of Athenian ideals in the *Panegyricus* illuminates communal valuations not merely in order to delight audiences in the glory of their city but, more importantly, to elucidate the kinds of ends that the proposed action was to serve and the kinds of valuations it was to safeguard.

Isocrates' unique approach to epideictic guided the rhetoric of praise to new aesthetic criteria, beyond the polarity of a surface or depth aesthetics maintained by the Sophists and Plato, respectively. As shown in the *Helen,* Isocrates assigns the art of display neither the task of uncovering the hidden truth, as Plato had done, nor the task of exhibiting truths on the surface of words, as the Sophists had done. For him, the art of display lends itself either to a formalistic aesthetic with a purely internal set of criteria, or to an extraformalistic aesthetic with extrinsic criteria derived from such notions as usefulness of purpose or benefit from consequences. It is on the basis of this divide that Isocrates critiques contemporary practices of epideictic rhetoric in the introduction of his *Helen.* The sophistic uses of epideictic, he remarks, are vacuous exercises in self-display that are neither beneficial to audiences nor challenging to orators: "No one who has chosen to praise bumble-bees and salt and kindred topics has ever been at a loss for words" (12). Likewise, philosophical displays amount to intellectual gymnastics, and philosophers attempting these displays "waste their time in captious disputations that are not only entirely useless, but are sure to make trouble for their disciples" (1). On the other side of the divide are epideictic speeches that address important issues and themes of general concern, speeches that display the orator's ability to deal "with subjects of real worth" (8) and to speak "on subjects recognized as good and noble" (12). The real art of display, then, lies not in the quality of the artistry exhibited by the speaker but in the benefit conferred on the audience.

Following his own criteria, Isocrates sets for himself the challenge of praising Helen in a way that would be meaningful to his contemporaries and beneficial to the Greek community. The practice of praising a mythical person, especially one with as tainted a reputation as Helen, is sophistic in origin, for inherent in such a practice is the orator's boast to make the trivial appear significant and the blameworthy praiseworthy. Isocrates takes the sophistic notion of display as a point of departure and adheres to its logic—namely, that trivial topics can be treated as occasions to exhibit one's rhetorical virtuosity. But he also extends the sophistic notion of display by adding the requirement of significance: it is not enough to treat a trivial topic with artistry and eloquence; one must also treat it so as to benefit the community in which one belongs. Accordingly, his praise of Helen espouses this requirement and adopts the following logic: Helen had a beauty of legendary proportions, a beauty unsurpassed by any mortal woman; her beauty not only attracted many suitors but, more importantly, united the Greeks in a common goal—to launch an expedition against Troy and to bring her back to Greece. Helen's beauty, in other words, must be understood as a symbol of unification; it succeeded in accomplishing what no Greek king had ever accomplished; therefore, the praise of Helen is justified—her beauty inspired the Greeks to unite and pursue a politically useful and economically beneficial goal.

The display of Helen's beauty as a symbol of Greek unification relies on the capacity of epideictic rhetoric to illuminate an ideal and reveal a generally accepted truth. As we have seen in the *Phaedrus,* it is this capacity that Plato exploits when trying to display by means of the myth of the charioteer the nature of true love and true beauty. To a certain extent, Isocrates' approach resembles that of Plato. Isocrates, however, discusses not only the truthfulness of beauty but also its usefulness in advocating a particular course of action. For Isocrates, beauty is not a universal idea but a useful notion that acquires its meaning from the project at hand—that is, the unification of the Greeks. As the following passage indicates, the exaltation of beauty in the *Helen* captures the significance of beauty, not for all times but in the specific context of political unification.

> We may learn how superior beauty is to all other things by observing how we ourselves are affected by each of them severally. For in regard to the other things which we need, we only wish to possess them and our heart's desire is set on nothing further than this; for beautiful things, however, we have an inborn passion whose strength of desire corresponds to the superiority of the thing sought. And while we are jealous of those who excel us in intelligence or in anything else, unless they win us over by daily benefactions and compel us to be fond of them, yet at first sight we become well-disposed toward those who possess beauty, and to these alone as to the gods we do not fail in our homage; on the contrary we submit more willingly to be the slaves of such than to rule all others, and we are more grateful to them when they impose many tasks upon us than to those who demand nothing at all. We revile those who fall under the power of anything other than beauty and call them flatterers, but those who are subservient to beauty we regard as lovers of beauty and lovers of services. (56–57)

This is no praise of a universal good, no inquiry into the essence of beauty regardless of context. Rather it is praise of a specific ideal in the light of a particular situation. Unlike ideals such as courage or justice, beauty could be used to bring about Greek unification. For Isocrates, beauty can act like a good leader: it can unite people under a single purpose, provide an ideal they are willing to serve, and make them put aside their own personal interests for a greater cause. In the absence of a great leader, the ideal of beauty can be a reliable substitute that responds effectively to the demands of unification.

Isocrates' treatment of epideictic rhetoric, then, shifts the terms of the debate between Plato and the Sophists over the function of the epideictic genre. The link between epideictic and competition, fostered by the Sophists, is a link that Isocrates' practice maintains. But the ground of competition shifts as the emphasis now goes to the orator's capacity to use the art of display for the benefit of the larger community. Rhetorical contests are now to be judged not on the basis of formal criteria provided by the art of rhetoric itself, but on the basis of the potential benefit that the orator's use of the art would render to the community. In other words, the competition is no longer over eloquence but over the uses and purposes to which eloquence is put.

Isocrates' treatment of epideictic rhetoric also preserves Plato's link between epideictic and the revelation of the truth. Unlike Plato, however, Isocrates does not adhere to the criteria of philosophical thought. This is so because for him knowledge of the idea of beauty itself is not especially useful. Accordingly, he follows a process by means of which the truth about beauty is disclosed in terms of what it can do. Isocrates reasons that if our knowledge of beauty can guide our conduct, we should submit to beauty in the same way we submit to a leader. In other words, insight on beauty does not amount to a universal notion, something that obtains in every instance. Rather, it amounts to a provisional and situational understanding, an understanding that colors the ideal of beauty with the colors of the particular situation.

In the hands of Isocrates, then, epideictic rhetoric maintains the Sophists and Plato's practices of display even as it employs new criteria for their use and significance. The Isocratean version of epideictic points beyond its own artistic ends to the pressing needs of the community. Accordingly, the praise of Helen ends on a contemporary note and a timely plea. At a time when a united Greek expedition against the Persians seems to be the most beneficial course of action, and at a time when no leader has emerged to unify the Greeks, Isocrates identifies a commanding ideal in the Greek heritage, an ideal that can fulfill the lack of leadership. Specifically, he projects the cultural ideal of beauty onto the political purpose of leadership and the need for unified action. In so doing, he tries to accomplish in his contemporary Athens the same goal Helen's beauty had accomplished in mythical times. Through the praise of Helen, Isocrates' use of epideictic rhetoric suggests a notion of display as an art whose significance lies in its capacity to transcend the artistic demands of its own form and to serve grand political purposes and beneficial forms of action.

It should come as no surprise, then, that some modern commentators have found the *Helen* lacking in formal criteria. According to these commentators, Isocrates' praise of Helen is compromised because he also engages in the praise of other mythical heroes. Why praise Theseus, they ask, in a work purporting to praise Helen? One response is that even if the object of praise shifts, the mode of display Isocrates follows does not. The following passage illustrates the point:

> In the first place, the scattered settlements and villages of which the state was composed he [Theseus] united, and made Athens into a city-state so great that from then even to the present day it is the greatest state of Hellas. . . . And he was so far from doing anything contrary to the will of the citizens that

he made the people masters of the government, and they on their part thought it best that he should rule alone, believing that his sole rule was more to be trusted and more equitable than their own democracy. . . . In consequence, Theseus passed his life beloved of his people and not the object of their plots, not preserving his sovereignty by means of alien military force, but protected, not by virtue of his authority ruling as a king, but by his benefactions as a popular leader. (35–37)

Like the display of Helen's beauty, the display of Theseus' effectiveness unfolds by illuminating simultaneously the ideal of leadership and by exhibiting the benefits it conferred upon the Athenians. As in the case of Helen, so in the case of Theseus Isocrates uses display neither in the way the Sophists had done, in order to exhibit their own virtuosity, nor in the way Plato had done, in order to uncover the essence of a hidden truth. Rather, he uses display aesthetically and pragmatically, both to exhibit the excellence of an ideal and to explain the usefulness of that ideal to the community.

Under Isocrates, then, epideictic rhetoric developed not independently, as a separate genre with its own artistic norms, but in close relation to political oratory. As a result of his efforts to fuse the two genres, he shaped the art of display into an art capable of serving a mixed purpose and a double function. Accordingly, the excellence he displays and the ideals he exhibits continued to observe the aesthetic criteria established by earlier uses of the epideictic genre. At the same time, they also conform to criteria of utility shaped by practitioners of political oratory. In effect, Isocrates argues that praising the virtues of the community and speaking for its welfare are two rhetorical functions that should not be separated.

ARISTOTLE

Aristotle undertakes in the *Rhetoric* to discuss the epideictic genre of rhetoric by abstracting its common features from the various examples available to him. As a result, he necessarily minimizes some of the differences among instances of display and downplays the various directions epideictic had followed as it evolved in practice. His objective in the *Rhetoric* is to describe what all epideictic practices have in common and to distinguish epideictic rhetoric from the other two kinds, the forensic and the deliberative.

Aristotle notes that the subject matter of epideictic rhetoric is praise or blame; its end is the honorable or the disgraceful; and the time appropriate to it is the present. Aristotle also observes that audiences of epideictic rhetoric differ from those of legal and political orations. While forensic and deliberative speeches are given to hearers who act as judges of things past or things to come, epideictic speeches are given to hearers who act as spectators of the speaker's ability to perform. Like the other two kinds, epideictic speeches also solicit the listeners' judgment, since they "are put together with reference to the spectator as if he were a judge" (II. xviii. 1). Thus, even as the content of an epideictic speech may vary, and even as the speaker's praise may be serious, the audience always consists of spectators invited to behold the display before them and to make judgments concerning the speaker's talent for rhetorical exhibition.

For Aristotle, then, what gets displayed through epideictic rhetoric is the ability of the speaker. Through this claim, Aristotle does not agree with the thinking according to which epideictic rhetoric offers a display either of the speaker or of the content of the speech. To him, the two appear indistinguishable or, at the very least, closely interrelated. Thus, even as he claims that the audience of epideictic oratory makes a judgment about the speaker's ability, he devotes more time to discussing the content of epideictic and less to the approach of the speaker. The assumption behind his discussion is that speakers display their ability best when they handle the topic of their praise appropriately. The most appropriate manner of handling praise depends on the way a speech exhibits greatness and nobility, as well as on the way the qualities of excellence are attached to the actions of the person praised. Thus, the challenge for epideictic orators lies in their ability to bring together the general end of epideictic (the honorable or the noble) with the particular case (the praise of the specific individual).

In order to explain how this challenge can be met, Aristotle divides his discussion into two parts. The first describes what is the honorable and the noble (I. ix. 1–31); the second shows how the actions of an individual can be made to appear honorable and noble (I. ix. 32–41). The most interesting feature of the first discussion is Aristotle's conflation of the noble with the virtuous. As he puts it,

> The noble, then, is that which, being desirable in itself, is at the same time worthy of praise, or which, being good, is pleasant because it is good. If this is the noble, then virtue must of necessity be noble, for, being good, it is worthy of praise. (I. ix. 3)

Aristotle goes on to define virtue as "the faculty of providing and preserving good things" and the greatest of virtues as "those which are most useful to others," since virtue is by definition "the faculty of conferring benefits" (I. ix. 4–6). From these definitions it follows that, in order to portray a person as noble, the orator must demonstrate that the person's actions coincide with virtuous conduct. As Aristotle puts it, "Praise is language that sets forth greatness of virtue; hence it is necessary to show that a man's actions are virtuous" (I. ix. 33).

The second part of Aristotle's discussion points out how an orator can best handle a person's actions so that they will appear virtuous. For it is only through self-willed actions that a person may have a justified claim to virtue, and it is only by focusing on actions that an orator can make a person appear virtuous:

> Since praise is founded on actions, and acting according to moral purpose is characteristic of the worthy man, we must endeavor to show that a man is acting in that manner, and it is useful that it should appear that he has done so on several occasions. (I. ix. 32)

The focus of praise, therefore, must be on a person's deeds and achievements, since achievements "in fact, are signs of moral habit" (I. ix. 33). Even if a person has not achieved anything noteworthy, Aristotle goes on, the praise should still be made on the grounds of potential achievements. The orator, in other words, should make the case that the person discussed is on the verge of achieving many virtuous things. By contrast, the orator should avoid praising on the basis of such circumstantial factors as noble birth or virtuous parents. On the other hand, Aristotle advises, a skillful orator can make accidents of good fortune appear to be willful actions and, therefore, signs of virtue. The idea in such a case is to make the accidental appear to be willed.

> For this reason also one must assume that accidents and strokes of good fortune are due to moral purpose; for if a number of similar examples (of acting according to moral purpose) can be adduced, they will be thought to be signs of virtue and moral purpose. (I. ix. 33)

Since praise is always praise of virtuous deeds, anything virtuous due to circumstances or accidents must also be shown to have been a result of purposeful action. Praiseworthy acts, Aristotle underscores, should "appear to be due to the man himself, and not to be the result of chance" (I. ix. 38).

Aristotle's discussion of epideictic in general, and of the speech praising deeds in particular, advances a conception of display that distinguishes him from his predecessors. Unlike Plato, who saw display as the surface manifestation of something deeper, and who assigned display the function of uncovering what remains hidden from ordinary view, Aristotle sees display as a particular manifestation of something self-evident. As we have seen, action for Aristotle is a sign of moral purpose, the manifestation of virtue. In a culture in which most people understand what virtue is, the display of action amounts to an exhibition of the self-evident nature of virtue. Unlike the Sophists, who used display to expose the limits or contradictions of self-evident but competing truths, Aristotle sees display as exhibiting commonly accepted truths. And unlike Isocrates, who used display to link commonly held truths with particular notions of utility, Aristotle acknowledges a link between what is societally accepted and what is politically desirable without prescribing it. He only notes that "[p]raise and counsels have a common aspect; for what you might suggest in councelling becomes encomium by a change in the phrase. . . . Accordingly, if you desire to praise, look what you would suggest; if you desire to suggest, look what you would praise" (I. ix. 36–37).

Unlike his predecessors, then, Aristotle looks to display as an instrument of cultural change. For him, the main problem with display is how to make a particular case fit the general rule, how to construe the actions of the person being praised in accordance with normative conceptions of virtue. We have already seen that in Aristotle's theory of deliberation, particular cases modify the general rule. In encomiastic praise, however, the actions praised reflect, without altering, the community's established standards of excellence. Part of the reason Aristotle treats the art of display conservatively comes from the formal demands of the particular subgenre of epideictic he considers—encomiastic praise. As he sees it, the form of the encomium serves a communal function: bestowing approbation on an individual whose conduct has upheld the standards of excellence set by the community, and whose actions have been motivated by the general welfare rather than by personal interest. This becomes apparent in the list of the praiseworthy qualities that an encomium might include:

> Those things of which the reward is honour are noble; also those which are done for honour rather than money. Also, those desirable things which a man does not do for his own sake; things which are absolutely good, which a man has done for the sake of his country, while neglecting his own interests; things which are naturally good; and not such as are good for the individual, since such things are inspired by selfish motives. (I. ix. 16–17)

Thus conceived, encomiastic praise can only generate a specific type of display, one that exhibits a particular case of excellence as an example of communal excellence.

Aristotle's epideictic orator, then, begins with a set of existing standards of excellence and tries to show how the actions of the individual praised exemplify those standards. And since the actions performed are also a given, the space for finessing the connection is limited primarily to the methods of amplification: the orator magnifies an action to the point where its excellence, extended and amplified, falls within the parameters of the communal understandings of excellence. Aristotle describes the process of amplification in epideictic in the following manner:

> Amplification is most suitable for epideictic speakers, whose subject is actions which are not disputed, so that all that remains to be done is to attribute beauty and importance to them. (I. ix. 40)

Amplification, then, enables the orator to exaggerate great and small things and to accentuate their significance. By amplifying the subject matter, orators can augment the degree of its importance and give it an aura of superiority. In Aristotle's words, "Amplification is with good reason ranked as one of the forms of praise, since it consists in superiority, and superiority is one of the things that are noble" (I. ix. 31).

Clearly, Aristotle's conception of epideictic rhetoric issues from an understanding of display as the process of exhibiting societal standards of excellence through the representation of individual cases that illustrate these standards. Even though this conception appears to echo Plato's view, a close look at Aristotle's description of the form of epideictic shows otherwise. Far from adhering to criteria of internal consistency, the form of encomium Aristotle has in mind is flexible, loose, and episodic. In his words, "Epideictic speeches should be varied with laudatory episodes, after the manner of Isocrates, who is always bringing someone in" (III. xvii. 11). Like Isocrates, Aristotle proposes a formal pattern organized around various laudatory moments scattered strategically throughout the narrative. Such a pattern breaks the narrative logic of the speech and places the emphasis on individual moments of praise. Accordingly, Aristotle argues that "the narrative should not be consecutive, but disjointed," and encourages epideictic speakers "not to narrate all the facts consecutively, because a demonstration of this kind is difficult to remember. From some facts a man may be shown to be courageous, from others wise or just" (III. xiv. 1–2).

The looseness in the form of the encomium is further accentuated by the flexible structure Aristotle proposes for the introduction of encomiastic speeches, or proemium. In fact, the structure he has in mind is so flexible that he compares the proemium to the prelude in flute playing:

> For as flute-players begin by playing whatever they can execute skillfully and attach it to the key-note, so also in epideictic speeches should be the composition of the proemium; the speaker should say at once whatever he likes, give the key-note and then attach the main subject. And all do this, an example being the proemium of the *Helen* of Isocrates; for the eristics and Helen have nothing in common. At the same time, even if the speaker wanders from the point, this is more appropriate than that the speech should be monotonous. (III. xiv. 1)

As with the main body of the speech, then, so with the proemium—there is no single principle of organization, no single logic under which all the parts of the speech must be subordinated.

Conceived in this way, the form of encomiastic praise allows much room for creative design and idiosyncratic expression. With the freedom to wander from the main path and digress from the central point of the speech, epideictic speakers have many choices of how to introduce a laudatory episode, and of how to prepare the audience to receive particular moments of praise. Thus, even as epideictic speakers may be constrained by cultural conceptions of excellence, the path to excellence they follow remains, according to Aristotle, a path of their own making.

SUMMARY

In this chapter we have examined the ways in which epideictic rhetoric developed in the context of the classical Greek culture. We have traced its development to its connection to civic occasions and societal functions such as religious and athletic festivals. We have also seen that it grew out of such cultural practices as competition, exhibition, exaggeration, and the perpetuation of dominant values. Finally, we have observed that epideictic rhetoric was preoccupied with the aesthetic dimension of language and the ways in which this dimension can entertain, delight, and edify audiences.

With this background in mind, we have explored the conceptions of epideictic rhetoric advanced by the Sophists, Plato, Isocrates, and Aristotle. We have noted that the Sophists' conception was shaped by an aesthetics that focuses on the appearance of words and treats language as a surface phenomenon. Using Prodicus' *The Choice of Heracles* as a representative sophistical work, we have pointed out that the Sophists often put epideictic rhetoric in the form of a public lecture designed to entertain the audience, exhibit the speaker's rhetorical virtuosity, and advertise a particular approach to rhetorical education. In contrast to the sophistical conception, we have shown that Plato's view of epideictic rhetoric is founded on an aesthetics of depth, an aesthetics that treats language as a poor imitation of the truth of ideas. Using the *Phaedrus* as a case study, we have observed that Plato is interested in epideictic rhetoric for its potential in moral education and for the discovery of the hidden principles in the conceptual order of the world. Our discussion of Isocrates has shown that he attempts to combine epideictic with political rhetoric. In so doing, he posits that beautiful discourse in itself is limited because it does not address the issue of utility. As his *Helen* demonstrates, epideictic rhetoric should not confine itself to the praise of culturally accepted values. Rather, it should point to concrete forms of action and should articulate specific benefits for the community. Finally, Aristotle's conception of epideictic rhetoric in his *Rhetoric* constitutes a theoretical statement highlighting the common features of the epideictic genre and differentiating it from the political and the forensic kinds. The distinguishing mark of Aristotle's conception is that the praise of a particular individual's actions should take place within the parameters of the cultural standards of virtue. Accordingly, Aristotle offers a discussion of what constitutes virtue and how a set of actions can be made to appear virtuous.

CHAPTER 4

RHETORIC AND LANGUAGE

Any examination of rhetoric includes a discussion of language as the medium of rhetoric, the instrument of communication, and the prompt to action. Such a discussion typically includes an account of the origin of language, its communicative functions, and its normative uses. Further, it generally contains considerations of its structure and its meaning, as well as its relationship to its users and the things it names. Last, it usually addresses such issues as correct usage, stylistic elegance, and persuasive appeal. These topics, however, are important not in themselves but for the ways in which they can help us refine our own rhetorical practices and understand the rhetorical practices of others. If painters and potters become better artists by learning more about paint and clay, respectively, speakers and writers can only stand to improve their linguistic repertoire by learning more than they already know about language, the ways it is used, the forms in which it may be put, the meanings it can set in motion, and the potential effects it might have. Knowledge of the medium of an art, then, is indispensable to the art at hand. Yet an art is much more than its medium. Accordingly, there can be no rhetoric without language; and even though all language is rhetorical, language and rhetoric are not the same thing. Rhetoric is a greater concern than language.

Greek rhetorical theorists have left us several interesting discussions about language. This chapter takes a look at some of the more central ones and examines their contribution to our understanding of rhetoric. More specifically, this chapter outlines four prominent views on language: the Sophistical, the Platonic, the Isocratean, and the Aristotelian. As we will see, these four views differ from one another significantly. At the same time, they all have at least one thing in common: each constitutes a foundation for a defensible theory of rhetoric. Briefly, the sophistical view treats language as a drug with beneficial or harmful effects on the human mind. The Platonic view considers language both as an imitation of and as an obstacle against the universe of ideas. The Isocratean view portrays language as the building block out of which human civilization is made. And the Aristotelian view regards language as a system of representation of the world in its actual reality.

Greek Culture and Rhetorical Theory

As we have noted in the Introduction, rhetorical theory is at once transhistorical and historically determined. Accordingly, the four views we explicate in this chapter resonate with much contemporary theorizing about language. At the same time, they find a historical grounding and specifically in the Greek culture of the fifth and fourth centuries B.C.E. But whereas their contemporary resonance can be discerned through the study of current theories, their historical determination is best shown by reference to three important realities in the Greek culture of that time.

The fifth and fourth centuries B.C.E. were a time of intense inquiry into all aspects of the world. This was an epoch in which no topic was left unexamined. The search for explanations encompassed natural phenomena, the relationship between humans and gods, the connections between nature and society, the various forms of political organization, the processes of growth and decay, the links between human thought and action, the purposes and methods of education, the meaning of law and human behavior, the differences between life and death, and a host of other issues. The issue of language was, of course, no exception. How explain the fact that people speak? Where did language come from? What is being said when one speaks? Is there a relationship between words and things? If so, what is it? What is the connection between speaking, thought, and action? What makes some ways of speaking more effective than others? What is one called to do when addressing others? These and other related questions were part of a larger mood of unrelenting inquisitiveness, self-confident speculation, adventuresome imagination, and bold intellectual experimentation. At the same time, these questions and their answers reflected sociopolitical anxieties felt by the people of that epoch.

Second, the Greek world of that period was a collection of relatively autonomous small communities geographically dispersed from the Black Sea to the Pillars of Heracles (Straits of Gibraltar). Despite the absence of a single centralized authority, each community felt a strong sense of belongingness to a common Greek culture defined by a more or less homogeneous language, a repertoire of common religious practices (processions, sacrifices), and a set of relatively uniform customs (oracles, ostracism). This is not to downplay differences between these communities. The differences were considerable and manifested themselves most often in war, a common occurrence in the Greek world. The same can be said about life within a given *polis,* community or city-state. Claims to internal uniformity notwithstanding, the unequal relations between the few and the many (the wealthy and the poor, the rulers and the ruled, the cultured elites and the common masses) were often strained to the point of full-fledged civil war. Differences between city-states were most apparent to those who traveled extensively—teachers, merchants, artists, and orators. As for the differences within a city-state, they were felt by all members of the society, especially the lower classes.

Third, one of the most innovative experiments in the Greek world was the implementation of the idea of democracy—rule by the many. Initially and most fully tried in Athens, democracy was adopted in various forms by other city-states as well. It was a political system that transferred authority from the hands of one ruler (tyrant or king) or a small group of men (oligarchy), to all the citizens of a political community. The logic of this transfer was that if all citizens had a stake in the fortunes and future of their city-state, they would be more likely to take an active part in conducting its affairs, thus shaping its character and sustaining its vitality. But how were final decisions to be made in the face of multiple perspectives and disagreements on what course of action is best at any one time on any one issue? Here the hope was that if all citizens were granted the freedom to speak on public matters and compete with their fellow citizens in an open forum, they would arrive at the best decisions. It soon became apparent, however, that majoritarian thought, democracy's principal engine, is seldom the best thought. When democracy began showing signs of decline, the leading intellectuals of the culture started having second thoughts about the capacity of the many to rule themselves effectively.

The Sophists' Theory of Language

The awareness of the tension between sameness and difference on the one hand, and oneness and multiplicity on the other, found itself in the theories of language that emerged out of the Greek experience. Specifically, the sophistical theory, which grounds itself in individual perception and local determination, allows for a multiplicity of languages (and there were several dialects in the Greek world) and, by extension, a variety of different meanings and conceptions of the world. In so doing, it implicitly recognizes the possibility of misunderstandings and conflicts among city-states, classes, or individuals. According to the Sophists, misunderstandings and conflicts can be either negotiated or resolved by means of persuasion.

The Platonic Theory of Language

By contrast, the Platonic theory, which insists on the correct use of language and dismisses conventionally negotiated meanings, allows variations in linguistic use, but only if they do not deviate from the one essential truth of the conceptual nature of things. By positing a one-to-one correspondence between what exists conceptually and what is spoken, Plato's theory supports the notion of a central authority and control in all domains of life—political, social, and cultural. This theory recognizes the existence of differences among city-states, classes, and individuals but explains it in terms of their lack of the truth, which is one. If all could have access to the truth, Plato thought, there would be no differences, no misunderstandings, and no conflicts. In effect, Plato's theory denies the very things that the Sophists encourage and permit. While the Sophists favor multiplicity and accommodate difference, to be resolved by means of rhetorical persuasion, Plato privileges oneness and emphasizes identity on the basis of the oneness of the truth.

The Isocratean Theory of Language

The Isocratean and Aristotelian theories of language offer two compromises to the extreme positions articulated by the Sophists and Plato. The Isocratean theory, which considers language as the element and force required to build human civilization, acknowledges people's capacity to make their world out of language. At the same time, it recognizes that some ways of making worlds are better than others. As such it makes allowances for a multiplicity of perspectives at the political, class, and individual levels; even so, it posits that a given perspective at a given time in history is preferable to all others. Generally favoring unity over diversity and cooperation over conflict, the Isocratean theory of language privileges that discourse which combines eloquent expression with wise judgment. By implication, it privileges that city-state, class, or individual that can offer the rest the most useful and beneficial option. In effect, the Isocratean theory of language deals with the issue of unity and multiplicity by recognizing multiplicity as an intermediate step to unification.

The Aristotelian Theory of Language

Aristotle's theory looks at language as a natural phenomenon, an instrument of knowledge, a prompt to practical action, and a medium of artistic expression. As such it stipulates linguistic differences according to use and purpose. Positing the simultaneous existence of universal ideas and particular cases, Aristotle argues that while universals supply the unchanging structure of things across time, people, and circumstances, particulars provide the variant forms of universals in their actual specificity. In the case of language, this means that while all people use language, the particular ways in which they use it differ from city-state to city-state, from class to class, and from individual to individual. Likewise, all people exist within the confines of government, but the particular form of government they live under (monarchy, oligarchy, democracy) constitutes a specific manifestation of governance. In effect, Aristotle's theory of language addresses the problem of unity and multiplicity by advancing the proposition that any one idea assumes more than one linguistic form when it manifests itself in speech or writing. But if this is so, differences among city-states, classes, or individuals can be resolved by reference to the common idea behind the differences.

THE SOPHISTS:
PROTAGORAS, GORGIAS

The sophistical theory of language posits that much of our language is the result of our perceptual encounters with external reality. Gorgias in particular observes that humans experience their physical environment perceptually, by means of their senses. Subsequently, they transform their perceptual encounters into language. As he puts it in his treatise *On Non-being or On Nature* (85), "*Logos* [language] arises from external things impinging on us, that is, from perceptible things. From encounter with flavor, *logos* is expressed by us about that quality, and from encounter with color, an expression of color." To this statement we can naturally add that from encounter with sound, texture, or odor, language is expressed by us about those qualities respectively. More importantly for rhetoric, we can extend Gorgias' notion to encompass the perception of social phenomena (i.e., communication) and the expression of language about their qualities.

Precisely how or why perceptual content is transformed into language Gorgias does not say—the impression he gives is that it happens automatically. Nor does he say anything about the reverse process (that from encounter with a word our thought is directed back to the specific experience of perceiving a thing). His thesis revolves mainly around the observation that the meeting between the world and humans does not come to an end with the act of perception—there is a sequel to this meeting, and the sequel is language. Before we consider the issue of language, however, a closer look at perception and its objects is in order. In what follows, we combine Gorgias' views with those of another sophist, Protagoras.

For Gorgias and Protagoras, an object in itself and an object perceived are two different things. First, an object in itself is not subject to human perception and, as such, falls outside human awareness—philosophers might debate about its objective existence, but such a debate is largely irrelevant to the everyday life of most people. Second, an object perceived exists only as perceived, only for the one who perceives it, and only at the moment of perception. Moreover, one can perceive an object only partially, not in its factual totality; therefore, any one thing exists only in the light of the perceptual capabilities of its perceivers. Further, one's perceptual experience of something is subjective and therefore not necessarily shared by others. Last, one's perception of the same thing changes as a function of space, time, and conditions. Accordingly, from one location a thing is perceived in one way; from another location in another. Likewise, the same object can now be perceived as one thing and later as another. Similarly, under one set of conditions a thing may appear brilliant or taste sweet, but under another it may appear dull or taste bitter.

The above discussion of perception has important implications for language. Insofar as language emerges from perception, it would seem that language is about, or refers to, perceived things—with the possible exception of the word *nothing,* we have no specific words for things of which we are unaware. Insofar as the perception of a thing is not identical with the thing itself, language would seem to refer to the thing perceived, not the thing itself. And insofar as perception is subjective, it would seem that language refers to the contents of our own private perception, not some universally objective reality equally accessible to all. In all three cases, however, language exceeds its referential function and assumes the status of an independent entity, an entity that "differs from all other substances" (*On Non-being or On Nature,* 86). That this is so becomes apparent when we consider that the act of speaking to one another involves us most directly in the exchange of words—we cannot exchange things in themselves or things as we perceive them. As Gorgias notes, "That by which we reveal [our perceptions] is *logos,* but *logos* is not substances and existing things. Therefore, [when we communicate] we do not reveal existing things to our neighbors, but *logos,* which is something other than substances" (84). Gorgias further notes that words also differ radically from actions, thus stressing again the non-identity between language and everything else. As he points out in *The Defense of Palamedes* (35), it is not "possible for the truth of actions to become free of doubt and clear to hearers." But if this is so, actions done and words about those actions are two different things; or, words spoken simply do not reflect perfectly the actions they purport to describe.

Despite their differences, however, words and things are related to one another. Things provide an external stimulus for words, and words are signs of our perceptual encounters with things. Gorgias does acknowledge that, strictly speaking, things have their own nature, not the one we wish them to have (*Encomium of Helen,* 15). But as we have seen, he also suggests that in their own nature or in the way we perceive them, things stand outside the domain of human meaning and significance. But the moment we name them, we bring them within that domain and begin treating them in relation to ourselves and others. To name something, then, is to disregard its nature as it might be or as we perceive it, and to change it into something else, according to our wishes. In other words, naming is the act through which we alter perceptual reality into linguistic reality. In and through language, then, we generally replace things we perceive with words and, in so doing, establish the sphere of human communication, a sphere in which words are more important than things.

For Gorgias, then, perception is a natural process, a process through which we get access to physical objects. At the same time, perception leads to the artificial process of creating language. And the moment we create language, we move from the province of nature to the province of society. Put differently, the natural world affords us access to physical objects, while the social world affords us access to language. While, then, people's contact with the physical world is mediated through their senses, their contact with the social world is mediated through words. And while the outcome of perception is language, the outcome of language is information and persuasion. The precise workings of persuasion are addressed in Chapter 1. In this chapter, we are concerned more with the link between language and things.

For Gorgias, language points both away from itself and toward itself; in other words, it is both referential and self-referential. In its referential capacity, it refers both to things to which we have perceptual access (i.e., trees, mountains, rivers) and to nonexisting things, things that are fabrications of the imagination (i.e., chariots racing on the sea, monsters, flying men). In the first instance, language is imitative or representational, as its stimulus comes from the outside; in the second, it is creative, as its stimulus comes from within. In its self-referential capacity, language operates with itself as the object of perception. This is another way of saying that we generally use words to refer to other words or to language. As we have seen in the few passages cited above, the referent to Gorgias' discussion of logos is logos itself.

From Gorgias' observations it follows that language works so as to point listeners back to past perceptual and linguistic experiences, or to create in them new virtual experiences. In the first instance, language directs the audience to relive something from its past; in the second, it invites them to experience something new. In the first case, language prompts the audience's memory, whereas in the second it counts on their ability to associate experiences with words, and the reverse. The apparent result in both cases is that listeners respond to language as if it were an object of actual perception. As Gorgias explains in his *Encomium of Helen* (16–18), people's responses to actual perceptions, especially sights, are virtually identical to their responses to words.

Accordingly, people react to frightful or pleasant words the way they do to frightful or pleasant perceptions. In the above two senses, then, language not only refers listeners to their past perceptions but also expands the horizon of their experiences by supplying them with linguistic stimuli.

More than his account of the origin of language, and more than his explanation of the distinction between words and things, Gorgias is concerned with the impact language has on humans. In his *Encomium of Helen,* he extends his discussion of language to include people's susceptibility to logos, especially oral speech. Logos, Gorgias observes, affects people in two ways: psychologically (by means of emotional excitation) and intellectually (by means of artful deception). In the first instance, language can evoke emotions, heighten them, or allay them altogether. In this regard, Gorgias notes that "speech is a powerful lord, which by means of the finest and most invisible body effects the divinest works: it can stop fear and banish grief and create joy and nurture pity" (8). When put in the form of dramatic poetry, Gorgias continues, language can make listeners experience powerful emotions by internalizing the exaggerated feelings exhibited by actors enacting poetical discourse on stage. This is how Gorgias describes this phenomenon: "Fearful shuddering and tearful pity and grievous longing come upon its [poetry's] hearers, and at the actions and physical sufferings of others in good fortunes and in evil fortunes, through the agency of words, the soul is wont to experience a suffering of its own" (9). Last, when language is put in the form of incantation, it affects people much like magic does: mysteriously and irrationally. As Gorgias puts it, "Sacred incantations sung with words are bearers of pleasure and banishers of pain, for, merging with opinion in the soul, the power of incantation is wont to beguile it and persuade it and alter it by witchcraft" (10).

In his attempt to explain the psychological influence of rhetorical prose on audiences, Gorgias relies on the earlier traditions of sacred magic and inspired poetry. In doing so, he attributes to the language of rhetorical prose a power much like the one magic and poetry were thought to have—the power of leading listeners to feel what the speaker wishes them to feel. In this regard, the orator for Gorgias is the direct descendant of the magician and the poet. Speaking words so as to influence audiences—this is what all three figures (magician, poet, orator) have in common. In effect, Gorgias observes that language— be it in the form of rhetorical prose, dramatic poetry, or sacred incantation—can affect humans in powerful ways. So much so, Gorgias thinks, that words can be likened to drugs. As he puts it in the *Encomium of Helen*:

> The effect of speech upon the condition of the soul [mind] is comparable to the power of drugs over the nature of bodies. For just as different drugs dispel different secretions from the body, and some bring an end to disease and others to life, so also in the case of speeches, some distress, others delight, some cause fear, others make the hearers bold, and some drug and bewitch the soul [mind] with a kind of evil persuasion. (14)

When Gorgias likens speech to a drug (*pharmakon*, from which comes the word *pharmacy*), he is attributing to oral language both positive and negative characteristics. Just as a certain drug might cure an illness or kill the patient, so too language might affect its listeners positively or adversely. What the precise effect of a speech might be on a particular audience depends on their emotional makeup as well as their capacity for response. In addition, it depends on the potency of the speech—certain audiences can tolerate only mild words, whereas others can withstand harsher ones. Last, the same speech might affect one audience in one way and a different audience in another. In and through the drug-body and speech-mind analogy, Gorgias succeeds in portraying orators as linguistic physicians who prescribe particular speeches to audiences. At the same time, he succeeds in depicting speech as a mood-altering agent that can either improve or worsen the emotional condition of listeners. Last, Gorgias succeeds in presenting audiences as sensitive beings whose emotional constitution is affected by the kinds of language they are exposed to.

That certain kinds of language can affect people emotionally is an interesting observation but may not seem especially profound. However, the significance of this observation for rhetoric becomes apparent the moment we realize that the kind and intensity of feelings felt by an audience affects its perceptions, judgments, decisions, and ultimately its actions. Accordingly, a political orator favoring the declaration of war would speak so as to arouse in the audience feelings of confidence in themselves and hostility against their enemies. Likewise, a forensic orator (i.e., a prosecutor) wishing to have a defendant convicted of a crime would speak so as to awaken in the jury feelings of horror for the crime, indignation against the defendant, and pity for the victim(s). If, then, one accepts Gorgias' premises (people are capable of feeling emotions; language can evoke particular emotional responses; and people's emotions affect their perceptions, judgments, decisions, and actions), it follows that an orator's linguistic choices are often made in order to arouse in the audience specific feelings, which, in turn, can lead them to the kinds of action the orator deems desirable.

As we noted earlier, speech can influence audiences not only psychologically but also intellectually. Gorgias recognizes the significance of reasoned argument in demonstrating the validity of one's claims. Accordingly, he advances in his *Encomium of Helen* four arguments to support his claim that Helen is not blameworthy for having eloped with Paris to Troy. The particular arguments aside, Gorgias notes that proof in rhetoric generally amounts to some form of deception. As he puts it in his *Encomium of Helen* (11), "All who have and do persuade people of things do so by molding a false argument." At one level, the falsehood of every argument can be explained by people's vulnerability to language as well as the general feebleness of their mental powers. Gorgias observes that most people cannot recall the past accurately, consider the present satisfactorily, or predict the future reliably—all they can do is formulate opinions and maintain beliefs, both of which are functions of rhetorical persuasion. At another level, the same phenomenon can be explained by the fact that most people operate as if words were identical to the things they name. But as we have seen, this is not the case. Deception in rhetoric, then, is possible because people do not have a firm grasp of external reality and because they are under the illusion that there is no difference between words and things. But if this is so, the orator is an artist whose artistry consists of two kinds of linguistic manipulation: substituting a name for a thing, and substituting one word for another. By extension, success in rhetoric is nothing more than having an audience accept the orator's substitutions.

PLATO

Like the Sophists, Plato considers language an important area of inquiry and devotes a great deal of attention to the relationship between names and things. In one of his dialogues, the *Cratylus,* he presents us with two competing theories of language. The first posits that language in general, and the correctness of names in particular, is determined by human convention and requires the agreement of the members of a particular linguistic community. As Hermogenes, one of the characters in the dialogue, says, "There is no name given to anything by nature; all is convention and habit of the users" (384d). The second theory posits that language should reflect the nature of the things it represents. Accordingly, names are correct only to the extent that they succeed in expressing the nature of the things they aim to express. As Cratylus, another character in the dialogue, is said to maintain, each thing has by nature a name, which one must discover and articulate by means of letters and syllables (390e).

Like Gorgias, Plato asserts that things have their own nature apart from human perception and language. But while Gorgias sees the independence of things themselves as a useless notion, Plato makes it the starting and central point of his philosophy of language. Thus he has Socrates declare that things "must be supposed to have their own proper and permanent essence; they are not in relation to us, or influenced by us, fluctuating according to our fancy, but they are independent and maintain their own essence the relation prescribed by nature" (386d–e). For Socrates, the same applies to actions, which can be done either rightly or wrongly, the right way being the natural way. According to this line of thought, neither perception nor language can offer us a reliable understanding of things or actions as they truly are—perception only mediates our access to them, while language only represents them. Therefore, perceptual and linguistic access to things is at best secondary to knowledge of things themselves.

Plato recognizes that people are born into a linguistic environment and are soon introduced to the language spoken by those around them. He also recognizes that a linguistic community cannot sustain itself unless its members agree on common meanings. Even so, he seriously doubts that the language people learn is correct. And he doubts whether conventions about linguistic usage and meaning attend to the way the world is in its essence. People may agree on the use and meaning of a name, but that is no guarantee that the name they use is the right one, the one corresponding to the thing it supposedly names. Accordingly, Plato dismisses the position that stipulates that "he who knows names knows also the things which are expressed by them" (435d) and contends that those who rely on language to learn about the nature of the world do the exact opposite of what they should. For him, the knowledge of things must precede the knowledge of language because it is impossible to know something (the thing) in terms of something else (the name) (438e). Thus he has Socrates say that "the knowledge of things is not to be derived from names. No, they must be studied and investigated in themselves" (439b). This study and investigation, according to Plato's view, promises to yield the correct name for each thing.

Plato's discussion about language in the *Cratylus* identifies three interrelated problems. First, people commonly assume that there is a direct relationship between the names they use and the way things are. On this matter, Plato's position resembles that of Gorgias: "The name is not the same with the thing named" (430a). Plato, however, goes one step further by positing that the name is not simply an utterance totally unrelated to the thing; rather, "the name is an imitation of the thing" (430b). As such, Plato suggests, the original (the thing) is primary, while its imitation (the name) is secondary. Plato also suggests that names are like pictures; both are imitations of the things they represent. The difference is that pictures appeal to the sense of sight whereas names appeal to the sense of hearing (430e–431a). Following this analogy, he defines a name as "vocal imitation of that which the vocal imitator names or imitates" (423b). But if this is so, Plato reasons, some imitations are correct, while others are wrong. Therefore, the basis of assigning names cannot be totally random or arbitrary—arbitrariness exacerbates the disparity between things and names, and leads to the generation of unfitting names, names that do not imitate faithfully the things named. However, all this can be avoided by first studying the nature of things, finding out what they are or do, and assigning them names only afterward and accordingly—in fact, the discovery of what a thing is and does includes the discovery of its natural name. If executed properly, such a program would not eliminate the difference between thing and name; however, it would infuse language with names that truly imitate or reflect the nature of things.

The second problem Plato identifies is that people generally make no distinction between fitting and unfitting names or correct and incorrect ways of speaking. For them, any name is as good as any other as long as the linguistic community to which they belong agrees to use it in specific ways and assign it a range of specific meanings. Similarly, most people believe that one way of speaking is as good as any other so long as it is acceptable to, and effective within, a particular society of speakers. The main focus of this theoretical attitude is language as it is used or can be used, not the nature of things as they are or the proper relationship between language and things. Consequently, the procedure (naming) that goes with this attitude is generally chancy, and its products (names) are typically defective—that is, erroneous. For Plato, however, the way language is used and the way it should be used are vastly different. For him, a name is an instrument by means of which we name something (388a); therefore, the function of a name should be "to express the nature [of the thing]" (396a). From this it follows that there are correct and incorrect ways of speaking. Because actions can be done rightly or wrongly, and because speaking is a kind of action, one should not speak any which way one pleases. When we talk, we should "give information to one another and distinguish things according to their natures" (388b). Put another way, language should tell us what things are and how they differ from one another.

The third problem Plato identifies in his discussion of language is the problem of truth and falsehood. Here he points out that people often use imaginary names as if they had real referents in the world. The trouble with such names, however, is that they can lead one to believe that something is the case when in fact it is not (i.e., "the world is a man who has a running at the nose" 440c). Worse, people call things what they are not. But to give something an unfitting name, to call it by a wrong name, or to say what is not is to speak falsely (429d). Conversely, to give something a fitting name, to call it by the right name, or to say what is in fact is to speak truthfully. Once again, the test of truth or falsehood is not convention—a name can be in circulation within a community of speakers and still be incorrect. Rather, the test is whether a name does express the nature of the thing it names. Accordingly, Plato has Socrates declare: "If I can assign names . . . to objects, the right assignment of them we may call truth, and the wrong assignment of them falsehood" (431a–b).

In the light of the above considerations, Plato asks three important questions. First, if convention and custom are not reliable in producing correct words and fitting names, how is one to rehabilitate language so as to reestablish its proper relationship to the things it names? Second, if most people cannot be trusted to make correct names, who should be the maker of such names? Third, if most people cannot discern the appropriateness or correctness of names, who is to decide this matter? In response to the first question, Plato has Socrates make the case for etymology, the study of the historical evolution of words from their earliest forms. Etymology assumes that many words are derivations of earlier, truer words (in fact, the term *etymology* itself is derived from two Greek terms: *etymos* [true, real] and *logos* [language, word]). Going back and discovering the meaning of the earliest forms of words is important because it can reaffirm the proper connections between word and thing, word and idea, word and action. According to Plato, these connections are forgotten over time as language changes for such reasons as euphony and convenience (414c). Eventually, however, people may come to understand the words themselves but lose sight of the things the words are originally meant to signify. To know the etymology of a word, then, is to know more than conventional use allows; it is to know how a word came to mean what it does today.

Etymology, however, can take us only so far. When we have discovered the earliest form of a word and its meaning, we still have no account of how that earliest form came to be made. Here Plato introduces for the consideration of his readers the onomatopoetic function of language, the function that underlies the process of articulation. Specifically, he posits that letters and syllables, the elements out of which words are made, are forms of gesture performed by the vocal apparatus. At the heart of this theory is the observation that the letters and syllables humans can utter are analogous to the sounds that things in their natural state make. By combining letters and syllables, humans formulate the earliest nouns and verbs, and through combinations of these the whole of a language. The fact that words change over time, or the fact that words for the same thing differ from one language to the next do not negate this explanation. On the contrary, both facts make the case for etymology even stronger. Thus Socrates points out that "whether the syllables of the name are the same or not the same makes no difference, provided the meaning is retained; nor does the addition or subtraction of a letter make any difference so long as the essence of the thing remains in possession of the name and appears in it" (393d). Clearly, the essence of the same thing and its meaning can be carried out by different words. That this is so, according to Plato, can be seen by comparing words to drugs:

> The syllables may be disguised until they appear different to the ignorant person, and he may not recognize them, although they are the same, just as any of us would not recognize the same drugs under different disguises of color and smell, although to the physician, who regards the power of them, they are the same, and he is not put out by the addition. And in like manner the etymologist is not put out by the addition of transposition or subtraction of a letter or two, or indeed by the change of all the letters, for this need not interfere with the meaning. (394b–c)

The usefulness of etymology notwithstanding, the language of contemporary usage still needs to be corrected, and new, fitting names have to be coined to replace current, unfitting ones. This task, according to Plato, cannot be left to just any one person: "Not every man knows how to give a thing a name" (388e, 390e, 391b). Even the poets and the rhetoricians, the two classes usually associated with linguistic expertise and innovation, are not to be trusted—the former invent names for imaginary things, while the latter manipulate names already in circulation. Plato would, instead, have the legislator charged with the task of reforming language. This should be so because the legislator is the one expert who, more than anyone else, knows the essence of things; and as we have seen, the knowledge of things is the most fundamental prerequisite for the creation of a correct language. The legislator, who, for Plato, virtually coincides with the philosopher, is uniquely qualified "to make and give all names with a view to the ideal name"—the name, that is, that inheres in the thing (389d).

Even after the legislator makes the names, there remains the issue of whether any given name has received the right form. For Plato, it is not the maker but the user of names who must make that determination. While, then, the legislator makes names, it is the dialectician who must decide whether the legislator has provided the right names. This is so because the dialectician is the one who knows how to ask the right questions and can answer them well (390b–d). There are two principles operating here. First, names have to be useful. But their usefulness involves a judgment that cannot be left to the maker (the legislator). Second, the maker has to make instruments (words) according to the specifications given by the user. Specifications, in other words, cannot come from the maker. By employing the maker-user (legislator-dialectician) pair, Plato, in effect, places two safeguarding mechanisms in his scheme for the production of language: the user provides the proper specifications, and the maker follows them precisely. In and through the expertise of the dialectician and the legislator, then, language can become, once again, what it was meant to be all along: a means of imitating accurately the reality of the world as it is.

The Platonic view of language has important implications for rhetoric. First, it calls on rhetoricians to be mindful of the ways they speak and the words they use. A rhetoric that would place a premium on speaking correctly and using fitting names would commit itself not to the perpetuation of existing linguistic norms but to the right and proper connection between the nature of things and language as an instrument of imitation. In effect, the Platonic version of rhetoric would strive to strengthen the connection between things and words and, in the process, would give priority to things over words. Second, the Platonic view of language challenges the priority of persuasion as the main goal of rhetoric. Orators who operate from within the theory of convention employ the common language most people already understand because they wish to be understood by them. In doing so, however, these orators do nothing to reform language. By contrast, orators who would adopt Plato's view of language would seek to instruct their listeners on the way the world is. As such, they would be critical of the ways language is used and take it upon themselves to arrest its continual disconnection from the reality of things. In effect, orators inspired by the Platonic view of language would value instruction more than persuasion.

ISOCRATES

Unlike the Sophistical view, which links language to individual perception, or the Platonic view, which presumes a natural connection between things and words, the Isocratean view posits that language is the building block of human civilization. Isocrates focuses neither on the displacing nor on the imitative functions of language. Rather, he concentrates on its constructive potential, on the idea that people can make by means of language what does not already exist in nature. In contrast to the Sophists, he does not discuss language as an independent reality, a reality that displaces the objects of human perception, one that can exercise an enormous power over one's emotions and intellect. And in contrast to Plato, he does not consider language as a vocal imitation whose function should be to reiterate what the world is in its truth. Instead, his focus and starting point is the products of human toil. Working as it were in reverse, so as to explain how the culture of his time had come to be what it was, he arrives at language as the force responsible for everything a culture is. More specifically, he arrives at language as the element that accounts for the existence of social and political institutions, ethical and aesthetical standards, and deliberative and epistemological processes. In short, language for Isocrates explains the fact of all human accomplishments.

A great deal of what Isocrates has to say about language appears in his rhetorical composition *To Nicocles,* a work written for his student Nicocles, the young king of Cyprus. In this work, he asserts that the faculty of speech is inborn. Humans are naturally endowed with the gift of language, a gift that distinguishes them from animals. Comparing humans with animals, Isocrates notes that some animals are superior when it comes to speed, physical strength, and other instinctual resources that animals possess for survival in their natural environment. On the other hand, he points out that humans are superior when it comes to language, which enables them to transcend the life of animals by creating a civilized life for themselves. In this regard, Isocrates states that, with the exception of speech,

> we are in no respect superior to other living creatures; nay, we are inferior to many in swiftness and in strength and in other resources; but because there

has been implanted in us the power to persuade each other and to make clear to each other whatever we desire, not only have we escaped the life of wild beasts, but we have come together and founded cities and made laws and invented arts; and, generally speaking, there is no institution devised by man which the power of speech has not helped us to establish. (5–6)

In this passage, Isocrates assigns language two specific functions: the persuasive and the expressive. In so doing, he resembles but also differs from the Sophists and Plato. Like the Sophists, he recognizes that language has the potential to persuade a person to think and act in certain ways. But instead of limiting persuasive acts to discrete, individual occurrences, he suggests that in and through language people persuade one another continuously, with communal life and concerted action being the primary goals. If, then, the Sophists understand the persuasiveness of language psychologically and individually, Isocrates understands it culturally and collectively. Like Plato, Isocrates acknowledges that speech serves an instrumental, expressive function. But instead of confining this function to the vocal imitation of the nature of things, he points out that people use language in order to express what they want and wish to one another. If, then, Plato employs language to give voice to the essence of things and actions, Isocrates tries to do the same to people's needs and desires.

In the passage quoted above, Isocrates directs our attention to the fact of social forms of togetherness as the most fundamental consequence of human language. Unlike Protagoras, who explains via an elaborate myth the establishment of the earliest human communities (see Chapter 2), Isocrates suggests that if there ever was a prelinguistic form of human existence, it must have been animal-like, either singular and isolated or in the form of small, scattered groups. But civilized life as we know it would simply be inconceivable without language. Precisely how the phenomenon of coming together originally took place Isocrates does not say. Leaving this matter to the imagination, he proceeds to assert that once humans came together they began working to found communities and agreeing to observe rules of their own making. That various cities may differ in the structure of their political organization, that there may be differences among their legal codes, technical achievements, or artistic styles, matters less than the fact of cities, the existence of laws, and the invention of arts. Simply put, civic, legal, technical, and artistic creations are all functions of language. Were it not for language, the societal and political organization of human life would not exist.

Having alluded to language as the necessary means to collective coexistence, Isocrates next refers to all the particular things humans have made in order to render civilized life possible. What tops his list are the legal and moral rules devised to regulate people's social behavior:

> For this [language] it is which has laid down laws concerning things just and unjust, and things base and honorable; and if it were not for these ordinances we should not be able to live with one another. It is by this also that we confute the bad and extol the good. (7)

In this part of his composition, Isocrates implies that it is simply not enough for people to come together. Working against the background of people's competing and conflicting interests, he suggests that unless a society has a strong legal and moral foundation, it cannot survive, let alone thrive. Echoing Protagoras' mythical account of human civilization, he places justice and morality at the center of all societal life. But in contrast to Protagoras, who had treated these two values as gifts from Zeus, Isocrates views law and morality as human creations motivated by necessity. In effect, Isocrates sees language as an instrument of normative ethics, a tool with which people draw lines of demarcation distinguishing between that which is fair and good and that which is unfair and evil. Thus by virtue of their membership in a linguistic community, people are constantly reminded of the community's sense of what is right and what is wrong. By listening to and speaking with one another, they are repeatedly exposed to what they as a society believe that they should or should not do.

Language, for Isocrates, is also a requirement for the kinds of *technai* (technologies, crafts, arts) people devise in order to sustain their lives and make them more enjoyable. These *technai* include the kind necessary for the procurement of food (farming, fishing, hunting) and shelter (building); the promotion and restoration of health (medicine); the defense or expansion of territory (war); as well as the kind needed for the preservation and welfare of the community (statesmanship, commerce, trade). Once a community secures the basic necessities of living, it begins to develop *technai* aiming at pleasure and enjoyment rather than need. These encompass such things as athletics, theatre, sculpture, painting, literature, and poetry. Over time, the accumulation of experience within a culture translates itself into practical and theoretical knowledge that is passed on from generation to generation. All these technologies, Isocrates suggests, are the result of collaboration, which, as we have seen, requires the use of language. As people tell one another what they need and desire, they construct the things and devise the procedures that take care of their collective needs and wishes.

In addition to its legal, moral, and technical functions, language for Isocrates also has a pedagogical one. In and through language people are educated and demonstrate their learning: "Through this [language] we educate the ignorant and appraise the wise; for the power to speak well is taken as the surest index of a sound understanding, and discourse which is true and lawful and just is the outward image of a good and faithful soul" (7). Here language is presented both as a means and a goal of education. At the same time, it is portrayed as the vehicle through which that which is presumably internal to the person (thoughts, sentiments, desires) becomes externalized. Last, it is depicted as a good indicator of one's character. Considering that Isocrates was a teacher of rhetoric, it is not surprising that he should make the refined use of language a goal of education. Nor is it surprising that he should posit a certain correspondence between what manifests itself in a person's language and what supposedly lies hidden within the person. Nor, finally, is it surprising that he should advance a correspondence of personal character and intelligence with the person's words.

Although Isocrates does not explicitly discuss in the above passage the educational function of language, he posits that the two main functions of language (persuasion and expression) constitute the foundation of all education. Persuasion, Isocrates suggests, constitutes the receptive mode of language. Accordingly, to be exposed to language means to learn from others not only words and their meaning, but also ways of thinking, feeling, and wishing. Persuasion, in other words, works so as to shape a person's capacity for ideas, sentiments, and desires in specific ways. Expression, on the other hand, constitutes the expressive mode of language. To express oneself linguistically means to use words so as to tell others that which has already been shaped in oneself. But the expressive mode of language does not complete the cycle of communication once and for all. Because one's language can have impact on one's listeners, one person's expression might become another person's persuasion. In this way, persuasion and expression succeed one another in a constant movement of receptivity and expressivity, a movement whose outcome is the ongoing education of the person. By being persuaded through the expressions of others, and by persuading others through one's own expressions, in short by listening and speaking, people simultaneously acquire and promote mainly a political education, an education on how to be a good citizen within the polis. The evidence of one's goodness as a citizen is, once again, to be found in one's words. Because language reflects one's way of thinking and because language obeys grammatical and syntactical rules, those who use it properly—that is, carefully and precisely—show themselves to be fair-minded, respectful, and faithful. By contrast, those who use it carelessly and imprecisely show themselves to be inconsiderate, confused, and disorderly.

Isocrates continues his discussion of language by noting that language serves people both in their public and private affairs by enabling them to arrive at decisions on collective issues that demand resolution. Moreover, he observes that eloquence and wisdom are the two most prized ideals one can pursue while using language. Finally, he points out that it is language that makes the pursuit of knowledge possible:

> With this faculty [speech] we both contend against others on matters that are open to dispute and seek light for ourselves on things which are unknown; for the same arguments which we use in persuading others when we speak in public, we employ also when we deliberate in our own thoughts; and, while we call eloquent those who are able to speak before a crowd, we regard as sage those who most skillfully debate their problems in their own minds. (8)

In this passage, Isocrates argues that both in its outward and inward operations language works in essentially identical ways. In both cases, it initially appears in the form of two or more opposing arguments. But because self-consistent and noncontradictory action requires that only one argument prevail over all others, the way to the one argument is through competition and debate among all the contending positions. Whether the debate is public or private, the process of argument and counterargument is the same. Once all the positions have been articulated, there begins the process of weighing the available options on the scales of personal or societal values (i.e., benefits, harm, utility, efficiency, prosperity, morality, etc.).

For Isocrates, the fact that differences in the public domain are often resolved by means of language rather than physical violence represents an enormous advancement in human civilization. Still, it is worth noting that at the end of any one debate there will be some winners and some losers as some arguments will have been judged better than others. According to Isocrates, those forms of language are likely to be favored that combine eloquence and wisdom. This is so because eloquent language appeals to the listeners' sense of beauty, and wise judgment appeals to their sense of reason. Clearly, the simple use of language is not sufficient. One has to cultivate the ideal of eloquence not only for aesthetical but also for practical purposes. Likewise, one has to aspire to wisdom by mastering linguistic forms of argument. Eloquent and wise arguments, however, do not resolve all societal and personal issues once and for all in a linear direction. Issues are mostly resolved provisionally and temporarily as resolutions are next put to the tests of action and experience. But regardless of the results of any one issue, public and private life are a constant source of new problems or old problems in a new form seeking workable solutions. In this way, language invites all its users to make and remake arguments, to defend them repeatedly against opposing arguments, and to test and retest them in the sphere of practical experience. Over time, the result of these linguistic practices is a living societal structure, a structure that time and again needs attention in terms of reconsideration, reconstitution, revision, and reform.

Isocrates concludes his discussion of language by restating the centrality of speech in all of human thought and action:

> If there is need to speak in brief summary of this power [the power to speak], we shall find that none of the things which are done with intelligence take place without the help of speech, but that in all our actions as well as in all our thoughts speech is our guide, and is most employed by those who have the most wisdom. (9)

At one level, this is an argument for a cultural approach to the practice and study of language—language should be examined for what it has done and can do, not for what it is and should do. At another level, it is an argument for rhetorical education—rhetorical education matters more than any other kind. In the first case, Isocrates calls for the awareness that people themselves are the makers of the worlds they inhabit, and that their capacity to make what they need and desire is directed by language. In the second case, he suggests that those who have better linguistic skills and can manipulate words in more sophisticated ways are more likely to become the architects of political, institutional, or technical designs for their communities. In and through their rhetorical know-how, they have the potential to articulate the visions and blueprints necessary for what would benefit all.

ARISTOTLE

The Aristotelian view of language represents a synthesis of many Sophistical, Platonic, and Isocratean notions. As such it is more comprehensive than any one of the three views we have considered thus far. At the same time, it has its own unique character as it approaches language in a more analytical and scientific manner than any one of the views preceding it. Like his predecessors, Aristotle acknowledges the profound significance language has for human life. But going beyond them, he first looks at language as a natural phenomenon, and then examines it more closely, this time according to its uses. Aristotle divides all uses of language into three categories: theoretical, practical, and productive. Working with this threefold division, he identifies areas of study that correspond to his three categories: the theoretical includes such areas as philosophy and science; the practical encompasses politics and ethics; and the productive contains rhetoric, literature, and poetry. With this scheme in place, Aristotle sets out to articulate standards by which the uses and purposes of language can be understood and judged. In other words, he attempts to identify what makes language "theoretically significant, practically effective, and poetically beautiful."[1]

To begin with, Aristotle views language as a natural phenomenon with a biological basis in human physiology. As such, he treats the sounds of words and the organs that produce and receive oral language as subjects of scientific investigation. In doing so, Aristotle extends the Sophists' theory of perception by discussing in greater detail each of the senses and their objects. This discussion can be found in his treatise *On Sense and Sensible Objects*. A more specific discussion of hearing and the voice can be found in another one of his treatises, *On the Soul*. By reading a section from this treatise, we can get a glimpse of his scientific approach to the phenomenon of sound as it pertains to human speech and hearing. The process of hearing, he notes, requires something that

> can produce movement in a body of air, which is single and continuous as far as the organ of hearing, and the air is physically one with the organ of hearing. . . . When the air outside is moved, the air inside is moved too. . . . The air itself is incapable of sound, because it is easily dissipated; only when there is something to prevent its dissipation does its movement result in sound. The air in the ears is lodged deep, so as to be unmoved, in order that it may accurately perceive all differences in motion. . . . A test of our hearing or not is the continual ringing in the ear like a horn; for the air in the ear always moves with a special movement of its own; but sound is from an outside source, and not

---

[1]Richard McKeon, "Aristotle's Conception of Language," *Classical Philology* 41 (October 1946), 195.

a property of the ear. . . . Now which makes the sound—the thing struck or the striker? Surely both, but in different senses; for sound is the movement of what can be moved. (420a3–420b5)

Aristotle continues his discussion of speech by turning to the production of sound by the voice. Voice, he says, is

the sound produced by a creature possessing soul; for inanimate things never have a voice; they can only metaphorically be said to give voice, e.g., a flute or a lyre, and all the other inanimate things which have a musical compass, and tune, and modulation. . . . Voice, then, is a sound made by a living animal, and that not with any part indiscriminately. But, since sound only occurs when something strikes something else in a certain medium, and this medium is the air, it is natural that only those things should have voice which admit the air. As air is breathed in Nature makes use of it for two functions: just as she uses the tongue both for taste and for articulation, of which taste is essential to life . . . and articulate speech is an aid to living well; so in the same way she employs breath both to conserve internal heat, as something essential . . . and also for the voice, that life may be of good standard. The organ of respiration is the throat, and the part which this is designed to serve is the lung. . . . Voice consists in the impact of the inspired air upon what is called the windpipe under the agency of the soul. . . . The voice is a sound which means something, and is not merely indicative of air inhaled, as a cough is; in uttering voice the agent uses the respired air to strike the air in the windpipe against the windpipe itself. (420b6–421a6)

Aristotle's discussion of the production of speech finds elaboration in his work *On Things Heard*. There he explains that differences in the qualities of the voice are due to the ways in which the windpipe, the lungs, and the mouth function normally but also to the conditions under which these organs operate. Aristotle couples his observations about the human voice to a parallel discussion of the sounds produced by different musical instruments (flutes, horns). Finally, he spends some time accounting for hard, sharp, rough, weak, shrill, and cracked voices. A central point in this discussion concerns the importance of accurate articulation: "Voices appear clear in proportion to the accuracy of the articulation. For unless there is perfect articulation the voices cannot be clear" (801b1–4).

The specific details of Aristotle's scientific discussion of language aside, it is important to note that he regards articulate speech as an aid to living well, and considers the voice as something that contributes to the quality of human life. Likewise, it is important to underline the primacy Aristotle assigns to hearing. Of all the senses, he claims, "hearing makes the largest contribution to wisdom. For discourse, which is the cause of learning, is so because it is audible; but it is audible not in itself but indirectly, because speech is composed of words, and each word is a rational symbol" (*On Sense and Sensible Objects,* 437a11–14). That Aristotle should hold oral language in such high esteem is understandable given that he lived in a predominately oral culture. At the same time, these judgments suggest that he, like Isocrates, considers speech as an outward manifestation of reason and a means of acquiring knowledge and wisdom, which set humans above animals. As Aristotle puts it in his *Politics:*

> Man alone of the animals possesses speech. The mere voice, it is true, can indicate pain and pleasure, and therefore is possessed by the other animals as well . . . but speech is designed to indicate the advantageous and the harmful, and therefore also the just and the unjust; for it is the special property of man in distinction from the other animals that he alone has perception of good and bad and right and wrong and the other moral qualities. . . . (1253a10–18)

Although a natural phenomenon, language cannot be fully explained by reference to the physical production of speech alone. A fuller explanation demands that one also address such matters as meaning, criteria for specific uses, and the purposes that language serves. When examining the theoretical or scientific uses of language, Aristotle notes that the end in this case is the formulation of principles and proofs regarding the nature of things as they are in actuality. Here language operates as an instrument of knowledge, recording and communicating facts, natural processes, and phenomena in the most accurate and precise way allowed by the nature of the linguistic symbols available. The criteria in the theoretical uses of language are the adequacy with which a subject matter is treated and the truth of the statements made in addressing a subject matter. Accordingly, the purposes of the theorists are instruction in and the understanding of the way things are. To achieve this purpose, the theorist seeks to make language correspond to or reflect the way things are. In his own discussion of the theoretical uses of language, Aristotle resembles Plato by privileging things and ideas over words. However, Aristotle does not go as far as Plato to assert that things have names by nature. On the contrary, he posits that meaning in general is established by convention and habit. In the particular case of theory, meaning is supplied by precise and unambiguous words that serve to define things and offer proofs that things exist, and that they exist in a particular way. The art par excellence in the theoretical uses of language is logic. This becomes apparent in Aristotle's *Prior Analytics, Posterior Analytics,* and *Topics,* three treatises devoted to the art of logic.

Turning to the practical uses of language, Aristotle points out that the end in this category is the formulation of reasoned discourse regarding people's conduct in the context of their sociopolitical relations with one another. Here language operates as a medium of communication designed to influence individual behavior and collective action. The criteria in the practical uses of language are to be found in the effectiveness of a given message and in the appropriateness of the message to the effect intended by the speaker. In the practical uses of language, the purpose of the speaker is persuasion, and the goal is prudential action. To achieve this purpose and reach this goal, the speaker seeks to shape language so as to resolve a communally significant issue, or to articulate possibilities the audience has yet to consider. By virtue of these observations, Aristotle resembles the Sophists, who see language as a force behind action, and who privilege words as they relate to real audiences rather than to abstract ideas. However, he does not go as far as the Sophists in asserting that language is an independent reality whose meaning is derived from the differences among words themselves. On the contrary, he posits that words are connected to thought by virtue of the fact that they represent it. Meaning in the practical uses of language is supplied by people's actions as the outcome of reasoned arguments. The two fields in which practical discourse predominates are politics and ethics. Aristotle wrote two treatises corresponding to these two fields, the *Politics* and the *Nicomachean Ethics*. The art par excellence in the practical uses of language is rhetoric, which Aristotle classifies as a productive art and defines as the ethical branch of politics. Aristotle also wrote the *Rhetoric,* a whole treatise devoted to the art of rhetoric.

When it comes to the productive uses of language, Aristotle claims that the end in this category is the formulation of artistic discourse that imitates human thoughts, personalities, and actions. Here language operates as the material out of which the artist constructs works designed to please the audience. The criteria in the productive uses of language are to be found in the qualities the work of art exhibits. In the productive uses of language, the purposes of the artist are the edification of the audience and the cultivation of its aesthetic sensibilities. To achieve these purposes, the linguistic artist (orator, poet) makes deliberate uses of the aesthetic resources of language (figures and tropes, metaphors, rhythm, rhyme) that make the encounter with linguistic forms of expression a delightful experience. On account of these views, Aristotle resembles Isocrates, who emphasizes the constructive character of language in the making of the products of human culture. However, he does not go as far as Isocrates in claiming that all political institutions and societal arrangements are due to language alone. Rather he posits that communal life is the outcome of the fact that humans are by nature political animals. Meaning in the productive uses of language is supplied by the linguistic innovations the artist puts forth and the ways in which these innovations deviate from the ordinary uses of speech. The art par excellence in the productive uses of language is poetry. Aristotle wrote the *Poetics*, a whole treatise devoted to the art of tragic poetry.

Insofar as all three of the above categories of linguistic use deal with language, they necessarily overlap. Accordingly, the language of a theoretical or scientific treatise might influence the behavior of its readers or exhibit unexpected elegance. Likewise, the words of a speech might articulate a set of political principles or display artistic merit. And the language of a play or a poem might have practical impact on the viewers' conduct or advance "proofs" of the way the world is. Aristotle, however, insists that, strictly speaking, different purposes call for different uses of language; and conversely, particular uses are informed by specific purposes. Therefore, one should expect to discern differences in the language of the logician, the orator, and the poet. This expectation, however, is not always met. That this is so is most evident in the discourse of the orator, whose language often brings together the forms of reasoning (arguments) of the logician and the stylistic devices of the poet in order to affect practical affairs. In fact, Aristotle himself devotes nine chapters of his *Rhetoric* to the discussion of arguments and twelve chapters to the discussion of style.

In his analysis of rhetorical reasoning, Aristotle points out that the proper function of arguments is to provide conclusive proofs. Proofs in rhetoric are important because they contribute to persuasion, a primary goal of rhetoric. As Aristotle puts it, "We are most fully persuaded when we consider a thing to have been proved" (1355a5–6). But the way the orator proves a case differs from that of the logician; while the logician employs the syllogism or induction, the orator uses the enthymeme or the example. The difference between the logical and rhetorical modes of proof lies in the formality of the propositions they use and the strictness of the procedures they follow. The syllogism uses true and valid statements that lead to necessary conclusions, whereas the enthymeme relies on generally held notions that lead to probable conclusions. Further, the syllogism consists of three interrelated propositions: a major premise, a minor premise, and a necessary conclusion. The enthymeme, on the other hand, is usually missing one or two of its propositions, which is/are supplied by the audience. The typical model of the syllogism comes in this form: All men are mortal (major premise); Socrates is a man (minor premise); therefore, Socrates is mortal (necessary conclusion). An example of an enthymeme would come in the following form: All politicians are crooks (a popular notion, serving as a major premise); John Smith is a politician (minor premise); therefore, John Smith is a crook (a likely conclusion).

The second form of rhetorical proof comes from the use of the example. The main difference between an enthymeme and an example is that the enthymeme proceeds deductively (from the general to the specific), whereas the example proceeds inductively (from the specific to the general). Examples are persuasive because they illustrate and support arguments and because they resonate with the experience of popular audiences. In addition to his discussion of the enthymeme and the example, Aristotle identifies four lines of general argument and twenty-eight lines of special argument used in rhetoric. The details of each line of argument aside, Aristotle's point is that rhetorical discourse has both a formal and a material aspect. The formal is furnished by the types of argument and the material by words (1359b16).

The same observation obtains in the case of style, except here the formal aspect of discourse is provided by stylistic devices. Aristotle notes that beyond the issue of argument, the orator must be concerned with how to set the facts of the case in words and how to deliver them in person. His rationale is that "it is not enough to know *what* we ought to say; we must also say it *as* we ought; much help is thus afforded toward producing the right impression of speech" (1403b16–17). Even though Aristotle generally prefers arguing and proving a case on the basis of relevant facts alone, he acknowledges that the manner of delivery is necessary: "We cannot do without it" (1404a2) because "the way in which a thing is said does affect its intelligibility" (1404a10). In the context of this discussion, Aristotle notes that when it comes to the subject of delivery rhetoric and poetry are similar: "It is plain that delivery has just as much to do with rhetoric as with poetry" (1403b24). He further observes that while delivery is a matter of managing one's voice, style is a matter of good diction.

According to Aristotle, the two chief qualities of good style in rhetoric are clarity and appropriateness. Clarity can be secured by the use of current, ordinary words, which convey a plain meaning. On the other hand, appropriateness is achieved by using a balanced combination of everyday language and uncommon terms, which give speech an unfamiliar air. This should be so, Aristotle claims, because "people like what strikes them and are struck by what is out of the way (extraordinary)" (1404b12). Even though style varies according to subject matter, occasion, and purpose, in all cases the orator should strive to speak naturally, not artificially: "Naturalness is persuasive, artificiality the contrary" (1404b19). In addition to these general stylistic qualities, Aristotle brings into his discussion some of the ways in which a speech can be impressive, vivid, dignified, memorable, and in good taste. He discusses such stylistic devices as metaphor, antithesis, simile, and so forth. Of these, metaphor receives the most attention. Aristotle defines a metaphor as the giving of a thing a name that belongs to something else (*Poetics,* 1457b6) and claims that metaphors render the style of an oration clear, charming, and distinguished (*Rhetoric,* 1405a7–8). Finally, he counsels that the materials of a metaphor must be beautiful to the ear (by virtue of their sound), to the understanding (by virtue of their meaning), to the eye (by virtue of the things they depict), or to some other physical sense (1405b18).

SUMMARY

In this chapter we have seen that the Sophists treat language as the medium of rhetoric, the medium the orator manipulates artistically for the purpose of creating specific impressions on the minds of the audience and evoking particular reactions from them. According to this view, language is largely the result of people's perceptual experiences of external reality. While external reality is what it is, perception mediates human access to it, and language names it and makes it meaningful. The most important feature of language for rhetoric is its impact on people. People are influenced emotionally and intellectually by words. Rhetorical influence is largely the result of the artistry of linguistic substitutions. The orator exploits people's capacity for emotional feeling, their susceptibility to language, their uncertainty about the nature of the world, and their illusion that language coincides with the things it names.

We have also seen in this chapter that Plato's view of language finds expression along the lines of two theoretical perspectives: the conventional and the natural. The conventional posits that language is the collective creation of a linguistic community, which assigns names to things arbitrarily and maintains their use and meaning on the basis of custom and habit. The natural posits that because names inhere in things naturally, they should be assigned consciously by those who know the nature of things as they truly are. According to Plato, language consists of vocal gestures meant to imitate the essence of things. The purpose of language should be to capture the nature of things in the elemental sounds of letters and syllables, and to instruct about the differences among things. Because language changes over time, the original connection between thing and word weakens. Etymology is helpful in recovering that connection. Beyond etymology, those who know things as they are should strive to rehabilitate language and instruct others how to use it correctly.

Isocrates' view of language posits that language constitutes the element and force responsible for human civilization and all cultural accomplishments. By using their inborn capacity for speech, humans bring about social forms of togetherness and concerted forms of action. Language serves an instrumental function. Through it people not only persuade and inform one another of their needs and wishes; they also make what is necessary for and desirable to their collective lives. Among the things language helps create, the most important are moral sensibilities, technical expertise, and political education. Although acquired and practiced naturally, language must be cultivated. Eloquence and wisdom are the two ideals worth pursuing and combining in the public and personal spheres of one's life.

Finally, Aristotle's view of language is organized along four different lines. First, it treats language as a natural phenomenon and then examines it on the basis of its three general uses: theoretical or scientific, practical, and productive. In its theoretical uses, language serves as an instrument of knowledge; in its practical uses it acts as a means of communication and a prompt to action; and in its productive uses it functions as a form of artistic expression. Each use is distinguished from the rest on the basis of its subject matter, ends, criteria, sources of meaning, and intended purposes. Although Aristotle discriminates between three different language arts (logic, rhetoric, and poetry), rhetoric combines elements of logic (found in types of argument and modes of proof) with elements of poetry (found in stylistic devices). In and through this combination, rhetorical prose mobilizes truth and beauty in the interest of effectiveness in the domain of practical affairs.

CHAPTER 5

RHETORIC AND KNOWLEDGE

❧

Traditionally, the idea of knowledge has been one of the central concerns of philosophy. During the fifth and fourth centuries B.C.E., however, philosophy did not differ much from other disciplines, and its concern with knowledge was shared by other areas of thought, especially rhetoric. Ever since then, knowledge and its relation to rhetorical persuasion have preoccupied not only philosophers but also rhetorical theorists. Today, many examinations of rhetoric include discussions of knowledge as the basis of informed choice, the foundation of rational deliberation, and the guide to intelligent action. Generally, these discussions cover such topics as the production of knowledge, its transmission, and its uses. At the same time, they include such issues as the authority, the meaning, and the impact of knowledge.

This chapter examines four theoretical positions on knowledge and points out their implications for rhetoric, how each colors our understanding of the art of persuasion. Briefly, the sophistical position posits that knowledge is a human creation whose elements are furnished by the contents of our perception and the possibilities of our language. The Platonic position equates knowledge with the mental discovery of the conceptual order of the universe. The Isocratean position considers knowledge as a function of insight into the historical past and the enduring legacies of a culture. And the Aristotelian position views knowledge as the result of the interaction between an intelligent animal (the human being) and an intelligible world (the "real" world). As we will see, each position is more or less different from the rest. At the same time, they all share one thing in common: all four seek to provide an orientation to the world and situate rhetoric within it.

In the last chapter, we characterized the Greek culture of the fifth and fourth centuries B.C.E. by reference to three defining realities: first, intense intellectual inquiry into all aspects of nature and society; second, keen interest in the problem of commonalities and differences among a collection of autonomous communities; and third, serious concern over the issue of oneness and multiplicity in the context of the political experiment of democratic governance. We also suggested that these realities are reflected in the theories of language articulated in that period. In this chapter, we are making the same case with the theories of knowledge formulated in that epoch.

The intellectuals of ancient Greece posed many questions regarding knowledge. Is knowledge possible? What does it mean to know something? Are all things knowable? How do human beings come to know? Are all people capable of knowing? Are some better at knowing than others? How does the mind apprehend external reality? Do the senses play a significant role in its apprehension? What are the sources of knowledge? How is knowledge generated? What forms does it take? Are there proper methods of acquiring and using knowledge? How are they determined? How is knowledge tested and validated? Who authorizes knowledge in a society? What are the essential characteristics of knowledge? Is knowledge determined by the object of study at hand? What accounts for error? These and similar questions intrigued many a thinker of the period we are considering and led to a variety of answers. Many of these questions are still being asked, and many of the answers proposed by the thinkers of Greek antiquity are seriously entertained by contemporary thinkers.

The Sophists' Theory of Knowledge

By construing the act of knowing as a creative act, the Sophists emphasize differences and downplay sameness. In doing so, they tacitly acknowledge distinctions between cities, classes, or individuals and attribute them to circumstantial factors. Explained in terms of such variables as tradition, chance, and specific needs or capacities, circumstantial factors determine the collective knowledge of a city-state or class as well as the individual knowledge of a person. According to this way of thinking, a particular city-state might know a great deal about tyranny and nothing about democracy; by contrast, another city-state might know the exact opposite. Likewise, a particular class might know much about luxury and nothing about necessity while another might know the reverse. In the same spirit, one individual could be said to know more about medicine, another more about music, and still another more about sculpture. In effect, the Sophists' theory of knowledge is relativistic—what and how people know depends on many factors. As such, it gives primacy to personal and local knowledge and dismisses the claim that something might be known universally and for all time. Even so, the Sophists do conceive of instances in which differences between epistemic claims have to be resolved, overcome, or temporarily put aside for the benefit of the greatest number of people. Those instances demand a special instrumentality that works by imposing persuasion, forging agreements, or creating consensus. For the Sophists, that instrumentality is rhetoric.

The Platonic Theory of Knowledge

In contrast to the Sophists, Plato posits that knowledge is the outcome of conceptual discovery, not an experiential or situationally grounded invention. The truth of any one thing is singular and absolute, not subject to particular circumstances or perspectives. For Plato, the foundation of knowledge is the abiding ideational reality of things, not their changing appearances—whereas appearances are accessible to us through the senses, ideas can be pursued and discovered only through the systematic exercise of one's reason. Essentially, Plato's theory sides with the oneness of the truth and the identity of truth and knowledge. Predictably, it also dismisses differences in and multiple versions of the truth as functions of ignorance and error, or instances of illusion. From this theory, it follows that such things as warfare between city-states, strife between classes, and conflict between individuals could be eliminated if only all would relinquish their partial perspectives and seek the singularity of what is true. For Plato, this would mean abandoning the practices of rhetoric, which perpetuate questionable beliefs and opinionated ignorance, and turning to philosophy, which is dedicated to the pursuit of true knowledge.

The Isocratean Theory of Knowledge

As with the case of language, the Isocratean and Aristotelian theories of knowledge occupy the space between the sophistical and Platonic positions. Like the Sophists, Isocrates views knowledge as an invention motivated by human need and desire; and like Plato, he regards ideas as the driving and sustaining force in the world. However, Isocrates shifts the site of knowledge from the particular individual, class, or city-state to the entire culture. Unlike the Sophists, he holds that knowledge is not simply a function of the moment, the mood, the circumstances or the interests of an individual or a group, and unlike Plato, he maintains that knowledge is not the result of a purely rational intelligence at work. For him, knowledge is the outcome of thoughtful judgment and seasoned experience, both in the context of one's cultural horizon. In this regard, Isocrates accepts differences among people, but only as long as they genuinely contribute to the vitality of a common cultural life. Isocrates also recognizes multiple versions of knowledge, but only on the condition that they issue from and support a unified cultural ideal. In effect, the Isocratean theory of knowledge acknowledges differences in and multiple views of the world against a background of sameness and oneness provided by the unifying idea of culture. The task of rhetoric in this way of thinking is to instruct a people on that part of their cultural heritage that has proved beneficial to their collective identity, and to critique those ideas and practices that interfere with their common predicament.

The Aristotelian Theory of Knowledge

The Aristotelian theory of knowledge posits that knowledge is a function of the interaction between intelligent humans and an intelligible world. By so doing, it combines the sophistical view of the relativity of knowledge with the Platonic view of the independence of the truth. By virtue of their natural capacity for perception and reason, humans can experience the world both in its particular and universal features. The reality of universal notions is not a self-sufficient entity, but an entity that manifests itself in particulars. On the basis of the observation that people think thoughts, perform actions, and make things, Aristotle's theory discriminates between scientific, practical, and productive kinds of knowledge, respectively. In all cases, however, knowledge is a function of human capacities on the one hand and the limitations and possibilities of matter and form on the other. Accordingly, knowledge of matter tends toward uniformity and agreement, whereas knowledge of forms admits of wider variation and difference. The task of rhetoric in this way of thinking is to adjust ideas to people, and people to ideas.

THE SOPHISTS:
PROTAGORAS, GORGIAS, ANTIPHON

As teachers of rhetoric, the Sophists were interested primarily in teaching the skill of composing and delivering orations competently. At the same time, they were intent on presenting their students with the thinking behind rhetoric and explaining to them rhetoric's necessity and justification as well as its failures and successes. In short, they were concerned not only with the how but also with the what and the why of rhetoric. A great deal of that thinking resolved around the relation of rhetoric and knowledge—in particular, whether rhetoric requires or imparts knowledge. In addressing this issue, the Sophists asked whether true knowledge is possible in the first place, what counts for knowledge in the social and political spheres, and how knowledge is created and communicated.

We have already foreshadowed part of the Sophists' theory of knowledge while looking at the main propositions of their theory of language: language issues from and influences perception; people have access to things perceptually and linguistically, by means of their senses and language; each person's perceptions are subjective and relative; human action is most often guided by opinions; and opinions are adopted and changed through experience, a large part of which is linguistic. These propositions were articulated partly as a critical response to pre-sophistical thinking, which had assumed that perception records external reality as it truly is, and that a thing and its name are one and the same. By conceiving the perceiver as contributing actively to the thing perceived, and by viewing the speaker as constituting the thing named, the Sophists were instrumental in changing significantly their predecessors' idea of knowledge.

The starting point of the Sophists' theory is not a formal definition of knowledge, but the human being as a desiring, thinking, perceiving, feeling, speaking, willing, and acting being. Because knowing is a human act and because it is the knower who does the knowing, it apparently made no sense to the Sophists to consider the act without taking into account the actor. Thus Protagoras stipulates: "Of all things man is the measure; of things that are that they are and of things that are not that they are not (Plato's *Theaetetus* 152A)." Taken by most scholars as the most fundamental statement of sophistical thought, Protagoras' dictum suggests that the existence, meaning, and significance of things is decided by the person. By implication, knowledge is determined in each case not by some abstract, suprahuman authority, but by the individual knower. But if this is so, knowledge is subjective—that is, created and held by the individual subject.

The individual, however, does not live alone; and living with others eventually leads to the realization that knowledge varies from person to person, or from the individual to the society at large. Accordingly, the Sophists' theory of knowledge goes beyond the individual subject and includes the context of social and political relations among people living their lives in communities of their own making. In this regard, the Sophists conceive of knowledge as something constantly invented and negotiated in and through situated interactions between the individual and the collective. But if this is so, knowledge varies according to the agreements people reach in their attempts to address common concerns. As such it is never completely pure or perfectly objective; rather, it is always conditioned by the characteristic makeup and the peculiar circumstances of the single knower and the rest of the community of knowers. This is another way of saying that knowledge is social.

In addition to its subjective and social character, knowledge for the Sophists is perspectival—it is a function of the kind of perspective one adopts. During the fifth and fourth centuries B.C.E., the two perspectives explored extensively were the perspective of nature and the perspective of convention. The details of that exploration aside, its main point was that each perspective affords us the kind of knowledge not afforded by the other. For the Sophists, the perspective of nature enables us to see sameness across people, whereas the perspective of convention enables us to see differences among them. In effect, people are neither the same nor different; rather, by nature they are the same, while by convention they are different. Among the Sophists, Antiphon maintained that "by nature we all have the same constitution in all particulars, barbarians and Greeks. We have only to consider the things which are natural and necessary to all mankind. . . . For we all breathe out into the air by the mouth and the nose, and we [all eat with our hands]" (*On Truth*, Fragment B). Alcidamas held that "God has set all men free; Nature has made no man a slave (cited by W. K. C. Guthrie, p. 159)." And Lysias the logographer had one of his clients argue in court that "no man is by nature either an oligarch or a democrat, but each tries to set up the kind of constitution that would be advantageous to him" (*Defense Against a Charge of Subverting the Democracy*, 8).

These three statements support the following conclusions. First, knowledge depends on a large number of factors. One of them is the perspective from which we, as knowers, operate. A given perspective provides an orientation to the world. Each perspective disallows or excludes orientations afforded by other perspectives. Which perspective we adopt is determined by many variables, including our circumstances and purposes. But because these variables differ from situation to situation, our perspective might vary, too. Thus the conventional distinctions between Greeks and barbarians, free persons and slaves, or oligarchs and democrats disappear the moment we adopt the natural perspective (Greeks breathe in the same way that barbarians do, free persons need food in the same way that slaves do, oligarchs bleed in the same way that democrats do). Conversely, observations of sameness vanish the moment we espouse the conventional perspective (Greeks are superior to barbarians, slaves are inferior to free persons, democrats are more progressive than oligarchs). In the same vein, we would expect, say, a physician to hold the natural perspective and treat all patients with the same care; by contrast, we would expect a politician to operate from the conventional perspective and give preferential treatment to one group of people over another.

Second, knowledge is seldom, if ever, impartial or disinterested; more often than not, it is conditioned by specific interests. Accordingly, humans do not organize their social and political systems by following the self-evident dictates of a suprahuman intelligence—that is, nature or God. Rather, they organize them according to their cultural, economic, and political interests, which determine their perspective. Thus cultural superiority is normally inculcated to instill in a people the sense of positive identity required to hold them together; slavery is typically instituted for economic reasons; and political or social structures are generally put in place by those who stand to benefit from them the most. One need not go far to find modern examples of interested knowledge. We all have heard the claim that "the United States is the best country in the world"—so often, in fact, that we take it to be true unquestionably. We are all familiar with the arguments of pre–Civil War slave owners in favor of the "natural" inferiority of slaves. And we all are aware of the motivations of lobbyists supporting or opposing a particular piece of legislation.

Third, each perspective has a corresponding vocabulary, which both determines and reflects the perspective at work. Because language affords us ways of expressing qualitative discriminations, the words of the conventional perspective betray one set of preferences (it is better to be a Greek than a barbarian, a free person than a slave, a democrat than an oligarch). On the other hand, the words of the natural perspective reveal another set of inclinations, and this because language also affords us possibilities for expressing equality (all people are equal in the eyes of God) and identity (all Athenian citizens have the same rights). The kind of knowledge we acquire from a given perspective, then, manifests itself in a certain language. In turn, the language we are exposed to determines which perspectives we adopt.

Thus far we have seen that knowledge for the Sophists is invented individually and constructed socially, which makes it subjective and social. We have also seen that knowledge depends on perspective, interests, and language, which makes it relative. But if knowledge of any one thing depends on so many factors, there is no universal criterion of the truth. Consequently, knowledge is never stable or certain. Because our senses can be faulty, we cannot rely entirely on our perceptions; because our thinking can be dull, we cannot be positive that our conclusions obtain; because there are disagreements among authorities on a given subject, we are not sure whose account is the true one; and because the pursuit of knowledge is ongoing, today's inventions often expose yesterday's knowledge as an error. On the strength of these observations, the Sophists gave truth up as unattainable, and declared that the world of human affairs is driven and ruled by opinions, not knowledge. As Gorgias points out in his *Encomium of Helen* (11), "On most subjects most men take opinion as counselor to their soul."

The Sophists, however, do not set out to portray opinion as a superior alternative to the truth. On the contrary, they uphold truth as a preferable, even if an impossible, option. As the defendant in Gorgias' *The Defense of Palamedes* (24) states categorically, "It is not right to trust those with an opinion instead of those who know, nor to think opinion more trustworthy than truth, but rather truth than opinion." Even so, certainty in knowing for the Sophists is a luxury or an ideal, something that we rarely, if ever, achieve in the public sphere. On the other hand, all people maintain opinions and act on them even though they are highly uncertain. As Gorgias observes, "Opinion is slippery and insecure, [and] it casts those employing it into slippery and insecure successes" (*Encomium of Helen,* 11).

But if this is so, how is a society in which everyone holds different opinions to function? Can a community of people survive without a common set of truths or beliefs? How are we to resolve competing and conflicting opinions on matters of common interest? On what basis are societal decisions to be made and actions carried out? The Sophists' answer would be that every society needs rhetoric precisely because there are so many opinions and no universal agreement on any one issue; and what rhetoric does is to make one opinion prevail over all others in the minds of the majority of the people. The Sophists would also argue that in a society of knowledge there would be no room for rhetoric, as knowledge would be passed on by those who possessed it to those who lacked it. In such a society, the knowers would be unwilling to entertain any alternatives. In fact, there would be no alternatives, or alternatives would really be considered errors. This would be so because, once discovered, the truth has no alternatives; it is singular and not subject to change. Therefore, the position of the true knower would always be incontestable, incontrovertible, final.

On the other hand, the Sophists would argue that in societies of opinion the exact opposite obtains. Because opinions are tentative and provisional, those who hold them are necessarily ambivalent—they have not made their minds up once and for all. As such they are open to persuasion and have not ruled out the possibility of debate. Unlike knowledge, opinions cannot be true or false; they can only be shown to be stronger or weaker, popular or unpopular, appealing or repulsive, satisfactory or unsatisfactory, persuasive or unpersuasive. And this is precisely what rhetoric does. It portrays some opinions as more desirable than others. Because it generally regards knowledge as opinion in disguise, rhetoric does not claim to possess or impart knowledge. Rather, it banks on the prevalence of opinions in the world, and asserts the capacity to shape and alter them, or to make one opinion more authoritative than the rest.

The problematic character of knowledge in the domain of public affairs becomes apparent when we look at typical legislative, judicial, or ceremonial occasions. Legislative bodies such as the Parliament in England, or the Congress in the United States, meet to deliberate on issues of common interest to the public. During legislative sessions, the people's representatives present and listen to proposals and counterproposals, claims and counterclaims, evidence and counterevidence, arguments and counterarguments, all meant to persuade the majority. Eventually, a vote is taken. The views of the majority carry the day, and the policy or law goes into effect. But the role knowledge plays in such settings is negligible at best. Proposals are judged not for their truth or falsehood, but for their sensibility. Further, evidence is generally evaluated along such criteria as relevance and sufficiency, not truth. Moreover, legislators never have all the evidence they need in order to decide with certainty. Finally, they have no way of knowing for sure how a particular piece of legislation will play out in the future. They can only predict or imagine that it will or will not prove effective and beneficial. But if this is so, why act in the first place? Because public issues demand immediate attention and decisive action. Besides, should the legislation turn out to be ineffective, the legislators can always try to improve or abandon it.

The problematic character of knowledge is also apparent in judicial settings. Judicial bodies such as a panel of judges or a jury gather to listen to a legal dispute between two parties. During the trial, the two sides present their respective cases, the one accusing, the other defending but both trying to influence the jury's decision. The judges consider both cases and reach a verdict, siding with the one and against the other. Invariably, however, the judges cannot know what exactly happened; their main access to the events in question is through oral accounts by partial or interested witnesses. And even though all witnesses swear to tell "the truth, the whole truth, and nothing but the truth," their stories are often inconsistent and contradictory. Still, the jury must reach a decision, taking into consideration all they have heard, no matter how confusing or inadequate. As Antiphon has the defendant state in the *Second Tetralogy,* "It is from what is said that the truth of the matter must be deduced" (Defense, second speech, 1). But as we have seen in the Sophists' theory of language, there is no one-to-one correspondence between an event and the language about that event. On what grounds, then, is a jury to decide what happened? The Sophists would argue that because the grounds cannot be those of certainty, they must be those of probability. That linguistic account which sounds more plausible is the one that persuades the judges of the guilt or innocence of the defendant.

The Sophists were well aware of the enormous issue inherent in the jury's lack of certainty, especially for the defendant, whose life might be at stake. Accordingly, Antiphon has the defendant argue in the *First Tetralogy* against probability: "You would do best to convict the men who actually killed him, not those who had reason to do so"

(Defense: first speech, 10). On the other hand, he has the prosecution respond that in some cases probability may be the only one choice:

> In saying that not those who probably, but those who actually, killed are murderers, he [the defendant] is quite right as far as actual murderers are concerned, provided that it is clear to us who are the men who actually killed the victim. But where the men who actually killed the man have not been detected, we must rest on the findings of probability and declare that he and no one else is the murderer of the victim. Crimes of this sort, we must remember, are committed in secret, not before witnesses" (Prosecution: second speech, 8)

Antiphon also recognizes the difficult dilemma jurors face by virtue of their lack of knowledge and necessary reliance on words. Thus he has the defendant of a murder case remind the jury of the weakness of language to express the truth and its power to mislead:

> There have already been many cases where people, through inability to speak, have failed to win credence with a true story and have perished, truth and all, because they have not succeeded in making their story plain. There have also been many cases where people with the ability to speak have gained credence with a false story and have been acquitted through that very lie. (*On the Murder of Herodes*, 3)

Later on in the same oration, the defendant reiterates the two tragic consequences the jury's lack of knowledge might engender: "It is as unfair that a bad choice of words should cause a man of good behavior to be put to death as it is that a good choice of words should lead to the acquittal of a criminal" (5).

The problematic character of knowledge also becomes apparent in ceremonial settings. On ceremonial occasions people congregate to celebrate or commemorate special events or people. During these occasions, one or more speeches of praise are given. As the following passage from Gorgias' *Funeral Oration* illustrates, the purpose of these speeches is not to impart knowledge but to edify the audience.

> These men attained an excellence which is divine and a mortality which is human, often preferring gentle fairness to inflexible justice, often straightness of speech to exactness of law. They believed that the most godlike and universal law was this: in time of duty dutifully to speak and to leave unspoken, to act and to leave undone. They cultivated two needed qualities especially, judgment and strength, the one for deliberating, the other for accomplishing. They gave help to those unjustly afflicted and punishment to those unjustly flourishing. They were determined in regard to the expedient, gentle in re-

gard to the fitting, by the prudence of the mind checking the irrationality of the body, insolent with the insolent, decent with the decent, fearless with the fearless, terrible among terrors.

This passage contains many claims about the personality and deeds of the men who died. But the truth of any or all the claims made herein would be difficult, if not impossible, to prove. The purpose of a eulogy, however, is not to speak with epistemic certainty on matters that can be demonstrated to be true. Rather, the purpose is to bid the dead farewell and comfort the living. In other words, the point of speaking about those who have died is to cover the distance between sorrow and hope, not that between truth and falsehood. Plato recognizes this in the *Symposium* when he has Socrates say disapprovingly:

> The truth, it seems, is the last thing the successful eulogist cares about; on the contrary, what he does is simply to run through all the attributes of power and virtue, however irrelevant they may be, and the whole thing may be a pack of lies, for all it seems to matter. (198d)

On some occasions, then, "the truth of the matter" is an irrelevant consideration. Ceremonial occasions are a case in point.

PLATO

Plato's theory of knowledge is a complex and elaborate affair. In this section, we focus on that part of his theory that most directly pertains to rhetoric. Plato was, and to some extent still is, the most prominent critic of rhetoric. Unable to reconcile the idea of persuasion with his philosophical program, he critiques vehemently the rhetorical practices of his contemporaries in many of his works, and especially in the *Gorgias*. Thus a considerable portion of his theory of knowledge takes the form of an argument against the thinking of the Sophists and their view of rhetoric. Plato's argument says that rhetoric is a flawed art because it is grounded on trial-and-error practices, not true knowledge. Worse, rhetoric promotes ignorance by leading people to believe that they know something when in fact they do not. Plato goes to great lengths in describing what constitutes knowledge and explaining how it can be acquired. In addition, he proposes a plan by means of which rhetoric can become a more respectable enterprise. Articulated in the *Phaedrus,* this plan would have rhetoric avail itself of knowledge first, and only then attempt to persuade.

According to Plato, knowledge of something is the conceptual discovery of what the thing is, not what it appears to be. To know something is to have cognitive access to its idea and truth, not its appearance. The truth of any one or all things exists independently of human beings. As such it cannot be created or invented by them; it must be discovered. Knowledge, in other words, is neither subjective nor social. This means that it cannot be left up to individual ingenuity or societal agreements; and it cannot be subject to changing circumstances, varying perspectives, particular interests, or common linguistic uses. For Plato, most people do not know the truth but possess the requisite mental equipment to acquire it. The pursuit and acquisition of knowledge takes a disciplined and sustained search carried out by means of critical discussions (dialectic) with an accomplished philosopher. The expected outcome of these discussions is that students will at least realize that their thinking is based on superficial opinions and unjustified beliefs, which they have adopted uncritically. Students will also come to see that the views they hold are simplistic, partial, internally inconsistent, and often contradictory. With these realizations in place, students will begin anew the search for ideas that are complete, consistent with one another, logical, and, above all, true.

For Plato, knowledge is an endless pursuit, an unattainable goal, if you will. But the way to this goal is full of obstacles. One such obstacle is the appearances of things. Appearances come in three forms: empirical reality (objects); artistic representation (drawings, paintings, sculptures); and linguistic representation (words). While appearances are at the surface, the truth is at the core. As such, the ideas of things can be said to be hidden behind their appearances. While the ideas of things remain constant, their appearances change over time, and across situations. The appearances of things are perceived by the senses, whereas their truth can be apprehended by the mind. The senses are not especially trustworthy or reliable sources of knowledge; the mind, on the other hand, is much more dependable. The mind can be trained to discover the truth of things and to detect the errors of the senses as well as its own. Rhetoric, however, is not interested in the discovery of the truth. Because it concerns itself with the appearances of things to lay audiences, it focuses on what seems to be the case, not with what in fact is the case. As such, it does not instruct audiences on the truth of things. As a product of opinions itself, rhetoric seeks to replace the opinions audiences already hold with the orators' opinions. This manner of operation may suit the purposes of the orators but keeps the audience in a state of ignorance.

Another obstacle to knowledge is the pursuit of bodily pleasure

and the avoidance of pain. Pleasure, which is devoid of reason, yields
no permanent intellectual content and as such fails to enrich the mind.
It only satisfies people's physical appetites and does so only temporarily. Further, things that are pleasing may be and often are harmful to
the self. For Plato, rhetoric is in the business of pleasing audiences with
flattering compliments and entertaining them with charming language. Because people generally like those who flatter them and dislike
those who point to their shortcomings, audiences generally like orators. For their part, orators are not only master flatterers; they also do
not tell their audiences the truth because the truth is often painful. For
Plato, the orator is like the cook who cares about the way a meal looks,
smells, and tastes, not whether it will benefit the body. The virtue of a
meal, however, lies in its nutritional value, not its pleasing appearance.
Likewise, the virtue of a speech lies in its truthfulness, not its pleasing
effects. Regarding the avoidance of pain, Plato proceeds analogically
by observing that people generally are reluctant to submit to a doctor's
medical orders because they are often unpleasant. Likewise, they also
use rhetoric to escape justice because punishment is always painful. In
both instances, however, Plato notes that the corrective purposes of
medicine and justice are frustrated, as the patient or criminal are not
cured.

A third obstacle to knowledge is the pursuit of social and political
power. Orators generally seek power, and often gain it by virtue of
their eloquence, which captivates the multitudes and persuades them
to place the orators in positions of power. For Plato, however, power
over the masses amounts to no power at all. This is so because the orators cater to their unenlightened listeners, telling them what they
want to hear (the pleasant), not what they must know (the true), or
must do (the good). In effect, the orators play up to the audience's ignorance and misconceptions in order to gain its approval. But if this is
so, orators are not masters of, but slaves to, their audiences. Orators,
then, do not exercise power over their audiences because it is the audiences that dictate and control what the orators say. But if this is so, the
orators' presumed power turns out to be a form of subservience. The
ultimate form of power, for Plato, comes not from the control of ignorant others, but from the control of oneself. Controlling oneself
means subjecting one's appetites and emotions to the rationality of the
mind.

A fourth obstacle to knowledge is the commonly used language in
a society. We have already seen in Plato's theory of language that there
are correct and incorrect names, and that knowing things should come

before assigning them names. To know something means to know its essence, not its common name. Conversely, to know the common name of a thing is not the same as knowing what makes a thing be what it is. The language of the orators, however, is based on the arbitrarily normative use of words, not on the correct correspondence between words and the truth of things. Orators employ the familiar language of a community because they concern themselves with their relation to their audiences, not their relation to ideas. Because they wish to be understood and accepted, they speak in their listeners' improper and incorrect language. And because they seek to please their audiences, they speak by slighting or neglecting the truth about things.

With all these obstacles to knowledge, Plato observes that most people typically opt for an inferior alternative: opinion. In this regard, he agrees with Gorgias—on most subjects most people rely on opinion, a very slippery and nebulous standard. But as he states in the *Republic,* "Opinions divorced from knowledge are ugly things. The best of them are blind" (506c). Clearly, while Gorgias and other Sophists accept the prevalence of opinion among most people and make it the basis of their rhetorical theory, Plato rejects the efficacy of opinion and formulates a theory of rhetoric founded on knowledge. Most explicitly stated in the *Phaedrus,* Plato's program for a reformed rhetoric consists of an outline of what the art of persuasion must do if it is to become an art worthy of the name. To this program we now turn.

Plato argues that rhetoric is not a self-conscious *techne* (art), but a routine and a habitude acquired by repeated practice. In order to become an art, it must be able to define itself, explain its actions, and account rationally for its procedures. Because rhetoric does not do these things, it is irrational; and anything irrational does not qualify for the label *techne.* The purpose of all arts, Plato observes, is to seek to perfect themselves and to enrich the life of those they serve the best way possible. These two purposes, however, cannot be accomplished in the absence of deliberate thought and reflection about what an art is and how it functions.

To acquire the status of an art, rhetoric must reform itself. Plato's recommendations for reform are many, but we will focus only on the most central. First, rhetoric must know the subject matter it purports to address. In other words, it is not unreasonable to expect orators to command a high degree of expertise on the subjects they address. And it makes little sense that an audience might know as much or more than the orator on a given subject. Rhetoric, then, must approach its subject matter methodically and investigate it systematically. Instead of

operating haphazardly and reacting routinely to changing circumstances, rhetoric must also establish principles to be observed consistently across situations. Arguing analogically, Plato uses medicine as a
model of a practice based on knowledge. Just as medicine knows the
physiology of the body, rhetoric must come to know the psychology of
the soul. And just as the knowledgeable physician knows what sorts of
drugs or regimens are appropriate to make a body healthy, the knowledgeable orator must know what kinds of words and rules of conduct
will improve the condition of the soul. For Plato, then, the effort to influence human minds through words is too important to be left to
practices predicated on ignorance, chance, or trial-and-error; orators
need to know how to influence audiences rationally. This means that
rhetoric must also classify the types of discourses and the types of souls.
Such classification, Plato believes, will help orators know which type of
speech is appropriate to which type of soul.

To the requirements for knowledge of the soul and subject matter,
Plato adds another, this one regarding the right definition of words.
An outgrowth of his theory of language, this requirement reiterates his
idea of the correctness of names. Definitions, he notes, are significant
because they let us know what a thing is and what it is not, how it differs from other things. About terms on which people generally agree,
definitions are not especially necessary. But where there is confusion
about the meaning of key terms, definitions are of paramount significance. Important terms like *freedom, justice, love, wickedness, goodness,*
or *beauty* are often the objects of intense disagreement among people.
Left undefined, these terms not only perpetuate disagreements; they
also interfere with the communication between speaker and audience,
as the speaker is often working with one meaning and the audience
with another. To minimize or avoid misunderstandings among people,
orators, according to Plato, ought to define important terms and use
them consistently throughout their discourses. By extension, listeners
who know the right definition of important but ambiguous words will
be less vulnerable to an orator's linguistic manipulations.

The best way to acquire knowledge of things and their correct linguistic definitions is through dialectic, a question-and-answer process
that aims to establish the truth about doubtful propositions. By examining critically any and all claims, dialectic seeks to expose invalid ways
of thinking and thus refute erroneous ways of reasoning and groundless ways of believing. On its way to knowledge, dialectic employs two
procedures: collection, or synthesis; and division, or analysis. The purpose of the first procedure is to bring a dispersed plurality into a single,

unified whole, so as to see it all together. The purpose in the second is the reverse—to divide a single form into its constituent parts, so as to see how each part functions in relation to every other part. Regardless of what the subject under examination is, dialectic helps those who engage in it to discover whether something is simple or complex. If it is simple, one then needs to discover what it can do to other things and how, or what other things can do to it and how. If it is complex, one needs to reduce it to its most basic components and treat each component as a simple object.

Plato shows us dialectic at work in many of his dialogues. To see further how collection and division work let us consider the case of a speech or a composition. To compose the single form called "speech" or "composition," one must put together letters to make words, words to make sentences, sentences to make arguments, and arguments to make ideas. Ideas are then placed into the larger units of the introduction, the body, and the conclusion. Finally, the form is completed when these units are juxtaposed in the proper order. Conversely, to analyze the single form of a speech or composition, one must divide it into its units (introduction, body, conclusion), each unit into ideas, each idea into arguments, and so forth. Careful synthesis and analysis, then, help one see whether the whole has all the parts it needs, how each part functions inside the whole, why each part is necessary or desirable, and how it affects and is affected by the other parts. Whereas the procedure of synthesis is most helpful when composing a piece of rhetoric, that of analysis is most beneficial when reading or listening to it. Together, the two procedures stimulate one's intelligence and lead to rational thinking and precise speaking.

Plato's theoretical ideal for a rhetoric founded on knowledge may not be entirely realistic, but it does set up higher expectations for the ways in which rhetoric might function in the sphere of public affairs. In the assembly, for example, the primary question among political orators addressing a particular issue would be not whether a proposed piece of legislation is expedient or feasible but whether it is good. By extension, citizens deliberating on an issue would make their decisions according to the goodness of the proposed measure, keeping in mind that a popular decision is not necessarily a good decision. In the courts, defendants would not defend the indefensible and accusers would not accuse the virtuous. Rather, both defendants and accusers would argue so as to serve justice, not their private interests and personal preferences. Likewise, juries would render their verdicts by looking not at which side advanced the more ingenious argument, but at what justice is and what justice demands. And in the festivals or other public occasions, the orators would not praise what is blameworthy or blame what is praiseworthy. Armed with the knowledge of their subject matter and cognizant of the mental condition of their audience, they would instead praise or blame according to that which is irrefutably true.

ISOCRATES

In the previous two sections, we have seen that the Sophists' and Plato's positions on knowledge are diametrically opposed. As a successor to the Sophists and a contemporary of Plato, Isocrates sees strength as well as weakness in both positions. As such, he adopts some of their stipulations while rejecting others. At the same time, he also forges his own. As will become evident in this section, Isocrates' position on knowledge is tied to and issues from his educational program, a program that assigns rhetoric the task of shaping the character of a whole culture.

Strictly speaking, Isocrates does not advance a theory of knowledge in the same sense that Plato does. Even so, what he says about knowledge merits attention because it extends the sophistical and Platonic views. Like the Sophists, Isocrates does not define knowledge formally. He only characterizes it as personal or social, political or cultural, theoretical or practical, abstract or specific. Isocrates also resembles the Sophists by positing that the principal criterion of knowledge is not its truth or validity but its utility. But whereas the Sophists subject knowledge to the welfare of the individual person, Isocrates is more interested in employing what is known in order to improve the quality of life of the entire society.

Yet another similarity between Isocrates and the Sophists regards the crucial role rhetoric plays in shaping the sensibilities and aspirations of a culture. But whereas they see rhetoric as a source of knowledge, Isocrates views it as the art that evaluates knowledge and translates it into action. In effect, Isocrates does not tell us what knowledge is. Asserting that it can be acquired formally through education, he mainly concerns himself with the issue of the relative worth of the knowledge available. For him, some kinds of knowledge are better than others.

Unlike the Sophists, who focus on what rhetoric is and what it can do, Isocrates' major preoccupation is what rhetoric should do. In this regard, he resembles Plato, who is also interested in reforming rhetoric. Both thinkers recognize that rhetoric addresses trivial as well as momentous matters, serious as well as silly subjects; and they both grant that rhetoric trains students to argue both sides of an issue. But whereas Plato's program for a reformed rhetoric points in the direction of dialectically secured knowledge about subject matter, the soul, and correct definition, Isocrates' program stresses sensitivity to occasion, propriety of language, and innovation in the manner of handling a topic. As he puts it in *Against the Sophists* (13), "Oratory is good only if it has the qualities of fitness for the occasion, propriety of style, and originality of treatment." At the heart of their difference lies the question whether the facts speak for themselves. Plato thinks so; Isocrates does not. From the Isocratean perspective, someone has to speak for the facts; and the person who can do this better than anyone else is the accomplished orator.

Despite this difference, Isocrates and Plato hold a similar position on the requirements of becoming an accomplished orator. Plato's keys to a finished performance in rhetoric are natural talent, knowledge, and practice. None of these prerequisites can be missing in the work of the aspiring orator. As Socrates tells Phaedrus, "If you lack any of these three you will be correspondingly unfinished" (*Phaedrus,* 269d). For Isocrates, the conditions for rhetorical achievement are quite similar: "The student must not only have the requisite aptitude but he must learn the different kinds of discourse and practice himself in their use" (*Against the Sophists,* 17). Isocrates also declares, in the manner of Socrates, that if any one of the things he recommends is lacking, students will accordingly fall below the mark of complete success (18). Clearly, the difference between the Platonic and Isocratean requirements revolves around the issue of knowing. Whereas Plato emphasizes knowledge of the truth of ideas, Isocrates underscores learning the different forms of discourse.

Both Plato and Isocrates address the relationship between knowledge and action. Plato assumes that correct knowledge in all cases leads to good personal behavior and sound collective action. Isocrates, however, disputes that assumption. In his view, knowledge and action are separated by some distance, a distance that only rhetoric can cover by means of two steps: judgment and persuasion. Judgment assigns worth to particular knowledge; it assesses whether it is relevant, valuable, useful. The assignment of worth, however, does not happen arbitrarily or randomly. Thus knowledge cannot be good (or bad) in itself. It must be good (or bad) for something other than itself. As for persuasion, it translates evaluated knowledge into specific action. Persuasion tells us what to do on the basis of what we know and in the face of a situation that demands action. Thus simply knowing something is not enough.

One must also evaluate and activate what one knows. For Isocrates, ideas are only as good as the results they produce in action. Knowledge-in-itself may be an abstractly meaningful concept, but because it has no applicability in the domain of human affairs, it is useless. Having knowledge, then, is one thing; discerning its usefulness is quite another; and telling others what it means or how to apply it is still another.

By way of illustration, let us consider the case of elections. To know when an election is held, what its purpose is, why voting is a vital civic duty, where I must go in order to vote, and how to cast my vote: all these things do not suffice to make me carry out the act of voting. Before I do so, I must make certain judgments regarding the importance of exercising the right to vote, the significance of the particular election, the consequences of its potential results, the impact of my vote, and so forth. But these judgments are still not enough to make me vote. Ultimately, I must be persuaded (by myself or others) to do it. Clearly, all the knowledge in the world is not enough to lead me to action; similarly, the best judgment in the world does not automatically translate into a particular action. Seen from another perspective, an election is a time-bound demand on every citizen wishing to vote—if I want to vote, I must do so on a given day and by a certain time. More importantly, I must cast my vote by the specified time even if I am not entirely sure of the integrity of my choice, even if I do not know all I would need or like to know about the issues or the candidates in order to make a more intelligent decision.

Action always takes place in response to desire or demand. While responses to desire or demand happen in the present, the fulfillment of desire and the meeting of demand take place in the future. Essentially, people act in the present in order to affect some aspect of the future. The success of any one action, however, is never guaranteed. Even if one takes all the measures necessary and does everything humanly possible, failure is always a possibility. Operating from within this perspective, Isocrates notes that "foreknowledge of future events is not vouchsafed to our human nature." As such, the power to predict exactly the future "lies in the realms of the impossible" (*Against the Sophists*, 2). But if this is so, Isocrates reasons, the best one can do is try to increase the likelihood of the success of any one action. In his *Antidosis* he elaborates on this notion by observing that, given the unavailability of complete and accurate knowledge about right action, all we can do is guess: "Since it is not in the nature of men to attain a science by the possession of which we can know positively what we should do or what we should say, in the next resort I hold that man wise who is able by his powers of conjecture to arrive generally at the best course [of action]" (271). According to this way of thinking, action is generally a matter of both urgency and uncertainty. People often act in response to a situation that cannot wait; and when they do, their actions are marked by varying degrees of uncertainty and insecurity.

Like the Sophists and Plato, Isocrates acknowledges that most people believe what they believe and do what they do on the basis of opinion, a most slippery and insecure thing. As we have seen, the Sophists posit that any one opinion has, at least theoretically, an equal chance to prevail over all others by means of rhetorical force. Even so, the Sophists recognize that the opinion that counts the most in any given case is the one that persuades the greatest number of people. Over time, a prevailing opinion in society achieves the status of truth and, as such, becomes the ground for other opinions. We have also seen that this is the precise point of Plato's intervention and attempt to replace the prevalence of opinion by the true knowledge of ideas. For Isocrates, however, all opinions are not the same—some are better than others. As in the case of knowledge, those opinions are better that, when translated into action, contribute more to the quality of human life. For Isocrates, then, the choice is not between knowledge and opinion; nor is it between strong and weak opinions; rather, it is between what is useful and what is useless. Presumably, he would favor useful knowledge over the useless kind. But if the choice were between useless knowledge and useful opinion, he would prefer the latter.

Given the uselessness of knowledge in itself, the uncertainty of the future, the unreliability of opinion, and the need for wise judgment and action, how is one to proceed with any reasonable expectation of success? If the wisdom or efficacy of an idea can be discerned only after its implementation and only in the light of its results, how can one argue for the benefits of a course of action in advance? Where should one look for guidance when formulating a judgment and proposing a course of action? For Isocrates, the answers to these questions are pointing toward the past.

The past provides the most reliable index for predicting the future and guessing the outcome of a given course of action. This is so because the past includes a host of successful and unsuccessful stories from which we can discern how things tend to work. Although the past is not identical with the future, it does offer us some sense of the way various plans of action fare under different conditions. Assuming, then, that the past tends to repeat itself more or less in the future, Isocrates proposes that one turn to the past of a culture, pursuing instances of success and avoiding examples of failure. In so doing, he places considerable weight on discourses informed by history. He himself follows his own advice in his *Panegyricus* and *On the Peace*, two discourses trying to persuade Athens that the way to end her current political troubles is to stop her antagonistic and disrespectful treatment of her allies. In both cases, Isocrates' arguments rely heavily on Athens' history, reminding her that her past policies of cooperation and respect were the source of countless blessings.

Despite its centrality in Isocratean thought, then, knowledge of the historical past in itself is not enough. One must also know how to bring this knowledge to bear on the stakes of the present situation. The point, for Isocrates, is not to dwell in the past; nor is it to speak about the present without warrant; rather, it is to combine historical insight with contemporary proposals that promise to improve the collective life of a people in the future. To do so, one needs to stay away from mechanistic studies and undertake the study of the more creative art of discourse, rhetoric. What makes rhetoric creative is the fact that it has to take into account such complicated and indeterminate variables as audience, situation, and subject matter. At the same time, the rhetorician has to examine the past thoroughly, address the present effectively, and affect the future positively. Finally, the rhetorician must perform a balancing act by choosing only some of the available materials, joining them together, arranging them properly, responding to the demands of the occasion, adorning the speech with striking thoughts, and clothing it with flowing and melodious phrases (*Against the Sophists,* 16).

Against the background of his own position on rhetorical education, Isocrates criticizes repeatedly teachers of rhetoric who teach highly abstract subjects without applicability to the common concerns of society. Further, he disapproves the narrow focus of their curriculum on logical proof and refutation because its usefulness is limited to the few disputing a particular matter. Moreover, he rejects those who teach history for its own sake: "Those discourses are better and more profitable which denounce our present mistakes than those which praise our past deeds, and those which counsel us what we ought to do than those which recount ancient history" (*Antidosis,* 62). Effectively, the thrust of Isocrates' criticism is directed at those educators who neglect political culture. For him, teachers should try "to instruct their pupils in the practical affairs of our government and train to expertness therein, bearing in mind that likely conjecture about useful things is far preferable to exact knowledge of the useless, and that to be a little superior in important things is of greater worth than to be pre-eminent in petty things that are without value for living" (*Helen,* 5).

Despite his intense interest in political culture, Isocrates does not overlook the development of the individual person. For him, the development of the person is largely a function of the quality of political culture. Although he does not believe that the good and just life can be taught (it does not depend on knowledge of the ideas of goodness and justice, respectively), he claims that the study of political discourses can stimulate the positive development of a person's character (*Against the Sophists,* 20). Isocrates' reasoning is that the study of political discourse obligates one to see "the bigger picture." This picture includes but extends beyond the interests of the individual to encompass the collective concerns, interests, and aspirations of the whole community, and by extension the whole state in which one lives. In effect, the study of political discourses teaches that a person's life is intertwined with the lives of many others in a network of relationships of interdependence. Moreover, this kind of study points out that the interests of the individual and those of the state must be balanced—excessive individual freedom leads to anarchy, while excessive state control leads to tyranny. Last, political discourses provide students with many case studies from which they can generalize how political life unfolds and how it affects the common good. These lessons, according to Isocrates, help form the type of character who understands the tension between rights and responsibilities, self and others, opportunities and constraints. In a word, these lessons help shape the ideal citizen (*Antidosis,* 275; 278).

ARISTOTLE

In our discussion of Aristotle's view of language, we noted that he divides the uses of language into theoretical, practical, and productive. The same threefold classification applies to Aristotle's view of knowledge. For him, theoretical knowledge concerns the way things are always or for the most part. Practical knowledge is about the relative and contingent matters involved in living and acting in society. And productive knowledge is about the ways in which things can be made. Because Aristotle designates rhetoric as a productive art (it concerns itself with making speeches, orations), this section focuses on his theory of productive knowledge. Even so, a few remarks about his general theory of knowledge are in order.

Aristotle posits that humans are political and rational animals. This means that they live with one another in cities and that they have mental and linguistic powers. The most central and controlling postulate in Aristotle's view of knowledge is that people are intelligent by nature and that the world is intelligible, also by nature. This means that people have the capacity to know the actual world in which they live, a world that, in the last analysis, is knowable. An important correlate to this postulate is that all people desire to know by nature why things are the way they are.

In their search for explanations, people come to know by means of their senses and their intellect. The senses perceive particular things, whereas the intellect perceives universals. In order to function, the senses require the presence of perceptible objects, whereas the mind can think at any given time what it wants, in the absence of a real object. Sense perception is a physical or natural process, whereas thinking is a mental one. Perception is activated by means of a sensible object, whereas thinking is set into motion by means of an object of thought. The process of knowing entails two movements: the one from the knower to the object, the other from the object to the knower. In other words, things are knowable because there are people who can know them; conversely, people can know because there are things that can be known. We can know things as they are, in their actuality, because they have the capacity to impress themselves on our senses and mind, and because our senses and mind are receptive and sensitive to what they encounter. As Aristotle explains it in the case of the senses, "Sense is that which is receptive of sensible forms apart from their matter, as wax receives the imprint of the signet-ring apart from the iron or gold of which it is made" (*On the Soul*, 423a18–20). To know something, then, is to have its form without its matter.

Knowing includes the capacity to retain both images and intelligible forms. Knowing and having images is not the same thing; but knowledge is not possible without images. This means that one cannot know something without having a perceptual image of the thing. Put differently, all knowing initially requires some kind of perceptual observation. Unlike Plato, who posits that one can directly know the purely conceptual forms of all things, Aristotle stipulates that we can know the intelligible aspect of only those things that have first been observed in sense experience. In other words, knowledge begins by first observing the actual world and then reflecting on what one has observed. As Aristotle puts it in *On the Soul*, "Without sensation a man would not learn or understand anything: at the very time he is actually thinking he must be seeing a sense image" (432a7–9). Even so, the aim of knowledge is to advance from sense experience, which tells us that something is, to an understanding of the reasons why something happens to be what it is and why it has the form it does. Accordingly, the knowledgeable person is the person who knows not only that something is, what and how it is, but also why it is the way it is.

To know a particular thing in one specific instance does not enable us to generalize about its truth in most or all other instances. The way we arrive at general or universal truths is through repeated observations of particular things. Repeated observations give rise to memory, and repeated memories give rise to experience. Experience provides the starting point of art and science: art in the case of process, and science in the case of facts.

Against this brief background of Aristotle's general theory of knowledge, let us turn to his view of productive knowledge, the kind needed for rhetoric. Like other productive arts, rhetoric is engaged in making something (an oration, a speech) out of certain materials (logos, language) in order to effect some change. And like other arts, rhetoric produces what it does under the guidance of experience and intelligence. Aristotle posits that the making of something requires experience with materials and forms (in the case of rhetoric, words and forms of reasoning). However, he also insists that experience alone is insufficient—having experience of what worked in one instance provides no assurance that the same thing will work in another. For such assurance, one also needs to know the reasons why something worked in a given case and why it will work in most cases like it. In addition to experience, then, one also needs to know universal rules. Conversely, knowledge of universal rules alone is generally insufficient. One must also have experience of particular cases—this because what rhetoric makes in each case is a particular thing (a single speech). While knowledge of universal rules can come mainly through oral instruction, experience with particular cases can come only through practice at making particular things (in the case of rhetoric, composing and delivering speeches). Insofar, then, as Aristotle equates productive knowledge with a blend of experience, intelligence, and practice, he generally agrees with Plato and Isocrates on what it takes to become accomplished in rhetoric.

Aristotle defines rhetoric as the art of observing in any given case the possible means of persuasion. He further explains that the function of rhetoric is "not simply to succeed in persuading, but rather to discover the means of coming as near such success as the circumstances of each particular case allow." Unlike the Sophists, who assign rhetoric a predominately practical character, Aristotle joins Isocrates and Plato in identifying the preparatory steps leading to rhetorical action. Specifically, Aristotle notes that, like all other arts, rhetoric aims at success but is not guaranteed it—there are simply too many variables to consider, and our considerations are mostly informed by probability, not certainty. Aristotle clarifies rhetoric's function by reference to the art of medicine: "It is not the function of medicine simply to make a man quite healthy, but to put him as far as may be on the road to health; it is possible to give excellent treatment even to those who can never enjoy sound health" (*Rhetoric,* I.i.14). The orator's question in all cases, then, is this: What factors do I need to consider in order to make my message to the audience persuasive?

The answer to this question varies according to the kind of rhetoric one has in mind. For Aristotle there are three kinds of rhetoric: political, forensic, and epideictic. Political rhetoric deals with deliberation, making decisions about unsettled issues, issues that an audience has the power to resolve. Political rhetoric always urges us either to do or not to do something. Its purpose is to influence decisions that affect the well-being of one person or all the citizens of the state. The time of political rhetoric is the future (whether something will or will not happen as the orator says), and its end is expediency or inexpediency. The political orator needs to be knowledgeable in the subjects about which people deliberate. These subjects include ways and means, war and peace, national defense, imports and exports, legislation, and the main kinds of government (democracy, oligarchy, aristocracy, monarchy) as well as their characteristic customs and institutions. The political orator also needs to know the public's view of happiness and its understanding of what is good. This is so because in urging listeners to do something, the orator aims at maintaining or increasing their happiness, and at upholding their notion of what is good.

Forensic rhetoric deals with adjudication, rendering a decision that settles a legal dispute. It always attacks or defends somebody. Its purpose is to influence the verdict of the judge(s). The time of forensic rhetoric is the past (whether something did or did not happen), and its end is justice or injustice. Forensic rhetoric demands knowledge of the laws of the state, as well as the character of wrongdoing (its motives, its perpetrators, and its victims). It also requires knowledge of such subjects as the causes of human action, the nature of pleasure and advantage, and the dispositions and circumstances that generally lead people to commit wrong.

Epideictic rhetoric deals with display, the portrayal of virtuous and admirable things. It always praises or blames something or someone. Its purpose is to shape the audience's perception of the worth of a quality, a deed, or a person. The time of epideictic rhetoric is the present (whether something or someone is as the speaker says), and its end is honor or dishonor. Epideictic rhetoric requires knowledge of the public's view of virtue and vice, honor and dishonor, and their causes and effects. It also requires an understanding of what values people most cherish, the sources of their pride, and their notion of heroism.

Aristotle devotes fourteen chapters in Book I of his *Rhetoric* to the discussion of the three kinds of rhetoric. The details of each chapter aside, it is important to recall that his discussion of all three kinds is founded on the idea that knowledge manifests itself in interrelated linguistic propositions, and that formally shaped language affects people's senses, minds, and emotions. At the perceptual level, the speaker constitutes an object of sight and hearing for the listeners. The physical appearance and language of the speaker are grounds on which the audience concludes whether the orator is honest, sensible, and friendly *(ethos)*. At the intellectual level, the propositions of the speech become the object of the listeners' thinking as they determine whether the propositions advanced prove the case argued *(logos)*. At the emotional level, the language of the orator can arouse in the listeners a range of feelings (anger, fear, shame, pity, indignation, etc.) that affect the kinds of judgments they make *(pathos)*.

Essentially, Aristotle's view of rhetoric places the orator in command of linguistic propositions the totality of which seeks to create in the audience a favorable impression of the speaker, to prove the speaker's case, and to place the audience in an emotional frame of mind that is sympathetic to the arguments proffered. Aristotle's view also places the audience in the position of judgment—they are the ones who ultimately decide whether the speaker is trustworthy, the case is proved, and their interests are served well. Even though each kind of rhetoric has its own special requirements, all three share a common goal: to bring the orator's discourse into alignment with the listeners' experience of how the world works and their understanding of what makes sense. Insofar, then, as the orator's speech confirms the listeners' experience of the world, validates their perceptions, and upholds their views of reality, they will be persuaded.

This, however, is not to say that Aristotle's orator becomes persuasive by catering to the audience. Aristotle's view of popular audiences is that they are unenlightened, inattentive, more emotional than rational, and unable to follow complicated arguments. Even so, he does not dismiss them altogether, in the manner of Plato, as totally ignorant. Although generally unaware of scientific truths, they are quite aware of the truths their experience in the world has taught them. Popular audiences, for Aristotle, consist of ordinary citizens who bring the truths of their experience to rhetorical events. When they function as critics (in political rhetoric), or judges (in forensic rhetoric), or spectators (in epideictic rhetoric), they try to test what the orator says by reference to what they know and believe. Conversely, they test what they know and believe by reference to what the orator says. On the other hand, the orator tries to address the listeners, bearing in mind their views and sensibilities. But if this is so, Aristotle's theory of rhetoric emphasizes neither the orator nor the audience but the interaction of the two. In and through this interaction, orator and audience attempt to adjust their respective views of the world, and in so doing get closer to the truth of the world in its actuality.

SUMMARY

In this chapter we have seen that knowledge for the Sophists is multifaceted and highly conditioned, in other words, relative. Insofar as it is determined by individual perceptions, it is subjective. To the extent that it is the outcome of situated interactions and negotiations among people, it is social. And inasmuch as it depends on perspective, interests, and language, it is perspectival, interested, and linguistic. Positing a distinction between certainty and probability on the one hand and truth and opinion on the other, the Sophists suggest that rhetoric attends to ever-shifting appearances. As such, rhetoric neither requires nor imparts true knowledge. Rather, it seeks to persuade by shaping and changing people's opinions on all domains, but especially in the domain of practical affairs.

In contrast to the Sophists, Plato equates knowledge with the discovery of the ideational order of reality. The truth of things is independent of human beings; it is singular, abiding, and universal. Knowledge is not readily available but it can be acquired through dialectic. Consisting of collection and division, dialectic helps one overcome the obstacles to knowledge, which include the domain of appearances, the pursuit of physical pleasures, the pursuit of social and political power, and the uncritical uses of common language. To become a true art, rhetoric needs to abandon opinions, avail itself of knowledge, and develop a set of principles. Moreover, it needs to learn about the interaction between the human soul and language. Finally, it needs to concern itself with the right definition of ambiguous words.

Isocrates' view of knowledge constitutes a unique synthesis of sophistical and Platonic notions. According to Isocrates, the basis of knowledge is opinion and its criterion is utility. Unless knowledge can be translated into meaningful and beneficial action, it is useless. Although the future is unpredictable, one can assume that it generally resembles the past. Rhetorical success requires historical insight, wise judgment, and serious study of political discourses. Political discourses help one understand political culture and pursue lines of personal growth and development.

Finally, the Aristotelian theory of knowledge posits that knowledge is a function of the interaction between intelligent humans and an intelligible world. People come to know through their senses and intellect. The senses know particular things whereas the intellect knows universals. Rhetoric requires productive knowledge, knowledge of how to make a speech out of the materials of language and the forms of reasoning. Productive knowledge is a function of both experience and intelligence. Rhetoric is the art of observing in any given case the possible means of persuasion. There are three kinds of rhetoric (political, forensic, and epideictic); each requires a wide range of knowledge. The speaker's character, the proof of the case argued, and the audience's emotional feelings are the grounds on which persuasion happens.

ROMAN RHETORICAL THEORY

CHAPTER 6

RHETORIC
IN
ROME

&

The concentrated and elaborate production of rhetorical practice and theory, so abundant in the Greek culture of the fifth and fourth centuries B.C.E., came to a virtual halt with the end of the fourth century. During the next two centuries, the Hellenistic period, rhetoric became a regular part of secondary education while rhetorical theory did not break much new ground. Most theoretical activity centered around topics and issues already identified or suggested by earlier Greek theorists, especially Aristotle. Generally, Hellenistic rhetoricians made modest contributions to rhetorical theory—for the most part, they concerned themselves with working out the details or implications of particular aspects of the rhetorical structure the Greek theorists had created. The next time rhetorical theory received sustained and systematic attention was in the hands of two Roman rhetoricians. Cicero (first century B.C.E.) and Quintilian (first century C.E.).

Greek Influence on Roman Rhetorical Theory

The Romans were in many ways the heirs of Greek culture. They had been in contact with the Greeks for quite some time. Greece, which had colonies in the southern part of the Italian peninsula and Sicily, had shared its cultural accomplishments through its traveling intellectuals, teachers, artisans, and merchants. And Rome, which conquered Greece militarily in the second century B.C.E., had many opportunities to discover the products of Greek culture. The result of this interaction was a certain reciprocal influence, which often led to the partial adoption of one another's institutions, customs, and ways of thinking. In the particular case of rhetoric, the Romans, at first sceptical, eventually adopted a great deal of what the Greek rhetoricians had developed, and adapted it to their own realities. Specifically, they made it part of their schooling and cultivated it in the fields of politics and law. Speaking about Rome's early encounter with rhetoric, Cicero notes:

> To say nothing of Greece, which has ever claimed the leading part in eloquence, and of Athens, that discoverer of all learning, where the supreme power of oratory was both invented and perfected, in this city of our own [Rome] assuredly no studies have ever had a more vigorous life than those having to do with the art of speaking.
>
> For as soon as our world-empire had been established, and an enduring peace had assured us leisure, there was hardly a youth, athirst for fame, who did not deem it his duty to strive with might and main after eloquence. At first indeed, in their complete ignorance of method, since they thought there was no definite course of training or any rules of art, they used to attain what skill they could by means of their natural ability and of reflection. But later, having heard the Greek orators, gained acquaintance with their literature and called in Greek teachers, our people were fired with a really incredible enthusiasm for eloquence. (I.iv.13–14)

Cicero and Quintilian are not the only figures in Roman rhetorical theory, but they are the most central ones. Their works are important sources of information about, and insight into, the practical uses and theoretical understandings of language for the purposes of persuasion. Their combined thinking was instrumental in preserving the Greek rhetorical heritage and shaping humanistic education in Europe for many centuries to come. Cicero had considerable experience as a pleader (lawyer) in the courts and as a politician. He is the author of several treatises covering such topics as political theory, law, ethics, and rhetoric. In addition to these treatises, his preserved writings include many legal and political orations and a large number of letters. Quintilian was primarily a teacher of rhetoric, but he also worked as a pleader in the courts. His only surviving work is the treatise *Institutio Oratoria,* a treatise on rhetorical education mainly concerned with the composition of an oration.

As we will see, the thinking expressed in the Roman works we examine often reflects views and notions already encountered in the Greek rhetoricians. Cicero and Quintilian repeatedly pay homage to their Greek predecessors and openly acknowledge their indebtedness to them. However, they also disagree with them, and describe the prevailing rhetorical views of their own times. In so doing, they demonstrate both the continuity of the rhetorical tradition and its changes under the circumstances of the Roman culture. The fact that these two Roman authors frequently follow the lead of their Greek counterparts does not mean that they did not have anything new to say. Rather, it means that much of what the Sophists, Plato, Isocrates, and Aristotle had identified in their study of rhetoric was found by Cicero and Quintilian to be still applicable and relevant to their epoch.

Throughout this book, we have stipulated that rhetorical theory develops from a set of particular practices and within a context of specific situations. Applied to this chapter, this stipulation means that a proper understanding of the Roman view of rhetoric requires some consideration of the character of Roman society and political institutions.

Roman Society and Political Institutions

In its earlier days, Rome was a small-city state ruled by a succession of kings. Later on, it adopted a republican form of government and grew considerably both in size and population. The collapse of the republican form of government in the last quarter of the first century B.C.E. led to the emergence of the Roman Empire. Thus in a period of seven centuries, Rome grew from a small city-state into a huge empire that dominated the Mediterranean world. The period we are most concerned with in this chapter is the late part of the Republic (first century B.C.E.) through the early part of the Empire (first century C.E.).

The population of the late Republic and early Empire consisted of three classes. The top of the hierarchy was occupied by a small but powerful aristocratic class of wealthy landowners (patricians). For all intents and purposes, the political and military affairs of Rome were in the hands of these men. The second class in Roman society was made up of well-to-do merchants, military officers, and members of prominent families in the different municipalities (equites). The third class consisted of various groups ranging from artisans to laborers, from the urban poor to prisoners of war brought into the country as slaves (plebeians). Interaction between the classes took the form of patronage. A wealthy patron would protect the interests of a large number of people from the lower strata; in turn, they would support his social status and political power.

The governmental structure of the Roman state was mainly aristocratic rule with limited popular participation. At the top of the political hierarchy was the senate, whose members came predominately from the wealthy aristocracy. Unlike the Greek assembly, the Roman senate did not legislate. Theoretically, its function was advisory, but in reality its powers were considerable on matters of legal and public policy. Convened only by a consul (the highest elected public official), the senate debated proposed legislation before sending it to popular assemblies for consideration. Occasionally, it passed laws by decree, voided legislation approved by an assembly, and asserted its power over the courts by fiat. The senate was also in charge of foreign affairs and appropriations. Finally, it defined the role of elected officials (the magistrates) in charge of important public duties (i.e., overseeing military operations, presiding over the courts, convening popular assemblies, conducting public works, and maintaining public order).

In addition to the senate, four popular assemblies represented four different groups of people divided according to wealth, territory, and status. Each assembly considered different questions. For example, the curial assembly considered religious and legal questions; the centuriate assembly elected public officials, declared wars, and ratified treaties; and the tribal assembly and the plebeian council concerned themselves with the representation of tribes (geographically determined units to which citizens belonged) and the lower classes (the plebeians). Each assembly was convened by the appropriate magistrate, who controlled its agenda. Unlike their Greek counterpart, Roman assemblies did not deliberate openly on issues of public interest; rather, they voted for public officials and legislation without much discussion or debate. After listening to the magistrate's appointees speak, the membership voted, not individually, but by groups. A majority of votes determined the vote of a given group, and a majority of groups determined the fate of a piece of legislation.

In the light of this sketchy outline of Roman society and institutions, our discussion in this chapter follows a modified version of the structure of the previous five chapters. Specifically, our examination of judicial and political rhetoric focuses on Cicero, while our discussion of epideictic rhetoric takes into account both Cicero and Quintilian's views. Although Quintilian has much to say about political and judicial rhetoric, it is not especially unique. When he does not follow the Greek rhetoricians, he follows Cicero. The next part of our discussion concerns itself with Cicero and Quintilian's understanding of language and its proper uses. As we will see, the Roman orientation to rhetoric is less philosophical or literary and more pragmatic than the Greek orientation. Accordingly, judicial and political oratory receives more attention than epideictic. Similarly, the discussion of language follows more a utilitarian and less a theoretical path. The Roman emphasis is not so much on what language is or how it operates as on what its effects are and how it should be approached and used.

RHETORIC AND LAW: CICERO

Law occupied a special place in the Roman culture. If it is true that the Greeks were interested primarily in philosophy, it is equally true that the Romans' predominant interest lay in law. The result of this interest was an impressive legal theory whose principles have been instrumental in shaping the legal orientation of many Western nations. In Rome, the making and administration of law was mainly the province of the rich aristocratic classes. For them, dealing with legal questions was a form of pastime, while engaging with legal practice was a form of public service. Law in the Roman culture, however, went beyond pastime and public service as it shaped and was shaped by politics. A career in law was often a big step toward the acquisition of political power. Accordingly, Cicero rose to political prominence partly on account of his good reputation as a pleader in the courts. In turn, the political and military power of the ever-expanding Roman state demanded new and effective laws for the administration of newly conquered territories and peoples. Addressing the importance of law in Roman society, Cicero has Crassus, one of the characters in *De Oratore,* observe that to study comparative law means to discover the superiority of the Romans over all other peoples:

> You will win from legal studies this further joy and delight, that you will most readily understand how far our ancestors surpassed in practical wisdom the men of other nations, if you will compare our own laws with those of Lycurgus, Draco and Solon [Greek lawmakers], among the foreigners. For it is in-

credible how disordered, and wellnigh absurd, is all national law other than our own; on which subject it is my habit to say a great deal in everyday talk, when upholding the wisdom of our own folk against that of all others, the Greeks in particular. (I.xliii.197)

Unlike the Greeks of the fifth century B.C.E., whose understanding of law was a mixture of religious precept, popular superstition, traditional custom, and secular thought, the Romans sought to separate law from morality or religion. They insisted that judicial decisions should be made on the basis of legal principle rather than the prevailing moral attitudes of the society. This separation meant that societal needs and communal customs were kept from becoming a major factor in the development of law—in effect, law was mostly in the hands of the aristocratic authorities, not in the hands of the populace. It also meant that legal reform was initiated and effected by expert jurists, not the masses. Of course political factors did enter the sphere of lawmaking. However, this was hardly a problem since lawmakers, politicians, and the authorities were all generally patricians. The point is that law was handled mostly by the ruling class for the benefit of its members.

During the late phases of the Roman Republic, the court system included appointed magistrates who heard cases initiated by citizens. The system also included various standing courts, each concerned with particular crimes (i.e., high treason, murder and poisoning, embezzlement, extortion, bribery in elections, and forgery of documents). Juries for these courts came not from one's peers but from the senatorial or the equite classes. As in the case of the Greek judicial system, any citizen could bring suit against another. But the course of the suit was determined by the litigants and their advocates, not the magistrate in charge. Unsuccessful suits ran the risk of accusation for false complaint. Successful suits included handsome rewards, such as a share of the criminal's property.

One of the more interesting innovations in the Roman judicial system was the introduction of the pleader (lawyer, advocate) in legal proceedings. Unlike the Greek system, which required that the accused appear in person and defend himself, the Roman system allowed a pleader (usually a wealthy patron) to accuse someone on behalf of a client or the state, or to defend his client. This innovation had at least three important consequences for judicial rhetoric. First, the average citizen no longer needed to be knowledgeable about the law or effective in addressing a judge or jury. In Rome, the technicalities of law and court procedure became the concern of experts. Likewise, the polish of rhetorical skills became part of the training of the orators, most of whom were court pleaders. Second, the mediation afforded by the pleaders distanced the litigants from each other and from the judges. Instead of representing themselves, they were now represented by someone else. For their part, the jurors had to evaluate the relative merits of the two sides of a dispute by maintaining a distinction between pleaders and litigants, something they could not always do. In effect, then, a jury often reached its verdict by weighing the arguments of two discourses divorced from the persons most immediately concerned. Third, litigants unhappy with the verdict could now blame the pleaders rather than themselves.

Cicero was not only a prominent and successful pleader in Roman courts but also a man of wide learning and culture. On the one hand, his forensic speeches illustrate the particular uses to which he put rhetoric while pleading specific cases. On the other hand, his rhetorical treatises (i.e., *De Inventione, De Oratore*) and his philosophical works (i.e., *De Legibus, De Officiis*) provide a sense of his understanding of forensic rhetoric and his conception of justice respectively. While we, like Cicero, recognize the distance between rhetorical practice and theory, and while we are aware of the quarrel between philosophy and rhetoric in his time, we agree with his view that theory and practice are two sides of the same coin and that rhetoric and philosophy are two interdependent areas of learning. Although we do not consider in this section Cicero's particular speeches of accusation and defense, our guiding supposition is that his understanding of judicial rhetoric is predicated on his conception of justice.

Cicero's conception of justice resembles Plato's. Following what Plato does in his *Laws,* Cicero posits in *De Legibus* that law is the ruling principle of all things. Part of God's divine intelligence and the highest expression of reason, law regulates the universe and nature, as well as human societies and individual behavior. Because humans are part of nature, they are bound to its laws, which they cannot escape or alter. A well-regulated and lawful state is one that models its legal system after the laws of nature. Justice consists of those laws of nature that apply to human beings. Justice is the foundation of every society and the most essential element of human relationships. Because justice issues from natural law, all forms of justice in their essence are matters of nature, not human convention. Human convention can strengthen the application of natural justice in a state by means of custom and usage.

Cicero is quite aware that this conception is opposed by the view that justice is simply a matter of human convention based on expediency. However, he is unwilling to go as far as the Greek Sophists and subject justice to the whim of circumstances and the force of persuasion. For him, even convention has its foundation in justice. As he explains in *De Inventione,* conceptions and practices of justice become over time customary by virtue of the advantages they yield to those who discover and learn them (II.liii.60). Cicero's argument, then, suggests that justice is not contrary to, but rather consistent with, individual or collective advantage. Cicero is also cognizant that some teachers teach the specifics of law as if it had nothing to do with justice. Asserting that Roman civil law is only a very small part of the idea of justice, he observes that these teachers "are teaching not so much the path of justice as of litigation" (*De Legibus* I.v.18). In effect, these teachers have adopted the view of the masses, who think that justice is a set of commands and prohibitions written in law books and enacted in the courts. Justice, however, transcends both law books and court performances.

In the light of Cicero's conception of justice, forensic rhetoric is nothing but an institutionalized attempt to discover that which is specifically just and lawful in a particular case. All the elaborate studies and prescriptions of rhetoric as it applies to judicial matters have this one purpose: to correct human transgression and, in so doing, restore the scales of justice to their true and original position of perfect balance. The rhetoricians' concern with the invention of arguments, models of composition and delivery, the character of the orator, the classifications of human motivation and action, the quality of evidence, the examination of witnesses, the dispositions and emotional makeup of the judges, and so forth—all these things have been devised for a singular end: the realignment of imbalanced human situations with natural justice. Of course, it goes without saying that determining what is just and lawful in a particular case is far from simple. People seem to have competing conceptions of justice and conflicting interpretations of the laws because in a court of law their interests are diametrically opposed. Cicero does not address the problems arising out of the conflict between a universal notion of justice and a set of specific individual interests. He simply counsels that judicial oratory should serve, rather than frustrate, justice; or, conversely, justice is not to be manipulated, but rather upheld, by oratory.

Of course, Cicero would readily admit that if all people followed the path of justice, there would be no need for forensic rhetoric. As it is, however, some disobey the dictates of reason and believe that their advantage lies outside the boundaries of law. These people, Cicero claims, deny the truth about human nature and will ultimately suffer the severest of penalties even if they escape all forms of human punishment (*De Republica* III.xxii.33). Cicero would also admit that despite the orator's best intentions and despite rhetoric's advancements, the attempt to restore justice at times fails—in fact, it can even lead to further injustice—that is, when transgressors are declared innocent and victims pronounced guilty. Even so, he, like Aristotle, seems to have faith that things that are true and just eventually triumph over their opposites. This faith is supported by the rules of the rhetorical art, which, as we have seen, amount to a useful guide to help justice prevail. Rhetoric cannot, any more than law itself, safeguard and guarantee justice.

One of the more interesting issues that emerges out of Cicero's concern with justice is the relationship between rhetoric and law. In *De Oratore*, he has Crassus and Antonius consider whether the forensic orator needs to be thoroughly versed in law in order to plead cases in the courts. The background against which this question is raised is first, the Romans' intense interest in, and awareness of the centrality of, law in any society, and second, Cicero's own view of the nature of justice.

De Oratore presents us with two answers to the question. The first argues that the forensic orator needs to know about the law pertaining to the case tried because such knowledge identifies the parameters within which he can select particular arguments—arguments outside those parameters will generally fail to win the case at hand. Advanced by Crassus, this position is an argument for professional competence. At the same time, it rests on the insight that the judges' perception of the pleader as a knowledgeable person is more likely to carry conviction. The same position, however, constitutes a response to the practice of some careless pleaders who were undertaking to defend clients without knowing what provisions the law made for their cases. In addition, then, to its theoretical merit, this position seeks to stipulate who should and who should not be allowed to practice rhetoric in the courts.

The second and opposite answer is that the forensic orator does not need to know the specific details of the law pertaining to his case. Advanced by Antonius, this position distinguishes the legal specialist from the orator. The former is "the man who is an expert in the statutes, and in the customary law observed by individuals as members of the community, and who is qualified to advise, direct the course of a lawsuit, and safeguard a client" (*De Oratore* I.xlvii.212). On the other hand, the orator is "a man who can use language agreeable to the ear, and arguments suited to convince, in law-court disputes and in debates of public business" (I.xlix.213).

Antonius' rationale is that knowledge of common law is not inherent in oratorical ability. The fact that one can excel in two or more fields of human endeavor does not establish a necessary connection between the fields of one's excellence. What the forensic orator needs is not legal knowledge, but a good sense of social life and the general practices of mankind. In the accomplished orator, he says, "we require a man of sharpness, ingenious by nature and experience alike, who with keen scent will track down the thoughts, feelings, beliefs and hopes of his fellow citizens and of any men whom on any issue he would fain win over by his word" (I.li.223). When it comes to the particular instance of pleading, Antonius continues, it is well known that it is not legal knowledge but eloquence that wins cases; and if this is so, a general knowledge of law suffices—details and technicalities can always be had from the experts. Antonius concludes by noting that the art of eloquence is hard enough as it is, and that the orator cannot possibly acquire all the knowledge available in all the different departments of learning (law, politics, ethics, history). Therefore, he should concentrate on the perfection of his art.

Because we live in a society of specialists, Antonius' answer makes more sense to us. However, Crassus' answer is informed by a submerged ethical attitude according to which a pleader's primary obligation is neither to himself nor to his client but to justice. He is its servant first and foremost. But if this is so, a pleader would not prosecute the innocent and would not defend the unjust. In this regard, Cicero would approve of Quintilian's view that the ideal orator would generally prefer defense over prosecution but would not hesitate to prosecute cases involving "the complaints of our allies, the death of friends or kinsmen, or conspiracies that threaten the common weal to go unavenged." Moreover, the ideal orator "will not defend all and sundry." Nor will he undertake to plead a case guided by the client's social status. Finally, he will desert a case he has undertaken if he finds out that carrying on would mean defending injustice (*Institutio Oratoria* XII.vii.1–7).

RHETORIC AND POLITICS: CICERO

Roman politics was no different from Greek politics. Both constituted spheres of power and influence. Both were arenas in which the interests of one group collided with those of another. Both were marked by violence on the one hand and rhetorical persuasion on the other— intense debates and prolonged negotiations preceded and followed domestic and foreign wars, betrayals, conspiracies, killings, and other acts of brutality. Both aimed at the resolution of public issues and the acquisition of advantage. And both sought to capitalize on opportunities and to anticipate the future by hammering out visions of order supposedly meant to better the life of the citizens and to preserve the state. All these similarities aside, the essential difference between Greek and Roman politics lies in the forms of their political organization. As we have noted, Greek politics was mainly democratic and relied on the full participation of the citizens. Roman politics under the Republic was mostly aristocratic, with limited popular participation.

Like Roman politics, Roman political rhetoric was similar to its Greek counterpart. Although the specific issues addressed by the Roman orators might have differed from those of their Greek colleagues, the Roman rhetoricians generally adopted most of Aristotle's discussion of the discourse of deliberation. But insofar as politics and rhetoric are interconnected, and insofar as Roman politics was structurally different from Greek politics, we should expect some difference between the two rhetorical understandings. As we examine in this section the Roman view of political rhetoric, we will see that Roman politics and rhetoric are expected to originate from, and be practiced by, the members of the upper class. In the hands of Cicero and Quintilian, this expectation finds expression in the ideal statesman on the one hand, and the ideal orator on the other.

Unlike the Greek political intellectuals, who never held public office, Cicero devoted much of his life to an active political career and held the highest governmental office in his country (consul). As with his judicial speeches, which indicate the legal uses to which he put rhetoric, his preserved political orations show us how he handled various political issues at various times and in various contexts. On the other hand, his rhetorical treatises (i.e., *De Inventione, De Oratore*) and his philosophical works (i.e., *De Republica, De Officiis*) give us some idea of the way in which he reduced his own and others' rhetorical practice in the domain of politics into a set of principles. Our arguments in the previous section regarding the relationship between practice and theory on the one hand and rhetoric and philosophy on the other apply in this section, too. Accordingly, our guiding supposition this time is that Cicero's understanding of political rhetoric is founded on his conception of politics.

Cicero's notion of politics combines elements of idealism and realism. On the ideal side, he claims in *De Republica* that the highest forms of human accomplishment are philosophy (the contemplation of ideas) and statesmanship (the creation of the state through institutions and laws), and that both forms are the result of the divine gifts of speech and reason. Statesmanship is the higher of the two because it requires the best forms of knowledge and action. By extension, the statesman is an ideal individual who, by virtue of his knowledge of, and care for, the common good, is much superior to most politicians, who are driven mainly by ambition and the pursuit of personal advantage. As Scipio, one of the characters in *De Republica*, argues, the ideal statesman is the most qualified man to carry out the greatest of human tasks:

> For just as the aim of the pilot is a successful voyage, of the physician, health, and of the general, victory, so this director of the commonwealth has as his aim for his fellow-citizens a happy life, fortified by wealth, rich in material resources, great in glory and honored for virtue. I want him to bring to perfection this achievement, which is the greatest and best possible among men. (V.vi.8)

A variation of Plato's philosopher-king in the *Republic*, Cicero's ideal statesman embodies a wide array of rare qualities. He is a man who combines philosophical insight with rhetorical eloquence, honor with integrity, prudence with practical wisdom, and rationality with imagination. He urges his fellow citizens to follow the path of justice and moderation. He prompts them to resist the temptations of their passions and to fulfill their duties to the best of their abilities. Serving as an example for imitation, his words and actions are meant to benefit the state and its citizens rather than himself. In short, everything the ideal statesman is, says, and does is motivated by the grandest idea: the good of the state.

Cicero, however, knows quite well that while the notion of the ideal statesmen posits what should be the case, the reality of actual politics reminds us what is the case. And he also knows that while an ideal is, by definition, unattainable, the actual is all too real. Even so, Cicero's realism does not lead him to condemn actual politics on account of its vast difference from an ideal version. Actual politics, he observes, is as good or wicked as the people who make and occupy it. The political sphere, in other words, reflects a mixed image of humanity in all its goodness and wickedness (*De Legibus* I.xi.31). Accordingly, unity and division, the two most crucial phenomena of political life, are a function of people's goodness and depravity respectively. As he puts it in one of the extant fragments of *De Legibus* (2), "By reason of their depravity they [people] quarrel, not realizing that they are of one blood and subject to one and the same protecting power [the power of Nature]. If this fact were understood, surely man would live the life of the gods!"

In the light of this conception of politics, rhetoric becomes an instrument for managing the affairs of the state by resolving public issues and securing consensus among citizens. Cicero, however, knows that rhetoric, like politics, is a mixed blessing because it can unite as well as divide people, and in so doing, benefit or harm the state. Addressing the doubleness of the art of persuasion in relation to politics, he claims that rhetoric's destructive potential can be tempered by the study of philosophy, which yields wisdom in the form of rational and moral knowledge. The opening lines of his *De Inventione* give us a glimpse of his thinking on the double-edged sword that is rhetoric:

> I have often seriously debated with myself whether men and communities have received more good or evil from oratory and a consuming devotion to eloquence. For when I ponder the troubles in our commonwealth, and run over in my mind the ancient misfortunes of mighty cities, I see that no little part of the disasters was brought about by men of eloquence. When, on the other hand, I begin to search in the records of literature for events which occurred before the period which our generation can remember, I find that many cities have been founded, that the flames of a multitude of wars have been extinguished, and that the strongest alliances and most sacred friendships have been formed not only by the use of the reason but also more easily by the help of eloquence. For my own part, after long thought, I have been led by reason itself to hold this opinion first and foremost, that wisdom without eloquence does too little for the good of the states, but that eloquence without wisdom is generally highly disadvantageous and is never helpful. Therefore, if anyone neglects the study of philosophy and moral conduct, which is the highest and most honorable of pursuits, and devotes his whole energy to the practice of oratory, his civic life is nurtured into something useless to himself and harmful to his country; but the man who equips himself with the weapons of eloquence, not to be able to attack the welfare of his country but to defend it, he, I think, will be a citizen most helpful and most devoted both to his own interests and those of his community. (I.i.1)

Rhetoric's potential for both good and evil finds further expression in Cicero's work. Following the realism of Aristotle, he designates that which is advantageous as the proper aim of political rhetoric. At the same time, however, Cicero follows the idealism of Isocrates when he makes the aim of political rhetoric include that which is honorable. In *De Inventione* (II.iv.12; lii.157–158), he explains that that which is advantageous (i.e., money) is sought as a means to an end. On the other hand, that which is honorable (i.e., virtue, knowledge, and truth) is pursued for its own sake. Interestingly, Cicero also includes in the area of political rhetoric things that are both honorable and advantageous (i.e., friendship and good reputation).

More than a follower of his Greek predecessors, however, Cicero is a representative of his own society and culture. As such, his addition of the honorable to political rhetoric reflects more than an accidental addition to the rhetorical theory he inherited. Specifically, it reflects the important distinction the Romans made between the aristocratic patricians and the common plebeians. As he points out in his *De Partitione Oratoria*:

> Mankind falls into two classes, one uninstructed and uncultivated, which always prefers utility to moral value, and the other humane and cultivated, which places true worth above all other things. Consequently the latter class of people give the first place to distinction, honor, glory, good faith, justice and all the forms of virtue, while the former class put the profits and emoluments of gain first. (XXV.90)

The clear implication of this passage is that when addressing cultivated audiences, the political orator foregrounds arguments for honor; when speaking to the ignorant masses, he uses arguments for advantage.

The fact that rhetoric is a mixed blessing does not prevent Cicero from searching for an ideal rhetoric, a rhetoric all orators would want to pursue. This search manifests itself in the portrait of the ideal orator much the same way that his search for an ideal politics manifests itself in the portrait of the ideal statesman. The portrait of the ideal orator emerges out of a debate between Crassus and Antonius in *De Oratore*. Cicero has Crassus point out that oratory affects the quality and direction of politics. Crassus observes that the orator, by virtue of his eloquence, influences not only the people themselves but also their political representatives in the popular assemblies and their rulers in the aristocratic senate. From this observation he moves to the argument that the orator could not influence audiences on political matters if he lacked knowledge of politics. Therefore, he concludes, orators who are influential in the political sphere must know something about politics. Conversely, the statesman who is deficient in eloquence cannot be the ideal statesman. In sum, Crassus' point is that the ideal statesman and the ideal orator are mirror images of one another.

Antonius opposes this line of thought by claiming that while oratory and statesmanship might coexist in the same person they are not necessarily interconnected:

> If a man is capable in both ways, such as the originator of national policy who is also a good senator, he is not just for that reason an orator; nor did the accomplished orator, who happens also to be outstanding in public administration, attain that special knowledge through his fluency in speaking. (*De Oratore* I.xlix.215)

For Antonius, "Whoever knows and uses everything by which the advantage of the State is secured and developed, is the man to be deemed the helmsman of the State, and the originator of national policy" (I.2xlviii.211). On the other hand, an orator is "a man of sharpness, ingenious by nature and experience alike, who with keen scent will track down the thoughts, feelings, beliefs, and hopes of his fellow-citizens and of any men whom on any issue he would fain win over by his word" (I.li.223).

Crassus is not persuaded. Although he grants that eloquence does not bestow political knowledge, he insists that the orator is much more than a technician of words. Beyond his talent in language, the ideal orator knows how to use it for the good of the state. Whether addressing military, legal, or political matters, he shows intelligence when describing how things are and insight when telling what should be done to change them for the better. That is why generals, jurists, and politicians seek his support and advice. He is a man of vision who can shape a national awareness and who can control through discourse people's emotional passions and channel their collective energy into productive forms of action. As Crassus puts it:

> We are not seeking some pettifogger, declaimer or ranter, but that man who, to begin with, is high priest of that art which, though unaided nature bestowed on mankind a great capacity for it, was deemed to have been the gift of a divinity, so that a property peculiar to humanity might seem no offspring of ourselves, but to be sent down upon us from heaven; who secondly can abide unharmed even on the field of battle, through the respect felt for his title or orator rather than any heraldic staff; who furthermore can by his eloquence expose to the indignation of fellow citizens, and restrain by punishment, the crimes and iniquities of the guilty; who also, by the shield of his talent, can deliver innocence from legal penalties; who again can either in-

spire a lukewarm and erring nation to a sense of the fitting, or lead them away from their blundering, or kindle their wrath against the wicked, or soothe them when they are excited against good men; who lastly can by his eloquence either arouse or calm, within the souls of men, whatever passion the circumstances and occasion may demand. (I.xlvi.202)

RHETORIC AND DISPLAY: CICERO AND QUINTILIAN

Cicero agrees with Aristotle that epideictic rhetoric differs from the deliberative and judicial kinds both in dignity and scope; it is more elevated and covers more ground than the other two genres. Even so, he observes, the Romans do not practice display rhetoric as much as their Greek predecessors had done. Cicero claims that unlike the Greeks, whose books are full of encomiastic speeches on some of their more notable public figures, the Romans have focused their rhetorical energies on the practical discourses of politics and the law, and, in so doing, have left a whole area of oratory unexplored. As Antonius reports in *De Oratore,* "Our Roman commendatory speeches that we make in the forum have either the bare and unadorned brevity of evidence to a person's character or are written to be delivered as a funeral speech, which is by no means a suitable occasion for parading one's distinction in rhetoric" (III.lxxxiv.341). For Cicero, this Roman lack of interest in oratorical display explains why nobody has laid down rules for epideictic discourse.

The absence of rules for epideictic oratory and the frequency of occasions for praising a person (i.e., bestowing honor on someone, defending the accused in court) prompt Cicero to address epideictic oratory at some length. Speaking through Antonius, he posits that the oratory of praise should mainly revolve around a person's character. However, he also points out that those qualities which are desirable and those which are praiseworthy in a person's character do not always coincide. Desirable qualities such as family, good looks, bodily strength, material resources, and wealth hardly constitute grounds for praise—the one who possesses them is usually not responsible for them. On the other hand, virtuous qualities are praiseworthy in themselves and constitute the basis for any kind of praise. But if this is so, desirable qualities can become topics of praise inasmuch as their particular manifestation demonstrates a person's virtuous qualities—that is, beneficence, temperance. For example, we would praise a rich person not for being rich, but for having used his wealth wisely or for the benefit of others rather than himself.

Cicero's perspective on epideictic oratory stipulates that the orator who praises must have knowledge of all the virtues. This is so because not all virtues are the same, and each one has its own demands. Although they all manifest themselves in some form of behavior, some virtues (i.e., intelligence, high-mindedness, inner strength, wisdom, magnanimity, eloquence) grace the one who possesses them while others (i.e., kindness, beneficence, mercy, justice, fidelity) benefit the human race in general. According to this division, the orator must realize that while audiences admire and derive pleasure from the praise of one's virtuous character, they especially appreciate hearing about deeds done without profit or reward. This is so, Antonius explains, because people believe that altruistic deeds "mark a man of outstanding merit" (*De Oratore* (II.lxxxv.346).

Cicero's advice for the epideictic orator issues not only from the number and kinds of virtues available, but more importantly from the audience's beliefs about the nature of virtue and the nature of a good man. In this regard, Cicero resembles Aristotle, who saw epideictic rhetoric as a way of praising in a person what the audience admires the most or blaming what it hates the most. Thus Cicero has Antonius add to the list of what audiences appreciate: "Also it is customarily recognized as a great and admirable distinction to have borne adversity wisely, not to have been crushed by misfortune, and not to have lost dignity in a difficult situation; and distinction is also conferred by offices filled, rewards of merit bestowed, and achievements honored by the judgment of mankind" (II.lxxxv.346–347).

Cicero's views on epideictic oratory find additional expression in some of his other works. In *De Inventione,* for example, part of his discussion of a legal defense is generated from the topics of praise. Thus the defense will sometimes have to praise the accused by showing that his life has been "upright in the highest degree," that he has performed difficult and dangerous services for the state out of a sense of duty, that he has generally treated other people well, and that he has repeatedly resisted the temptation to dishonesty (II.xi.35). Also in *De Inventione,* Cicero includes in his discussion of deliberative rhetoric a list of those things that people generally consider honorable, and therefore praiseworthy. Those things include wisdom, which is "the knowledge of what is good, what is bad and what is neither good nor bad"; justice, which is "a habit of mind which gives every man his desert while preserving the common advantage"; courage, which is "the quality by which one undertakes dangerous tasks and endures hardships"; and temperance, which is "a firm and well-considered control exercised by the reason over lust and other improper impulses of the mind" (II.liii.160–164). Finally, in *Topica*, Cicero observes that whenever the topic under discussion is honor and virtue, or dishonor and vice, the orator will need to resort to the epideictic categories of praise or blame (xxiii.89–96). To the extent that praise and blame serve the purposes of political and judicial oratory, Cicero's implicit argument is that the two main concerns of epideictic can and should be used when the orator addresses political issues or pleads cases in court. In other words, there is no reason why the epideictic genre should in practice be kept apart from the other two.

Following Cicero's footsteps, Quintilian seeks to expand the scope of epideictic oratory and keep it from becoming irrelevant to practical affairs. In this attempt, he adopts the Isocratean perspective, which subordinates the discourse of praise or blame to a higher goal, the good of the community. In this regard, he criticizes Aristotle for having separated the function of epideictic oratory from practical matters, thus limiting it to a display of the orator's rhetorical virtuosity for the delight of the spectators. Although Quintilian does acknowledge that epideictic oratory often aims at mere show and display, he also notes that the genre is used by Roman orators for utilitarian purposes as well. The examples he cites include funeral orations, which are generally treated as civic duties assigned to public officials; witness testimony, which can carry considerable weight in a legal case by virtue of the kind of praise or blame it pronounces; and praise or blame against one's political rivals, which can affect the outcome of an election. In effect, Quintilian's position supports Aristotle's observation that epideictic rhetoric is akin to the deliberative kind "inasmuch as the same things are usually praised in the former as are advised in the latter" (*Institutio Oratoria* (III.vii.28).

As we have seen, Aristotle had eliminated proof from the discourse of display on the grounds that the facts of the case are widely known. Quintilian, however, argues that some form of proof is always required by epideictic discourse because it generally has a practical dimension; but even when the purpose of epideictic oratory is display pure and simple, some semblance of proof is expected. For without the element of proof, a discourse, regardless of its goal, will fail to make its case. In any case, the proper function of epideictic oratory according to Quintilian is "to amplify and embellish its themes" (III.vii.6).

Unlike Cicero, whose treatment of epideictic oratory revolves around a person's character, Quintilian wishes to enlarge its range. For him, occasions for amplification and embellishment are virtually countless as they include praise directed to gods, heroes, and sometimes animals as well as inanimate objects. Depending on the object of praise, Quintilian notes, there are certain topics that must be addressed and certain steps that must be followed. Thus, in the case of the gods:

> Our first step will be to express our veneration of the majesty of their nature in general terms. Next we shall proceed to praise the special power of the individual god and the discoveries whereby he has benefited the human race. For example, in the case of Jupiter, we shall extol his power as manifested in the governance of all things, with Mars we shall praise his power in war, with Neptune his power over the sea; as regards inventions we shall celebrate Minerva's discovery of the arts, Mercury's discovery of letters . . . (III.vii.7–8)

Regarding the praise of specific individuals, Quintilian notes that the variety of topics to be considered is much wider. One such topic concerns the period prior to a living person's birth, another the period following a dead person's death. In the first case, reference should be made to the person's country, parents, and ancestors, showing that the person's achievements were such that he proved himself worthy of the greatness of his country, a credit to his parents, and an honorable descendant to his ancestors. In the second case, the orator should mention the contributions the departed made while alive. Praiseworthy contributions include offspring, artistic creations, public projects, communal service, and the like. When praising someone still alive, the themes of praise should revolve around the person's character, physical attributes, and external circumstances. Character can be praised along the lines of words and deeds in a chronological order or along the lines of the person's virtues (i.e., courage, fortitude, self-control, justice). Gifts of fortune or external and accidental advantages can be praised not in themselves but for the ways in which the person has used them. In this regard, Quintilian observes that audiences especially appreciate the celebration of deeds that the one praised was the first or the only one to perform; or that the deeds exceeded any normal expectation and were done for the benefit of others rather than oneself (III.vii.10–18).

A particular aspect of epideictic oratory concerns the praise of the audience. By praising one's listeners, Quintilian points out, the orator seeks to secure their good will and advance his case. On this issue, he follows Aristotle, who claims that a discourse of praise is more likely to be effective if it affirms what the audience values and denounces what it hates. Quintilian, however, takes issue with Aristotle's view that "since the boundary between vice and virtue is often ill-defined, it is desirable to use words that swerve a little from the actual truth, calling a rash man brave, a prodigal generous, a mean man thrifty." Quintilian responds that this is something "a good man will never do unless perhaps he is led to do so by considerations of the public interest" (III.vii.24–25).

Although, as we have seen, epideictic rhetoric covers a wide range of subjects, cities, public works, and places are three subjects in Quintilian's list that have contemporary relevance. Cities, he remarks, are praised in ways that resemble the praise of people. More specifically, the founders of a city are treated as its parents, its history carries a great deal of authority, and its virtues and vices are discussed like the virtues and vices of an individual. Cities are often assigned the role of the parents, while their citizens are given the role of the children. Public works are praised "in connection with their magnificence, utility, beauty and the architect or artist must be given due consideration." Finally, places are praised for their beauty and utility. As Quintilian puts it, "Beauty calls for notice in places by the sea, in open plains or pleasant situations, utility in healthy or fertile localities" (III.vii.27).

RHETORIC AND LANGUAGE: CICERO AND QUINTILIAN

Both Cicero and Quintilian understand language as a natural capacity developed and perfected by effort and study. For both, language finds its highest artistic form in rhetoric, the supreme power of all human accomplishments, the cause of the phenomenon of human civilization. Cicero's account of the origin and benefits of language to humankind resembles that of Isocrates. Like him, Cicero focuses on the crucial role language played in awakening human consciousness and unifying scattered individuals living like animals into ordered communities guided by the rule of law. Also in the manner of Isocrates, Cicero attributes to language two monumental transformations of human life: first, the translation of the survival instinct into the idea of the common good, and second, the conquest of physical force by persuasion. But unlike Isocrates, whose discourse focuses only on the upstanding and beneficial uses of *logos,* Cicero also mentions the potential for the corrupt and harmful uses of rhetoric. In a lengthy passage in *De Inventione,* he explains that rhetoric

> arose from the most honorable causes and continued on its way from the best
> of reasons. For there was a time when men wandered at large in the fields like
> animals and lived on wild fare; they did nothing by the guidance of reason,
> but relied chiefly on physical strength; there was as yet no ordered system of
> religious worship nor of social duties; no one had seen legitimate marriage nor
> had anyone looked upon children whom he knew to be his own; nor had they
> known the advantages of an equitable code of law. And so through their ig-
> norance and error blind and unreasoning passion satisfied itself by misuse of
> physical strength, which is a very dangerous servant.
>
> At this juncture a man—great and wise I am sure—became aware of the
> power latent in man and the wide field offered by his mind for great achieve-
> ments if one could develop this power and improve it by instruction. Men
> were scattered in the fields and hidden in sylvan retreats when he assembled
> and gathered them in accordance with a plan; he introduced them to every
> useful and honorable occupation, though they cried out against it at first be-
> cause of its novelty, and when through reason and eloquence they had lis-
> tened with greater attention, he transformed them from wild savages into a
> kind and gentle folk.
>
> To me, at least, it does not seem possible that a mute and voiceless wisdom
> could have turned men silently from their habits and introduced them to dif-
> ferent patterns of life. Consider another point: after cities had been estab-
> lished how could it have been brought to pass that men should learn to keep
> faith and observe justice and become accustomed to obey others voluntarily
> and believe not only that they must work for the common good but even sac-
> rifice life itself, unless men had been able by eloquence to persuade their fel-
> lows of the truth of what they had discovered by reason? Certainly only a
> speech at the same time powerful and entrancing could have induced one who
> had great physical strength to submit to justice without violence, so that he
> suffered himself to be put on a par with those among whom he could excel,
> and abandoned voluntarily a most agreeable custom, especially since this cus-
> tom had already acquired through lapse of time the force of a natural right.
>
> This was the way in which at first eloquence came into being and advanced
> to greater development, and likewise afterward in the greatest undertakings of
> peace and war it served the highest interests of mankind. But when a certain
> agreeableness of manner—a depraved imitation of virtue—acquired the
> power of eloquence unaccompanied by any consideration of moral duty, then
> low cunning supported by talent grew accustomed to corrupt cities and un-
> dermine the lives of men. (I.ii.2–3)

Cicero expands his discussion of language in *De Natura Deorum,*
a treatise in which he considers the faculty of speech alongside the capacity for reason. His claim there is that reason and speech are two different but complementary gifts from the gods. Balbus, one of the

characters in the treatise, singles out for praise the synthesizing function of reason, its ability to put together various elements (i.e., words,
propositions) and understand the results of its own connecting operations. At the same time, he credits reason for such accomplishments as
definition, the construction of knowledge, and the production of practical necessities as well as aesthetic delights. In his discourse on reason,
Balbus considers

> first our powers of understanding, and then our faculty of conjoining premises
> and consequences in a single act of apprehension, the faculty I mean that en-
> ables us to judge what conclusion follows from any given propositions and to
> put the inference in syllogistic form, and also to delimit particular terms in a
> succinct definition; whence we arrive at an understanding of the potency and
> the nature of knowledge, which is the most excellent part even of the divine
> nature. Again, how remarkable are the faculties . . . our sensory and intellec-
> tual perception and comprehension of external objects; it is by collating and
> comparing our percepts that we also create the arts that serve practical neces-
> sities or the purpose of amusement. (II.lix.147)

Immediately after discussing reason, Balbus considers the faculty
of speech and treats it, in the manner of Isocrates, as a means of discovering and transmitting knowledge, an instrument of persuasion, a
tool for regulating people's emotional energies, and a device for establishing rules for social behavior and political governance:

> Then take the gift of speech, the queen of arts . . . what a glorious, what a di-
> vine faculty it is! In the first place it enables us both to learn things we do not
> know and to teach things we do know to others; secondly it is our instrument
> for exhortation and persuasion, for consoling the afflicted and assuaging the
> fears of the terrified, for curbing passion and quenching appetite and anger; it
> is this that has united us in the bonds of justice, law and civil order, this that
> has separated us from savagery and barbarism. (II.lix.148)

As one might expect, the distance between the praise of language
in the above passages and the high status of the orator and his craft in
Roman society is quite short. In *De Oratore,* Cicero revisits the theme
of rhetoric's power, but this time he focuses on the person of the orator and his influence on the domains of social and political life. Using
Crassus as his mouthpiece, Cicero directs the readers' attention to the
personality of the accomplished orator. As the following passage indicates, the orator is a powerful figure because he can influence, and in
so doing control, people's thoughts and actions. In Crassus' words,
"There is to my mind no more excellent thing than the power, by
means of oratory, to get a hold on assemblies of men, win their good

will, direct their inclinations wherever the speaker wishes, or divert them from whatever he wishes" (I.viii.30).

Crassus continues praising the orator as an exceptional figure, one who excels in taking the capacity for language to admirable heights. Thanks to the genius of oratory, he notes, language transcends its instrumental and practical functions and becomes an object of aesthetic pleasure. The polished orator, he also observes, can affect by means of eloquent words the mood, the thought, and the behavior of crowds and leaders alike. Moreover, he can give voice to the voiceless, help the weak, and ensure the dignity and security of his fellow citizens. Finally, he can use oratory as a weapon to defend himself and accuse the wicked. In what reads like a soliloquy, Crassus wonders:

> What is so marvellous as that, out of the innumerable company of mankind, a single being should arise, who either alone or with few others can make effective a faculty bestowed by nature on every man? Or what so pleasing to the understanding and the ear as a speech adorned and polished with wise reflections and dignified language? Or what achievement so mighty and glorious as that the impulses of the crowd, the consciences of the judges, the austerity of the Senate, should suffer transformation through the eloquence of one man? What function again is so kingly, so worthy of the free, so generous, as to bring help to the suppliant, to raise up those that are cast down, to bestow security, to set free from peril, to maintain men in their civil rights? What too is so indispensable as to have always in your grasp weapons wherewith you can defend yourself, or challenge the wicked man, or when provoked take your revenge? (I.viii.31–32)

In his enumeration of the benefits of discourse, Crassus goes beyond rhetoric's pervasive presence in the public domains of law and politics to include conversation, yet another sign of the superiority of humans over animals:

> What in hours of ease can be a pleasanter thing or one more characteristic of culture, than discourse that is graceful and nowhere uninstructed? For the one point in which we have our very greatest advantage over the brute creation is that we hold converse one with another, and can reproduce our thought in word. (I.viii.32)

Despite all the praise he heaps on the person who is versed in the arts of speech, Cicero tries to dispel the notion that the orator is simply someone with an inborn talent and technical adeptness in language. In addition, Cicero insists, the orator is a cultured man of wide learning and broad intellectual horizons, an individual who consistently makes thoughtful and mature judgments, a dedicated student of human behavior in all its forms, a man of tested integrity and wisdom, and a person of virtuous character. In sum, Crassus points out, the accomplished orator embodies the ideal of the good citizen:

> The genuine orator must have investigated and heard and read and discussed and handled and debated the whole of the contents of the life of mankind, inasmuch as that is the field of the orator's activity, the subject matter of his study. For eloquence is one of the supreme virtues—although all the virtues are equal and on a par, but nevertheless one has more beauty and distinction in outward appearance than another, as is the case with this faculty, which, after compassing a knowledge of facts, gives verbal expression to the thought and purposes of the mind in such a manner as to have the power of driving the hearers forward in any direction in which it has applied its weight; and the stronger this faculty is, the more necessary it is for it to be combined with integrity and supreme wisdom, and if we bestow fluency of speech on persons devoid of those virtues, we shall not have made orators of them but shall have put weapons into the hands of madmen. (III.xiv.54–55)

While Cicero's discussion of language sounds more like a discourse of praise, Quintilian's looks more like the material one would expect to read in a textbook. This is hardly surprising if we recall that Cicero's remarks represent the thoughts of a seasoned orator reflecting on his illustrious career, whereas Quintilian's are meant to provide a pedagogical blueprint for the education of future orators. Like Cicero, Quintilian observes that speech is a natural endowment, one that over time and through much trial and error has achieved high levels of refinement: "Mankind," he points out, "received the gift of speech from nature at its birth . . . while the usefulness of speech brought improvement and study, and finally method and exercise gave perfection" (*Institutio Oratoria* III.ii.1). Elaborating on this brief explanation, Quintilian stresses neither the wisdom and grandeur of the first orator nor the earliest effects of speech on people, but the gradual accumulation of knowledge about language and its uses. In effect, the historical trajectory Quintilian draws out points to the development of an art the teaching of which can enhance the natural ability for language:

> It was . . . nature that created speech, and observation that originated the art of speaking. Just as men discovered the art of medicine by observing that some things were healthy and some the reverse, so they observed that some things were useful and some useless in speaking, and noted them for imitation or avoidance, while they added certain other precepts according as their nature suggested. These observations were confirmed by experience and each man proceeded to teach what he knew. (III.ii.3)

Quintilian proceeds to discuss language in terms of four interrelated categories: reason, antiquity, authority, and usage. Reason, he notes, finds support primarily in analogy and secondarily in etymology. Analogy requires a mental move from something familiar to something unfamiliar. It is a move that enables us to unlock the unfamiliar by the key of the familiar. This can be done if, once we discover that two different things are similar in some way, we begin looking for, and do discover, additional similarities between them. In effect, analogical thinking enables us to know that which we do not by means of that which we do. Accordingly, Quintilian posits that "the essence of analogy is the testing of all subjects of doubt by the application of some standard of comparison about which there is no question, the proof that is to say of the uncertain by reference to the certain" (I.vi.4). Analogies, for Quintilian, are not ready-made linguistic fixtures; rather, they are discoveries people make as they notice relationships between words and ideas in use. As he puts it:

> Analogy was not sent down from heaven at the creation of mankind to frame the rules of language, but was discovered after they began to speak and to note the terminations of words used in speech. It is therefore based not on reason but on example, nor is it a law of language, but rather a practice, which is observed, being in fact the offspring of usage. (I.vi.16)

Reason also finds support in etymology, which "inquires into the origin of words" (I.vi.28). Like Plato, Quintilian refers to etymology in connection with the correctness of names. But unlike Plato, who sought to establish a doctrine of correspondence between thing and word, he is more interested in the correct use of language. Accordingly, he points out that etymological inquiry is useful generally, but especially when we are seeking the currently correct definition of a word. In this regard, Quintilian claims that

> etymology is sometimes of the utmost use, whenever the word under discussion needs interpretation. . . . Consequently we find room for etymology when we are concerned with definitions. Sometimes again this science attempts to distinguish between correct forms and barbarisms . . . not to mention other words which depend on current usage. (I.vi.29–30)

But despite the merits Quintilian sees in etymology, he warns that some etymologists carry their task to such an extreme that their effort to restore words that have changed with usage to their true and original form "leads to the most hideous absurdities" (I.vi.32).

From the correctness of words Quintilian naturally moves to correctness in speaking, which he considers a rhetorical virtue. To speak correctly means to observe a balance between tradition and innovation. Tradition satisfies the need for stability, whereas innovation constitutes a response to the need for creativity. Given that language is always in the process of evolution, it always preserves what has traditionally proved useful (i.e., meaningful) and discards that which is no longer so. At the same time, it develops new words and forms of expression in order to maintain its efficiency and effectiveness. But if this is so, correct speaking demands that one combine a happy medium between old and new forms of linguistic use. As Quintilian puts it, "What can be more necessary than that we should speak correctly? Nay, I even think that, as far as possible, we should cling to correct forms and resist all tendencies to change. But to attempt to retain forms long obsolete and extinct is sheer impertinence and ostentatious pedantry" (I.vi.20).

From the issue of correctness Quintilian moves to that of clarity. Echoing Aristotle, he posits that clarity is one of the foremost virtues of language. Clear speech is immediately apprehensible and readily understood by the audience. By contrast, unclear speech is an embarrassment because it needs clarification if it is to succeed in conveying its meaning. To achieve clarity, the speaker must be ever so attentive to words whose derivation can be traced to antiquity as well as to words recently coined. The case for antiquity can be made on both fronts. First, antiquity reasserts itself before us every time we inquire into the etymology of a word. Second, antique words, like antique furniture, acquire value precisely because they have survived for so long and because they are being brought into the present by the user. The point is that words from antiquity strike us as novel because we have forgotten their earlier meanings and uses. As Quintilian puts it:

> Archaic words not only enjoy the patronage of distinguished authors but also give style a certain majesty and charm. For they have the authority of age behind them, and for the very reason that they have fallen into desuetude, produce an attractive effect not unlike that of novelty. But such words must be used sparingly and must not thrust themselves upon our notice, since there is nothing more tiresome than affectation. . . . (I.vi.39–40)

But since language is a mixture of both archaic and neological elements, Quintilian counsels that clarity is best achieved by using neither the most archaic nor the most recently coined words; both kinds risk leaving the audience in the dark. Addressing the issue of clarity vis-à-vis archaic and neological words, he notes:

> But what a faulty thing is speech, whose prime virtue is clearness, if it requires an interpreter to make its meaning plain! Consequently in the case of old words the best will be those that are newest, just as in the case of new words the best will be the oldest. (I.vi.41)

Authority in language involves the same arguments we have encountered while considering reason and antiquity. Quintilian suggests that the best forms of language have been authorized—that is to say, sanctioned by the masters of language. Their example can serve as a guide not only in the avoidance of errors but also as a model of imitation. Because their language has been recognized as the greatest by expert critics, reading these authors can help readers improve their own linguistic practices. As Quintilian remarks, "The same arguments apply to authority. For although the use of words transmitted to us by the best authors may seem to preclude the possibility of error, it is important to notice not merely what they said, but what words they succeeded in sanctioning" (I.vi.42). But as we have seen in Quintilian's earlier arguments, authority in language changes over time precisely because language changes. Thus the authority of a particular master of old may decline as that of another, more contemporary, may rise. This means that the student of language needs to have a good ear for the fall of older linguistic forms and the emergence of the newer ones.

The above considerations notwithstanding, Quintilian returns again and again to the cardinal importance of usage: "Usage however is the surest pilot in speaking and we should treat language as currency minted with the public stamp" (I.vi.3). By "public stamp" Quintilian does not mean the linguistic practices of the public at large. Unwilling to relinquish the last word on usage to the majority of speakers, he suggests that the language of the masses is neither virtuous nor enlightened, neither correct nor refined. Accordingly, the inspiration to speak well cannot come from the circles of the uneducated: "We must not accept as a rule of language words and phrases that have become a viscious habit with a number of persons" (I.vi.44). Quintilian grants that, like action, linguistic usage is regulated normatively. Yet, he maintains that regulation should be determined by the minority of the educated. Drawing a parallel between words and deeds, he defines usage in speech as "the agreed practice of educated men, just as where our way of life is concerned I should define it as the agreed practice of all good men" (I.vi.45).

SUMMARY

In this chapter we have seen that Cicero's view of the relationship between rhetoric and law is predicated on a conception of natural justice. According to this conception, laws are concrete manifestations of justice, whereas rhetoric is an instrumentality meant to uphold the laws and advance the cause of justice. Although Cicero is aware that rhetoric can be used to undermine the laws and frustrate the cause of justice, he nevertheless claims that the good pleader will not employ rhetoric wrongfully. This claim is based on two assertions; first, justice eventually prevails, and second, the philosophical study of justice and the professional knowledge of law are the best safeguards for the rightful use of oratory.

This chapter has also shown that Cicero's views on rhetoric and politics are both idealistic and realistic. At its best, politics is administered by the ideal statesman, whose only goal is the common good of the people and the good of the state. At its best, rhetoric is practiced by the ideal orator, whose primary purpose is to influence people's thoughts and actions in the direction of unity and cooperation. In its actuality, politics is corrupt, violent, and destructive; those engaged in it are driven by ambition and seek personal power and advantage. In its actuality, rhetoric exploits popular beliefs and sentiments in ways that lead to division and conflict. Although Cicero's ideal politics and ideal rhetoric are unattainable, statesmen and orators can approximate them by acquiring the rational and moral knowledge afforded by the study of philosophy.

Despite the relative dearth of epideictic oratory in Roman society, Cicero and Quintilian apparently believed that the genre merited attention. Whether epideictic oratory should be treated as a separate genre or in connection with the deliberative and judicial kinds is not the point of this chapter. Rather, the point is that the discourse of praise finds useful applications in both the political and the legal spheres. Likewise, whether the discourses of praise or blame should be directed at a person's character or any object whatsoever is not the issue. Rather, the issue is how to help the orator carry out the tasks of praising or blaming effectively.

Finally in this chapter we have seen that for Cicero and Quintilian the capacity for language is the human capacity par excellence, that capacity which makes human beings human. As the basic material of rhetoric, language can be formulated so as to become the driving force behind innumerable benefits. While Cicero's discussion points to many of these benefits and praises the orator as the consummate linguistic craftsman, Quintilian's provides four basic categories (reason, antiquity, authority, usage) through which the student can understand the permanent as well as the changing features of language. If nothing else, these categories call attention to the cognitive operations, the historical origins, and normative uses of language. And in so doing, they help students find their way to correctness and clarity.

QUESTIONS
FOR
DISCUSSION

CHAPTER 1

1. Discuss the relationship between the structure of the Athenian courts and the art of persuasion. How did the former affect the development of the latter?
2. Discuss the principles of *dissoi logoi* (twofold argument), *to prepon* (the appropriate), and *kairos* (the opportune moment). How did these principles affect the nature of persuasion?
3. Discuss the Sophists' approach to court oratory as exemplified by Gorgias' *Encomium of Helen.* What conclusions do you draw about their views on the nature of persuasion?
4. Discuss the grounds on which Plato bases his condemnation of rhetoric. What justification for this condemnation does Plato offer in the *Apology?*

5. Discuss Isocrates' critique of rhetoric as it was practiced in the courts. How does his critique differ from Plato's?

6. Discuss what contributions Aristotle's psychological explanations of human nature make to our understanding of the art of persuasion.

CHAPTER 2

1. Discuss the relationship between the structure of the Athenian assembly and the art of deliberation. How did the former affect the development of the latter?

2. Discuss the potential and limits of deliberation in regard to the improvement of democracy. How do relations among people become more or less democratic through deliberation?

3. Discuss the relationship between deliberation and knowledge. In what ways can deliberation compensate for the limits of human knowledge?

4. Discuss Plato's critique of public deliberation as practiced by orators in his day. Why does Plato regard public oratory as a flawed *techne*?

5. Discuss Isocrates' conception of deliberation as a practical art. In what ways does Isocrates believe deliberation can circumvent the limits of knowledge?

6. Discuss the grounds on which Aristotle regards the ability to deliberate as practical wisdom. How do these grounds extend Isocrates' conception of deliberation as a practical art?

CHAPTER 3

1. Discuss the relationship between religious and athletic festivals and the rhetoric of display. In what ways did the former contribute to the development of the latter?

2. Discuss the relationship between dominant valuations and the rhetoric of display. Can the genre of display also be used to promote alternative valuations?

3. Discuss what Prodicus' *Choice of Hercules* contributes to our understanding of rhetoric as the art of display.

4. Discuss Plato's critical attitude toward the rhetoric of display. What basis does the *Phaedrus* offer for that critique?

5. Discuss the relationship between display and politics as Isocrates conceived it. How does Isocrates' *Helen* illuminate this relationship?

6. Discuss the relationship between the rhetoric of display and the moral character of the speaker as Aristotle conceived it. How does Aristotle link surface and appearance with moral content?

CHAPTER 4

1. Discuss the sophistic view of language as the power to shape reality. How is this view supported by Gorgias' *Encomium of Helen*? Why was this view contested by Plato?
2. Discuss Plato's understanding of language as capable of conveying a sense of the world of ideas. On what basis does Plato defend his understanding?
3. Discuss Isocrates' view of language as the basis for human civilization and communal life. In what ways does language act as a force to bind humans together?
4. Discuss Aristotle's conceptions of practical and productive uses of language. How do these two concepts help us better understand the nature of rhetoric?

CHAPTER 5

1. Discuss the Sophists' view of relative knowledge. How does the Sophists' view of situated knowledge get around the problem of relativism?
2. Discuss the relationship between knowledge and truth as Plato conceived it. Given this view, how does Plato get around the problem of change?
3. Discuss the relationship between knowledge and judgment as Isocrates conceived it. What role does history play in that relationship according to Isocrates?
4. Discuss the relationship between universal rules and particular cases in Aristotle. What kind of interplay between the two leads, according to Aristotle, to productive knowledge?

CHAPTER 6

1. Discuss the relationship between Greek and Roman conceptions of law and justice. How would Aristotle respond to Cicero's view of judicial rhetoric?

2. Discuss the similarities and differences between Greek and Roman politics. How would the Greek Sophists respond to Cicero's view of political oratory?
3. Discuss the differences between Greek and Roman epideictic rhetoric. How can these differences be explained?
4. Discuss similarities between the Greek and Roman views on language. How would Isocrates respond to what Cicero and Quintilian have to say about language?

SUGGESTIONS
FOR
FURTHER
READING

Greek Rhetorical Theory

Benoit, William. "Isocrates and Aristotle on Rhetoric." *Rhetoric Society Quarterly* 20 (1990): 251–260.

———. "Isocrates and Plato on Rhetoric and Rhetorical Education." *Rhetoric Society Quarterly* 21 (1991): 60–72.

Benson, Thomas W., ed., and Michael H. Prosser. *Readings in Classical Rhetoric.* Ann Arbor: University Microfilms International, 1985.

Cherwitz, Richard A., ed. *Rhetoric and Philosophy.* Hillsdale, N.J.: L. Erlbaum Associates, 1990.

Clark, Norman. "The Critical Servant: An Isocratean Contribution to Critical Rhetoric." *The Quarterly Journal of Speech* 82 (1996): 111–124.

Cole, Thomas. *The Origins of Rhetoric in Ancient Greece.* Baltimore: Johns Hopkins University Press, 1991.

Corbett, Edward P. J. *Classical Rhetoric for the Modern Student.* 3rd ed. New York: Oxford University Press, 1990.

Guthrie, W. K. C. *The Sophists.* Cambridge: Cambridge University Press, 1971.

Haden, James. "Two Types of Power in Plato's *Gorgias*." *The Classical Journal* 87 (1992): 313–326.

Hauser, Gerard. *Introduction to Rhetorical Theory*. New York: Harper and Row, 1986.

Ijsseling, Samuel. *Rhetoric and Philosophy in Conflict*. The Hague: Martinus Nijhoff, 1976.

Jaeger, Werner. *Paideia: The Ideals of Greek Culture*. 3 vols. Trans. G. Norlin and L. Van Hook. New York: Oxford University Press, 1971.

Jarratt, Susan Carole Funderburgh. *Rereading the Sophists: Classical Rhetoric Refigured*. Carbondale: Southern Illinois University Press, 1991.

Kennedy, George Alexander. *A New History of Classical Rhetoric*. Princeton, N.J.: Princeton University Press, 1994.

Kerferd, G. B. *The Sophistic Movement*. Cambridge: Cambridge University Press, 1981.

———, ed. *The Sophists and Their Legacy*. Wiesbaden: Franz Steiner, 1981.

Matsen, Patricia, ed. *Readings from Classical Rhetoric*. Carbondale: Southern Illinois University Press, 1990.

Murphy, James J., ed. *A Synoptic History of Classical Rhetoric*. New York: Random House, 1972.

Poulakos, John. *Sophistical Rhetoric in Classical Greece*. Columbia: University of South Carolina Press, 1995.

Sheeks, Wayne. "Isocrates, Plato, and Xenophon Against the Sophists." *The Personalist* 56 (1975): 250–259.

Sprague, Rosamond. *The Older Sophists*. Columbia: University of South Carolina Press, 1972.

Sutton, Jane. "Rereading Sophistical Arguments: A Political Intervention." *Argumentation* 5 (1991): 141–157.

Vernant, Jean-Pierre. *Myth and Thought Among the Greeks*. London: Routledge, 1983.

———. *The Origins of Greek Thought*. Ithaca: Cornell University Press, 1982.

Wardy, Robert. *The Birth of Rhetoric: Gorgias, Plato and Their Successors*. New York: Routledge, 1996.

Woodman, A. J. *Rhetoric in Class Historiography: Four Studies*. London: Croom Helm, 1988.

Rhetoric and Law

Barrett, Harold. *Sophists: Rhetoric, Democracy, and Plato's Idea of Sophistry*. Novato, Calif.: Chandler and Sharp, 1987.

Bybee, Michael D. "Logic in Rhetoric—And Vice Versa." *Philosophy and Rhetoric* 26 (1993): 169–190.

Carawan, Edwin. "The *Tetralogies* and the Athenian Homicide Trials." *American Journal of Philology* 114 (1994): 235–270.

Cohen, David. "Law, Autonomy, and Political Community in Plato's *Laws*." *Classical Philology* 88 (1993): 301–317.

Dover, K. J. "The Freedom of the Intellectual in Greek Society." *Talanta* 7 (1976): 24–54.

DuVoisin, Jacques Antoine. "The Rhetoric of Authenticity in Plato's *Hippias Major.*" *Arethusa* 29 (1996): 363–388.

Feaver, D. D., and John E. Hare. "The Apology as an Inverted Parody of Rhetoric." *Arethusa* 14 (1981): 205–217.

Fowler, Alastair. "Apology for Rhetoric." *Rhetorica* 8 (1990): 103–118.

Gagarin, Michael. "The Nature of Proofs in Antiphon." *Classical Philology* 85 (1990): 22–32.

Garner, Richard. *Law and Society in Classical Athens.* London: Croom Helm, 1987.

Haden, James. "Two Types of Power in Plato's *Gorgias.*" *The Classical Journal* 87 (1992): 313–326.

Kennedy, George Alexander. *The Art of Persuasion in Greece.* Princeton, N.J.: Princeton University Press, 1963.

MacDowell, Douglass. *The Law in Classical Athens.* Ithaca: Cornell University Press, 1978.

Osborne, R. "Law in Action in Classical Athens." *Journal of Hellenic Studies* 105 (1985): 40–58.

Papillon, Terry L. "Isocrates on Gorgias and Helen: The Unity of *Helen.*" *The Classical Journal* 91 (1996): 377–391.

Poulakos, John. "Gorgias' and Isocrates' Use of the Encomium." *Southern Speech Communication Journal* 51 (1986): 300–307.

———. "Gorgias' *Encomium to Helen* and the Defense of Rhetoric." *Rhetorica* 1 (1983): 1–17.

Riggsby, Andrew M. "Appropriation and Reversal as a Basis for Oratorical Proof." *Classical Philology* 90 (1995): 245–255.

Robertson, N. "The Laws of Athens, 410–399 B.C.: The Evidence for Review and Publication." *Journal of Hellenic Studies* 110 (1990): 43–75.

Roochnik, David. "In Defense of Plato: A Short Polemic." *Philosophy and Rhetoric* 24 (1991): 153–158.

Sullivan, Dale L. "*Kairos* and the Rhetoric of Belief." *The Quarterly Journal of Speech* 78 (1992): 317–332.

Vickers, Brian. *In Defence of Rhetoric.* Oxford: Clarendon Press, 1988.

Worthington, Ian, ed. *Persuasion: Greek Rhetoric in Action.* New York: Routledge, 1994.

Zadrow, A. "Truth and Persuasion in Classical Rhetoric and in Modern Rhetoric." *Verifiche* 12 (1983): 31–50.

Rhetoric and Politics

Arnhart, Larry. *Aristotle on Political Reasoning: A Commentary on the Rhetoric.* DeKalb: Northern Illinois University Press, 1981.

Arnheim, M. T. W. *Aristocracy in Greek Society.* London: Thames and Hudson, 1977.

Austin, M. M., and P. Vidal-Naquet. *Economic and Social History of Ancient Greece.* Berkeley and Los Angeles: University of California Press, 1977.

Barrett, Harold. *Sophists: Rhetoric, Democracy, and Plato's Idea of Sophistry.* Novato, Calif.: Chandler and Sharp, 1987.

Benitez, Eugenio. "Argument, Rhetoric, and Philosophic Method: Plato's *Protagoras*." *Philosophy and Rhetoric* 25 (1992): 222–252.

Bosworth, A. B. "The Humanitarian Aspect of the Melian Dialogue." *Journal of Hellenic Studies* 113 (1993): 30–44.

Campbell, Blair. "Thought and Political Action in Athenian Tradition: The Emergence of the 'Alienated' Intellectual." *History of Political Thought* 5 (1984): 17–59.

Connor, W. R. *The New Politicians of Fifth-Century Athens*. Princeton: Princeton University Press, 1971.

Davidson, James. "Isocrates Against Imperialism: An Analysis of the *De Pace*." *Historia* 39 (1990): 20–36.

Davies, John. *Athenian Propertied Families*. Oxford: Oxford University Press, 1971.

———. *Wealth and the Power of Wealth in Classical Athens*. Salem, N.H.: Ayer, 1981.

Farrar, Cynthia. *The Origins of Democratic Thinking: The Invention of Politics in Classical Athens*. Cambridge: Cambridge University Press, 1988.

Finley, M. I. *Economy and Society in Ancient Greece*. New York: Viking, 1981.

———. *Politics in the Ancient World*. Cambridge: Cambridge University Press, 1983.

Fuks, Alexander. "Isokrates and the Social-Economic Situation in Greece." *Ancient Society* 3 (1972): 17–44.

Gillis, Daniel. "Isocrates, the *Philippos*, and the Evening of Democracy." *ATTI* 8 (1976–1977): 123–133.

Hansen, M. H. "Athenian Democracy: Institution and Ideology." *Classical Philology* 84 (1989): 137–148.

Havelock, Eric. "Plato's Politics and the American Constitution." *Harvard Studies in Classical Philology* 93 (1990): 1–24.

Heilbrunn, Gunther. "Isocrates on Rhetoric and Power." *Hermes* 103 (1975): 154–178.

Jones, A. H. M. *Athenian Democracy*. Baltimore: Johns Hopkins University Press, 1986.

Miller, Carolyn. "The *Polis* as Rhetorical Community." *Rhetorical* 11 (1993): 211–240.

Ober, Josiah. *Mass and Elite in Democratic Athens: Rhetoric, Ideology, and the Power of the People*. Princeton: Princeton University Press, 1989.

———. "The Nature of Athenian Democracy." *Classical Philology* 84 (1989): 322–324.

Padgug, Robert A. "Classes and Society in Classical Greece." *Arethusa* 8 (1975): 85–118.

Perlman, S. "Panhellenism, the Polis, and Imperialism." *Historia* 25 (1976): 1–30.

Renehan, R. "Polis, Plato, and Aristotle." *The Classical Quarterly* 45 (1995): 68–72.

Rhodes, P. J. "Political Activity in Classical Athens." *Journal of Hellenic Studies* 106 (1986): 132–145.

Ste. Croix, G. E. M. de. *The Class Struggle in the Ancient Greek World*. Ithaca: Cornell University Press, 1981.

Stockton, David. *The Classical Athenian Democracy*. Oxford: Oxford University Press, 1990.

Thompson, Wesley. "Isocrates on the Peace Treaties." *Classical Quarterly* 33 (1983): 75–80.

Vatai, Frank. *Intellectuals in Politics in the Greek World*. London: Croom Helm, 1984.

Yunis, Harvey. *Taming Democracy: Models of Political Rhetoric in Classical Athens*. Ithaca: Cornell University Press, 1996.

Rhetoric and Display

Bennett, Larry J., and William Blake Tyrell. "Sophocles' *Antigone* and Funeral Oratory." *American Journal of Philology* 111 (1990): 441–456.

Bowie, E. L. "Early Greek Elegy: Symposium and Public Festival." *Journal of Hellenic Studies* 106 (1986): 13–35.

Burger, Ronna. *Plato's Phaedrus: A Defense of a Philosophic Art of Writing*. University: University of Alabama Press, 1980.

Carter, Michael F. "The Ritual Functions of Epideictic Rhetoric: The Case of Socrates' Funeral Oration." *Rhetorical* 9 (1991): 209–222.

Connor, W. R. "Tribes, Festivals, and Processions: Civic Ceremonial and Political Manipulation in Archaic Greece." *Journal of Hellenic Studies* 107 (1987): 40–50.

Consigny, Scott. "Gorgias's Use of the Epideictic." *Philosophy and Rhetoric* 25 (1992): 281–297.

Coventry, L. J. "Philosophy and Rhetoric in the *Menexenus*." *Journal of Hellenic Studies* 109 (1989): 1–15.

duBois, Page. "Phallocentrism and Its Subversion in Plato's *Phaedrus*." *Arethusa* 18 (1995): 91–106.

Furley, W. D. "Praise and Persuasion in Greek Hymns." *Journal of Hellenic Studies* 115 (1995): 29–46.

Griswold, Charles L. *Self-knowledge in Plato's Phaedrus*. New Haven: Yale University Press, 1986.

Holt, Philip. "Ajax's Burial in Early Greek Epic." *American Journal of Philology* 113 (1992): 319–332.

Hopkins, Keith. *Death and Renewal*. Cambridge: Cambridge University Press, 1983.

Loraux, Nicole. *The Invention of Athens: Funeral Oration in the Classical City*. Trans. A. Sheridan. Cambridge: Harvard University Press, 1986.

Oravec, Christine. "Observation in Aristotle's Theory of Epideictic." *Philosophy and Rhetoric* 9 (1976): 162–174.

Poulakos, Takis. "Toward a Cultural Understanding of Classical Epideictic Oratory." *Pre/Text* 9 (1988): 147–166.

Stoeber, Michael. "Phaedrus of the *Phaedrus:* The Impassioned Soul." *Philosophy and Rhetoric* 25 (1992): 271–280.

Sullivan, Dale L. "The Ethos of Epideictic Encounter." *Philosophy and Rhetoric* 26 (1993): 113–133.

Vickers, Brian. "Epideictic and Epic in the Renaissance." *New Literary History* 14 (1982–83): 497–537.

Rhetoric and Language

Benardete, Seth. "On Plato's Sophist." *The Review of Metaphysics* 46 (1993): 747–780.

Bergren, Ann L. T; "Language and the Female in Early Greek Thought." *Arethusa* 16 (1983): 69–98.

Cahn, Michael. "Reading Rhetoric Rhetorically: Isocrates and the Marketing of Insight." *Rhetorica* 7 (1989): 121–144.

Clark, Norman. "The Critical Servant: An Isocratean Contribution to Critical Rhetoric." *The Quarterly Journal of Speech* 82 (1996): 111–124.

Cole, Thomas. *The Origins of Rhetoric in Ancient Greece*. Baltimore: Johns Hopkins University Press, 1991.

Crowley, Sharon. "Of Gorgias and Grammatology." *College Composition and Communication* 30 (1979): 279–284.

Dekerckhove, D. "Classical Rhetoric and Communication-Theory." *Communication* 7 (1983): 181–200.

Eades, Trent. "Plato, Rhetoric, and Silence." *Philosophy and Rhetoric* 29 (1996): 244–258.

Enos, R. L. *Greek Rhetoric Before Aristotle*. Prospect Heights, Ill.: Waveland Press, 1993.

Farrell, Thomas. *Norms of Rhetorical Culture*. New Haven: Yale University Press, 1993.

Gentzler, Jyl. "The Sophistic Cross-examination of Callicles in the *Gorgias*." *Ancient Philosophy* 15 (1995): 17–43.

Hays, Steve. "On the Skeptical Influence of Gorgias's *On Non-being*." *Journal of the History of Philosophy* 28 (1990): 327–337.

Kastely, James L. "In Defense of Plato's *Gorgias*." *PMLA* 106 (1991): 96–109.

Kennedy, George A. "A Hoot in the Dark: The Evolution of General Rhetoric." *Philosophy and Rhetoric* 25 (1992): 1–21.

Kerferd, G. B. *The Sophistic Movement*. Cambridge: Cambridge University Press, 1981.

Kirby, John T. "Aristotle's *Poetics:* The Rhetorical Principle." *Arethusa* 24 (1991): 197–218.

Lentz, Tony. *Orality and Literacy in Hellenic Greece*. Carbondale: Southern Illinois University Press, 1989.

Mailloux, Steven. *Rhetoric, Sophistry, Pragmatism*. New York: Cambridge University Press, 1995.

Nimis, Steve. "Aristotle's Analogical Metaphor." *Arethusa* 21 (1988): 215–227.

Noille, C. "The Analysis of Style in Classical Rhetoric." *Dix-septième siècle* 188 (1995): 389–406.

Ogden, D. "Crooked Speech: The Genesis of the Spartan Rhetra." *Journal of Hellenic Studies* 114 (1994): 85–102.

Rummel, Erika. "Isocrates' Ideal of Rhetoric: Criteria of Evaluation." *Classical Journal* 75 (1979): 25–35.

Sabry, R. "Digression in Classical Rhetoric." *Poetique* 79 (1989): 259–276.

Too, Yun Lee. *The Rhetoric of Identity in Isocrates: Text, Power, Pedagogy*. New York: Cambridge University Press, 1995.

Welch, Kathleen E. *The Contemporary Reception of Classical Rhetoric: Appropriations of Ancient Discourse*. Hillsdale, N.J.: L. Erlbaum, 1990.

Rhetoric and Knowledge

Barris, Jeremy. "The Foundation in Truth of Rhetoric and Formal Logic." *Philosophy and Rhetoric* 29 (1996): 314–328.

Bertelsen, Dale A. "Sophistry, Epistemology, and the Media Context." *Philosophy and Rhetoric* 26 (1993): 296–301.

Dodds, E. R. *The Ancient Concept of Progress*. Oxford: Clarendon Press, 1973.

Enos, R. L. "The Epistemology of Gorgias' Rhetoric: A Re-examination." *Southern Speech Communication Journal* 42 (1976): 35–51.

Flory, Dan. "Stoic Psychology, Classical Rhetoric, and Theories of Imagination in Western Philosophy." *Philosophy and Rhetoric* 29 (1996): 147–167.

Griswold, Charles L. *Self-knowledge in Plato's* Phaedrus. New Haven: Yale University Press, 1986.

Hays, Steve. "On the Skeptical Influence of Gorgias's *On Non-being*." *Journal of the History of Philosophy* 28 (1990): 327–337.

Rose, Peter W. "Sophocles' *Philoctetes* and the Teachings of the Sophists." *Harvard Studies in Classical Philology* 80 (1976): 49–107.

Schiappa, Edward. "Protagoras and Logos: A Study in Greek Philosophy and Rhetoric." *American Journal of Philology* 114 (1993): 623–628.

Vickers, Brian, ed. *Rhetoric Revalued*. Binghamton, N.Y.: Center for Medieval and Early Renaissance Studies, 1982.

Walters, Frank D. "Gorgias as Philosopher of Being: Epistemic Foundationalism in Sophistic Thought." *Philosophy and Rhetoric* 27 (1994): 143–155.

Zhao, Shanyang. "Rhetoric as Praxis: An Alternative to the Epistemic Approach." *Philosophy and Rhetoric* 24 (1991): 255–266.

Roman Rhetorical Theory

Anderson, Graham. *The Second Sophistic: A Cultural Phenomenon in the Roman Empire*. London: Routledge, 1993.

Burnyeat, Miles, and Frede, Michael. *The Original Skeptics: A Controversy*. Indianapolis: Hackett Publishing Company, 1997.

Clarke, M. L. *Rhetoric at Rome: A Historical Survey*. New York: Barnes and Noble, 1966.

Dominik, William J., ed. *Roman Eloquence: Rhetoric in Society and Literature*. London: Routledge, 1997.

Dyck, A. R. *A Commentary on Cicero*. Ann Arbor: University of Michigan Press, 1996.

Eden, Kathy. *Hermeneutics and the Rhetorical Tradition*. New Haven: Yale University Press, 1997.

Fortenbaugh, W. W., ed. *Peripatetic Rhetoric after Aristotle*. New Brunswick: Transaction Books, 1994.

Gleason, Maud W. *Making Men: Sophists and Self-Presentation in Ancient Rome*. Princeton: Princeton University Press, 1995.

Kennedy, George Alexander. *The Art of Rhetoric in the Roman World, 300 B.C.–A.D. 300*. Princeton: Princeton University Press, 1972.

———. *Classical Rhetoric and Its Christian and Secular Tradition from Ancient to Modern Times*. Chapel Hill: University of North Carolina Press, 1980.

————. *Quintilian*. New York: Twayne Publishing, 1969.

Meador Jr., Prentice A. "Rhetoric and Humanism in Cicero." *Philosophy and Rhetoric* 3 (1970): 1–12.

Winterbottom, Michael. *Problems in Quintilian*. London: University of London Institute of Classical Studies, 1970.

Wood, Neal. *Cicero's Social and Political Thought*. Berkeley and Los Angeles: University of California Press, 1988.

Rhetoric and Law: Cicero

Bauman, Richard A. *Crime and Punishment in Ancient Rome*. New York: Routledge, 1996.

Enos, Richard L. *The Literate Mode in Cicero's Legal Rhetoric*. Carbondale: Southern Illinois University Press, 1988.

Evans, Jane DeRose. *The Art of Persuasion: Political Propaganda from Aeneas to Brutus*. Ann Arbor: University of Michigan Press, 1992.

Fantham, Elaine. "Ciceronian 'Conciliaro' and Aristotelian 'Ethos'." *Phoenix* 27 (1973): 262–275.

Ferray, Jean-Louis. "The Statesman and the Law in the Political Philosophy of Cicero." In *Justice and Generosity*," edited by Andre Laks and Malcolm Schofield. New York: Cambridge University Press, 1992.

Frier, B. W. *The Rise of the Roman Jurists: Studies in Cicero's* Pro Caecina. Princeton, N.J.: Princeton University Press, 1985.

Harries, Jill. *Law and Empire in Late Antiquity*. New York: Cambridge University Press, 1998.

Honore, Tony. *Emperors and Lawyers*. New York: Oxford University Press, 1994.

————. *Law in the Crisis of Empire, 379–455 A.D.: The Theodosian Dynasty and Its Quaestors*. New York: Clarendon Press, 1998.

MacKendrick, P. L. *The Speeches of Cicero: Context, Law, Rhetoric*. London: Duckworth, 1995.

May, J. M. *Trials of Character: The Eloquence of Ciceronian* Ethos. Chapel Hill: University of North Carolina Press, 1988.

Robinson, O. F. *The Criminal Law of Ancient Rome*. Baltimore: Johns Hopkins University Press, 1995.

Rhetoric and Politics: Cicero

Arnheim, M. T. W. *The Senatorial Aristocracy in the Later Roman Empire*. Oxford: Clarendon Press, 1972.

Cape Jr., Robert W. "The Rhetoric of Politics in Cicero's Fourth Catilinarian." *American Journal of Philology* 116, no. 2 (1995): 255–277.

Corbeill, Anthony. *Controlling Laughter: Political Humor in the Late Roman Republic*. Princeton: Princeton University Press, 1996.

Craig, Christopher. *Form as Argument in Cicero's Speeches: A Study of Dilemma*. Atlanta: Scholars Press, 1993.

Eckstein, Arthur M. *Senate and General: Individual Decision Making and Roman Foreign Relations*. Berkeley and Los Angeles: University of California Press, 1987.

Ferray, Jean-Louis. "The Statesman and the Law in the Political Philosophy of Cicero." In *Justice and Generosity,* edited by Andre Laks and Malcolm Schofield. New York: Cambridge University Press, 1992.

Fuhrmann, Manfred. 1992. *Cicero and the Roman Republic*. Cambridge: Blackwell.

Gotoff, H. C. *Cicero's Caesarian Speeches: A Stylistic Commentary*. Chapel Hill: University of North Carolina Press, 1993.

Habricht, Christian. *Cicero the Politician*. Baltimore: Johns Hopkins University Press, 1990.

Lacey, W. K. *Cicero and the End of the Roman Republic*. London: Hodder and Stoughton, 1978.

Mitchell, T. N. *Cicero, the Senior Statesman*. New Haven: Yale University Press, 1991.

Ruebel, James S., ed. *Caesar and the Crisis of the Roman Aristocracy: A Civil War Reader*. Norman: University of Oklahoma Press, 1994.

Talbert, Richard J. A. *The Senate of Imperial Rome*. Princeton: Princeton University Press, 1984.

Rhetoric and Display: Cicero and Quintilian

Goar, R. J. *Cicero and the State Religion*. Amsterdam: Hakkert, 1972.

Kennedy, Duncan F. *The Arts of Love: Five Studies in the Discourse of Roman Love Elegy*. Cambridge: Cambridge University Press, 1993.

Ochs, Donovan J. *Consolatory Rhetoric: Grief, Symbol, and Ritual in the Greco-Roman Era*. Columbia: University of South Carolina Press, 1993.

Reece, Richard, ed. *Burial in the Roman World*. London: Council for British Archaeology, 1977.

Toynbee, J. M. C. *Death and Burial in the Roman World*. Ithaca: Cornell University Press, 1971.

Vasaly, Ann. *Representations: Images of the World in Ciceronian Oratory*. Berkeley and Los Angeles: University of California Press, 1993.

Walker, Susan. *Memorials to the Roman Dead*. London: British Museum Publications, 1985.

Wisse, Jakob. Ethos *and* Pathos: *From Aristotle to Cicero*. Amsterdam: Hakkert, 1989.

Rhetoric and Language: Cicero and Quintilian

Bloomer, Martin. *Latinity and Literary Society at Rome*. Philadelphia: University of Pennsylvania Press, 1997.

Dominik, William J., ed. *Roman Eloquence: Rhetoric in Society and Literature*. London: Routledge, 1997.

Fantham, Elaine. *Roman Literary Culture: from Cicero to Apuleius*. Baltimore: Johns Hopkins University Press, 1996.

Habinek, Thomas N. *The Politics of Latin Literature: Writing, Identity, and Empire in Ancient Rome*. Princeton: Princeton University Press, 1998.

Roberts, Deborah, Francis Dunn, and Don Fowler. *Classical Closure: Reading the End in Greek and Latin Literature*. Princeton: Princeton University Press, 1997.

Rudich, Vasily. *Dissidence and Literature Under Nero: The Price of Rhetoricization*. London: Routledge, 1997.

Woodman, Tony, and Jonathan Powell, eds. *Author and Audience in Latin Literature*. New York: Cambridge University Press, 1992.

SPEECHES

PERICLES • *Funeral Oration*

Many of those who have spoken here in the past have praised the institution of this speech   35
at the close of our ceremony. It seemed to them a mark of honour to our soldiers who have
fallen in war that a speech should be made over them. I do not agree. These men have
shown themselves valiant in action, and it would be enough, I think, for their glories to be
proclaimed in action, as you have just seen it done at this funeral organized by the state.
Our belief in the courage and manliness of so many should not be hazarded on the goodness or badness of one man's speech. Then it is not easy to speak with a proper sense of
balance, when a man's listeners find it difficult to believe in the truth of what one is saying. The man who knows the facts and loves the dead may well think that an oration tells
less than what he knows and what he would like to hear: others who do not know so much
may feel envy for the dead, and think the orator over-praises them, when he speaks of exploits that are beyond their own capacities. Praise of other people is tolerable only up to a
certain point, the point where one still believes that one could do oneself some of the
things one is hearing about. Once you get beyond this point, you will find people becoming jealous and incredulous. However, the fact is that this institution was set up and approved by our forefathers, and it is my duty to follow the tradition and do my best to meet
the wishes and the expectations of every one of you.

'I shall begin by speaking about our ancestors, since it is only right and proper on such   36
an occasion to pay them the honour of recalling what they did. In this land of ours there
have always been the same people living from generation to generation up till now, and
they, by their courage and their virtues, have handed it on to us, a free country. They certainly deserve our praise. Even more so do our fathers deserve it. For to the inheritance
they had received they added all the empire we have now, and it was not without blood
and toil that they handed it down to us of the present generation. And then we ourselves,
assembled here today, who are mostly in the prime of life, have, in most directions, added
to the power of our empire and have organized our State in such a way that it is perfectly
well able to look after itself both in peace and in war.

'I have no wish to make a long speech on subjects familiar to you all: so I shall say
nothing about the warlike deeds by which we acquired our power or the battles in which
we or our fathers gallantly resisted our enemies, Greek or foreign. What I want to do is, in
the first place, to discuss the spirit in which we faced our trials and also our constitution
and the way of life which has made us great. After that I shall speak in praise of the dead,
believing that this kind of speech is not inappropriate to the present occasion, and that this
whole assembly, of citizens and foreigners, may listen to it with advantage.

'Let me say that our system of government does not copy the institutions of our   37
neighbours. It is more the case of our being a model to others, than of our imitating anyone else. Our constitution is called a democracy because power is in the hands not of a minority but of the whole people. When it is a question of settling private disputes, everyone
is equal before the law; when it is a question of putting one person before another in po-

Source: From *History of the Peloponnesian War, Book 2,* by Thucydides, translated by Rex Warner (Penguin
Classics, 1954), pp. 144–151. Translation copyright © Rex Warner, 1954. Reproduced by permission of
Penguin Books, Ltd.

sitions of public responsibility, what counts is not membership of a particular class, but the actual ability which the man possesses. No one, so long as he has it in him to be of service to the state, is kept in political obscurity because of poverty. And, just as our political life is free and open, so is our day-to-day life in our relations with each other. We do not get into a state with our next-door neighbour if he enjoys himself in his own way, nor do we give him the kind of black looks which, though they do no real harm, still do hurt people's feelings. We are free and tolerant in our private lives; but in public affairs we keep to the law. This is because it commands our deep respect.

'We give our obedience to those whom we put in positions of authority, and we obey the laws themselves, especially those which are for the protection of the oppressed, and those unwritten laws which it is an acknowledged shame to break.

38   'And here is another point. When our work is over, we are in a position to enjoy all kinds of recreation for our spirits. There are various kinds of contests and sacrifices regularly throughout the year; in our own homes we find a beauty and a good taste which delight us every day and which drive away our cares. Then the greatness of our city brings it about that all the good things from all over the world flow in to us, so that to us it seems just as natural to enjoy foreign goods as our own local products.

39   'Then there is a great difference between us and our opponents, in our attitude towards military security. Here are some examples: Our city is open to the world, and we have no periodical deportations in order to prevent people observing or finding out secrets which might be of military advantage to the enemy. This is because we rely, not on secret weapons, but on our own real courage and loyalty. There is a difference, too, in our educational systems. The Spartans, from their earliest boyhood, are submitted to the most laborious training in courage; we pass our lives without all these restrictions, and yet are just as ready to face the same dangers as they are. Here is a proof of this: Where the Spartans invade our land, they do not come by themselves, but bring all their allies with them; whereas we, when we launch an attack abroad, do the job by ourselves, and, though fighting on foreign soil, do not often fail to defeat opponents who are fighting for their own hearths and homes. As a matter of fact none of our enemies has ever yet been confronted with our total strength, because we have to divide our attention between our navy and the many missions on which our troops are sent on land. Yet, if our enemies engage a detachment of our forces and defeat it, they give themselves credit for having thrown back our entire army; or, if they lose, they claim that they were beaten by us in full strength. There are certain advantages, I think, in our way of meeting danger voluntarily, with an easy mind, instead of with a laborious training, with natural rather than with state-induced courage. We do not have to spend our time practising to meet sufferings which are still in the future; and when they are actually upon us we show ourselves just as brave as these others who are always in strict training. This is one point in which, I think, our city deserves to be admired. There are also others:

40   'Our love of what is beautiful does not lead to extravagance; our love of the things of the mind does not make us soft. We regard wealth as something to be properly used, rather than as something to boast about. As for poverty, no one need be ashamed to admit it: the real shame is in not taking practical measures to escape from it. Here each individual is interested not only in his own affairs but in the affairs of the state as well: even

those who are mostly occupied with their own business are extremely well-informed on general politics—this is a peculiarity of ours: we not say that a man who takes no interest in politics is a man who minds his own business; we say that he has no business here at all. We Athenians, in our own persons, take our decisions on policy or submit them to proper discussions: for we do not think that there is an incompatibility between words and deeds; the worst thing is to rush into action before the consequences have been properly debated. And this is another point where we differ from other people. We are capable at the same time of taking risks and of estimating them beforehand. Others are brave out of ignorance; and, when they stop to think, they begin to fear. But the man who can most truly be accounted brave is he who best knows the meaning of what is sweet in life and of what is terrible, and then goes out undeterred to meet what is to come.

'Again, in questions of general good feeling there is a great contrast between us and most other people. We make friends by doing good to others, not by receiving good from them. This makes our friendship all the more reliable, since we want to keep alive the gratitude of those who are in our debt by showing continued goodwill to them: whereas the feelings of one who owes us something lack the same enthusiasm, since he knows that, when he repays our kindness, it will be more like paying back a debt than giving something spontaneously. We are unique in this. When we do kindnesses to others, we do not do them out of any calculations of profit or loss: we do them without afterthought, relying on our free liberality. Taking everything together then, I declare that our city is an education 41
to Greece, and I declare that in my opinion each single one of our citizens, in all the manifold aspects of life, is able to show himself the rightful lord and owner of his own person, and do this, moreover, with exceptional grace and exceptional versatility. And to show that this is no empty boasting for the present occasion, but real tangible fact, you have only to consider the power which our city possesses and which has been won by those very qualities which I have mentioned. Athens, alone of the states we know, comes to her testing time in a greatness that surpasses what was imagined of her. In her case, and in her case alone, no invading enemy is ashamed at being defeated, and no subject can complain of being governed by people unfit for their responsibilities. Mighty indeed are the marks and monuments of our empire which we have left. Future ages will wonder at us, as the present age wonders at us now. We do not need the praises of a Homer, or of anyone else whose words may delight us for the moment, but whose estimation of facts will fall short of what is really true. For our adventurous spirit has forced an entry into every sea and into every land; and everywhere we have left behind us everlasting memorials of good done to our friends or suffering inflicted on our enemies.

'This, then, is the kind of city for which these men, who could not bear the thought of losing her, nobly fought and nobly died. It is only natural that every one of us who survive them should be willing to undergo hardships in her service. And it was for this reason 42
that I have spoken at such length about our city, because I wanted to make it dear that for us there is more at stake than there is for others who lack our advantages; also I wanted my words of praise for the dead to be set in the bright light of evidence. And now the most important of these words has been spoken. I have sung the praises of our city; but it was the courage and gallantry of these men, and of people like them, which made her splen-

did. Nor would you find it true in the case of many of the Greeks, as it is true of them, that no words can do more than justice to their deeds.

'To me it seems that the consummation which has overtaken these men shows us the meaning of manliness in its first revelation and in its final proof. Some of them, no doubt, had their faults; but what we ought to remember first is their gallant conduct against the enemy in defence of their native land. They have blotted out evil with good, and done more service to the commonwealth than they ever did harm in their private lives. No one of these men weakened because he wanted to go on enjoying his wealth: no one put off the awful day in the hope that he might live to escape his poverty and grow rich. More to be desired than such things, they chose to check the enemy's pride. This, to them, was a risk most glorious, and they accepted it, willing to strike down the enemy and relinquish everything else. As for success or failure, they left that in the doubtful hands of Hope, and when the reality of battle was before their faces, they put their trust in their own selves. In the fighting, they thought it more honourable to stand their ground and suffer death than to give in and save their lives. So they fled from the reproaches of men, abiding with life and limb the brunt of battle; and, in a small moment of time, the climax of their lives, a culmination of glory, not of fear, were swept away from us.

43   'So and such they were, these men—worthy of their city. We who remain behind may hope to be spared their fate, but must resolve to keep the same daring spirit against the foe. It is not simply a question of estimating the advantages in theory. I could tell you a long story (and you know it as well as I do) about what is to be gained by beating the enemy back. What I would prefer is that you should fix your eyes every day on the greatness of Athens as she really is, and should fall in love with her. When you realize her greatness, then reflect that what made her great was men with a spirit of adventure, men who knew their duty, men who were ashamed to fall below a certain standard. If they ever failed in an enterprise, they made up their minds that at any rate the city should not find their courage lacking to her, and they gave to her the best contribution that they could. They gave her their lives, to her and to all of us, and for their own selves they won praises that never grow old, the most splendid of sepulchres—not the sepulchre in which their bodies are laid, but where their glory remains eternal in men's minds, always there on the right occasion to stir others to speech or to action. For famous men have the whole earth as their memorial: it is not only the inscriptions on their graves in their own country that mark them out; no, in foreign lands also, not in any visible form but in people's hearts, their memory abides and grows. It is for you to try to be like them. Make up your minds that happiness depends on being free, and freedom depends on being courageous. Let there be no relaxation in face of the perils of the war. The people who have most excuse for despising death are not the wretched and unfortunate, who have no hope of doing well for themselves, but those who run the risk of a complete reversal in their lives, and who would feel the difference most intensely, if things went wrong for them. Any intelligent man would find a humiliation caused by his own slackness more painful to bear than death, when death comes to him unperceived, in battle, and in the confidence of his patriotism.

44   'For these reasons I shall not commiserate with those parents of the dead, who are present here. Instead I shall try to comfort them. They are well aware that they have grown up in a world where there are many changes and chances. But this is good

fortune—for men to end their lives with honour, as these have done, and for you honourably to lament them: their life was set to a measure where death and happiness went hand in hand. I know that it is difficult to convince you of this. When you see other people happy you will often be reminded of what used to make you happy too. One does not feel sad at not having some good thing which is outside one's experience: real grief is felt at the loss of something which one is used to. All the same, those of you who are of the right age must bear up and take comfort in the thought of having more children. In your own homes these new children will prevent you from brooding over those who are no more, and they will be a help to the city, too, both in filling the empty places, and in assuring her security. For it is impossible for a man to put forward fair and honest views about our affairs if he has not, like everyone else, children whose lives may be at stake. As for those of you who are now too old to have children, I would ask you to count as gain the greater part of your life, in which you have been happy, and remember that what remains is not long, and let your hearts be lifted up at the thought of the fair fame of the dead. One's sense of honour is the only thing that does not grow old, and the last pleasure, when one is worn out with age, is not, as the poet said, making money, but having the respect of one's fellow men.

'As for those of you here who are sons or brothers of the dead, I can see a hard struggle in front of you. Everyone always speaks well of the dead, and, even if you rise to the greatest heights of heroism, it will be a hard thing for you to get the reputation of having come near, let alone equalled, their standard. When one is alive, one is always liable to the jealousy of one's competitors, but when one is out of the way, the honour one receives is sincere and unchallenged. 45

'Perhaps I should say a word or two on the duties of women to those among you who are now widowed. I can say all I have to say in a short word of advice. Your great glory is not to be inferior to what God has made you, and the greatest glory of a woman is to be least talked about by men, whether they are praising you or criticizing you. I have now, as the law demanded, said what I had to say. For the time being our offerings to the dead have been made, and for the future their children will be supported at the public expense by the city, until they come of age. This is the crown and prize which she offers, both to the dead and to their children, for the ordeals which they have faced. Where the rewards of valour are the greatest, there you will find also the best and bravest spirits among the people. And now, when you have mourned for your dear ones, you must depart.' 46

66 Now he concludes in the following way that nothing exists. If [anything] exists, either the existent exists or the nonexistent or both the existent exists and the nonexistent, But, as he will establish, neither does the existent exist nor the nonexistent, as he will make clear, nor the existent and [the] nonexistent, as he will also teach. It is not the case then that any-

67 thing exists. More specifically, the nonexistent does not exist; for if the nonexistent exists, it will both exist and not exist at the same time, for insofar as it is understood as nonexistent, it will not exist, but insofar as it *is* nonexistent it will, on the other hand, exist. It would, however, be entirely absurd for something to exist and at the same time not to exist. The nonexistent, therefore, does not exist. And to state another argument, if the nonexistent exists, the existent will not exist, for these are opposites to each other, and if existence is an attribute of the nonexistent, nonexistence will be an attribute of the existent. But it is not, in fact, true that the existent does not exist. [Accordingly], neither will

68 the nonexistent exist. Moreover, the existent does not exist either. For if the existent exists, it is either eternal or generated, or at the same time eternal and generated. But it is neither eternal nor generated nor both, as we shall show. The existent therefore does not exist. For if the existent is eternal (one must begin with this point) it does not have any be-

69 ginning. For everything which is generated has some beginning, but the eternal, being ungenerated, did not have a beginning. And not having a beginning it is without limit. And if it is without limit it is nowhere. For if it is somewhere, that in which it is, is something other than it, and thus if the existent is contained in something it will no longer be without limit. For the container is greater than the contained, but nothing is greater than the unlimited, so that the unlimited cannot exist anywhere. Moreover, it is not contained in it-

70 self. For in that case container and contained will be the same, and the existent will become two things, place and body (place is the container, body the contained). But this is absurd. Accordingly, existence is not contained in itself. So that if the existent is eternal it is unlimited, and if it is unlimited it is nowhere, and if it is nowhere it does not exist. Ac-

71 cordingly, if the existent is eternal, it is not existent at all. Moreover, neither can the existent be generated. For if it has come into being, it has come either from the existent or the nonexistent. But it has not come from the existent. For if it is existent, it has not come to be, but already exists. Nor from the nonexistent. For the nonexistent cannot generate anything, because what is generative of something of necessity ought to partake of positive

72 existence. It is not true either, therefore, that the existent is generated. In the same way it is not jointly at the same time eternal and generated. For these qualities are mutually exclusive of each other, and if the existent is eternal it has not been generated, and if it has been generated it is not eternal. Accordingly, if the existent is neither eternal nor gener-

73 ated not both at once, the existent should not exist. And to use another argument, if it exists, it is either one or many. But it is neither one nor many, as will be set forth. Therefore, the existent does not exist. For if it is one, it is an existent or a continuum or a magnitude or a body. But whatever of these it is, it is not one, since whatever has extent will be di-

Source: "On the Nonexistent" by Gorgias from Rosamond Kent Sprague, *The Older Sophists,* University of South Carolina Press (Columbia: 1972) © 1972, pp. 136–147. Reprinted by permission of the publisher.

vided, and what is a continuum will be cut. And similarly, what is conceived as a magnitude will not be indivisible. And if it is by chance a body it will be three-dimensional, for it will have length, and breadth and depth. But it is absurd to say that the existent is none of these things. Therefore, the existent is not one. And moreover it is not many. For if it is 74 not one, it is not many either, since the many is a composite of separate entities and thus, when the possibility that it is one was refuted, the possibility that it is many was refuted as well. Now it is clear from this that neither does the existent exist nor does the nonexistent exist. It is easy to conclude that both the existent and the nonexistent do not exist either. 75 For if the nonexistent exists and the existent exists, the nonexistent will be the same thing as the existent as far as existence is concerned. And for this reason neither of them exists. For it is agreed that the nonexistent does not exist, and the existent has been shown to be the same as the nonexistent and it accordingly will not exist. Of course, if the existent is 76 the same as the nonexistent, it is not possible for both to exist. For if both exist, they are not the same, and if the same, both do not exist. To which the conclusion follows that nothing exists. For if neither the existent exists nor the nonexistent nor both, and if no additional possibility is conceivable, nothing exists.

Next it must be shown that even if anything exists, it is unknowable and incompre- 77 hensible to man. For, says Gorgias, if things considered in the mind are not existent, the existent is not considered. And that is logical. For if "white" were a possible attribute of what is considered, "being considered" would also have been a possible attribute of what is white; similarly, if "not to be existent" were a possible attribute of what is being considered, necessarily "not to be considered" will be a possible attribute of what is existent. As 78 a result, the statement "if things considered are not existent, the existent is not considered" is sound and logically follows. But things considered (for this must be our starting point) are not existent, as we shall show. The existent is not therefore considered. And moreover, it is clear that things considered are not existent. For if things considered are ex- 79 istent, all things considered exist, and in whatever way anyone considers them. Which is absurd. For if one considers a man flying or chariots racing in the sea, a man does not straightway fly nor a chariot race in the sea. So that things considered are not existent. In 80 addition, if things considered in the mind are existent, nonexistent things will not be considered. For opposites are attributes of opposites, and the nonexistent is opposed to the existent. For this reason it is quite evident that if "being considered in the mind" is an attribute of the existent, "not being considered in the mind" will be an attribute of the nonexistent. For this is absurd. For Scylla and Chimaera and many other nonexistent things are considered in the mind. Therefore, the existent is not considered in the mind. Just as objects of sight are said to be visible for the reason that they are seen, and objects 81 of hearing are said to be audible for the reason that they are heard, and we do not reject visible things on the grounds that they are not heard, nor dismiss audible things because they are not seen (since each object ought to be judged by its own sense, but not by another), so, too, things considered in the mind will exist even if they should not be seen by the sight nor heard by the hearing, because they are perceived by their own criterion. If, 82 therefore, someone considered in the mind that chariots race in the sea, even if he does not see them, he should believe that there are chariots racing in the sea. But this is absurd. Therefore, the existent is not an object of consideration and is not apprehended.

83   But even if it should be apprehended, it would be incapable of being conveyed to another. For if existent things are visible and audible and generally perceptible, which means
that they are external substances, and of these the things which are visible are perceived by
the sight, those that are audible by the hearing, and not contrariwise, how can these things
84 be revealed to another person? For that by which we reveal is *logos,* but *logos* is not substances and existing things. Therefore we do not reveal existing things to our neighbors,
but *logos,* which is something other than substances. Thus, just as the visible would not become audible, and vice versa, similarly, when external reality is involved, it would not be-
85 come our *logos,* and not being *logos,* it would not have been revealed to another. It is clear,
he says, that *logos* arises from external things impinging upon us, that is, from perceptible
things. From encounter with a flavor, *logos* is expressed by us about that quality, and from
encounter with a color, an expression of color. But if this is the case, *logos* is not evocative
86 of the external, but the external becomes the revealer of *logos.* And surely it is not possible
to say that *logos* has substance in the way visible and audible things have, so that substan-
tial and existent things can be revealed from its substance and existence. For, he says, even
if *logos* has substance, still it differs from all the other substances, and visible bodies are to
the greatest degree different from words. What is visible is comprehended by one organ,
logos by another. *Logos* does not, therefore, manifest the multiplicity of substances, just as
they do not manifest the nature of each other.

THRASYMACHUS • *On the Constitution*

B. FRAGMENTS

THE CONSTITUTION

"I wish, Athenians, that I had belonged to that ancient time when silence sufficed for young people, since the state of affairs did not force them to make speeches and the older men were managing the city properly. But since our fortune has reserved us for this later time, in which we submit to <the government of> our city <by others> but <bear> its misfortunes ourselves, and of these the greatest are the work neither of gods nor of chance but of the administration, one really has to speak. That man is either lacking in feeling or outstanding in patience who will continue to present himself for mistreatment at the hands of anyone who likes and will himself endure the blame for the treachery and cowardice of others. The time gone by is enough for us: instead of peace, we are at war; danger <has brought us> to such a pass that we cling to the day that is ending and dread that which is to come; instead of comradeship, we have fallen into mutual enmity and turbulence. Other people are rendered violent and contentious by the abundance of their good fortune; but we were calm when we were fortunate, and in misfortune, which tends to calm other people down, we have gone wild.

"Why should anyone put off speaking <what> is in his mind, if <it has fallen> to him to be injured by the present situation and he thinks he is on to something that will put an end to such things?

"I shall begin by showing that in speaking against each other those of our politicians, and others too, who are at odds with each other, have undergone what inevitably happens to people who try to win without thinking. They think they are saying the opposite to each other, and fail to realize that they are pursuing the same policies and that their opponents' arguments are included in their own. Just consider, right from the start, what each of them is after. To begin with, our ancestral constitution troubles them, though it is very easy to understand and is what all our citizens have most in common. But surely, whenever anything is beyond the scope of our own judgment, we must abide by what our elders have said; and whatever the old-timers saw for themselves, we must learn of from those who beheld it. . . ."

Source: "On the Constitution" by Thrasymachus from Rosamond Kent Sprague, *The Older Sophists,* University of South Carolina Press (Columbia: 1972), © 1972, pp. 90–91. Reprinted by permission of the publisher.

A DEFENSE ON BEHALF OF PALAMEDES BY THE SAME AUTHOR

1   Prosecution and defense are not a means of judging about death; for Nature, with a vote which is clear, casts a vote of death against every mortal on the day on which he is born. The danger relates to dishonor and honor, whether I must die justly or whether I must die

2   roughly with the greatest reproaches and most shameful accusation. There are the two alternatives; you have the second within your power, I the first; justice is up to me, roughness is up to you. You will easily be able to kill me if you wish, for you have power over

3   these matters, over which as it happens I have no power. If then the accuser, Odysseus, made his accusation through good will toward Greece, either clearly knowing that I was betraying Greece to the barbarians or imagining somehow that this was the case, he would be best of men. For this would of course[1] be true of one who saves his homeland, his parents, and all Greece, and in addition punishes a wrongdoer. But if he has put together this allegation out of envy or conspiracy or knavery, just as in the former case he would be the

4   finest of men, so in this he would be the worst of men. Where shall I start to speak about these matters? What shall I say first? To what part of the defense shall I turn my attention? For an unsupported allegation creates evident perplexity, and because of the perplexity it follows that I am at a loss in my speech, unless I discover something out of the truth itself and out of the present necessity, having met with teachers more dangerous than inventive.

5   Now I clearly know that my accuser accuses me without <knowing> the matter clearly; for I know in my heart clearly that I have done no such thing; and I do not know how anyone could know what did not happen. But in case he made the accusation thinking it to be so, I shall show you in two ways that he is not speaking the truth. For I could not if I wished, nor would I if I could, put my hand to such works as these.

6   I come first to this argument, that I lack the capability of performing the action charged. There must have been some first beginning to the treason, and the beginning would have been speech, for before any future deeds it is necessary first for there to be discussions. But how could there be discussions unless there had been some meeting? And how could there have been a meeting unless the opponent sent to me or <someone> went

7   from me to him? For no message arrives in writing without a bearer. But this can take place by speech. And suppose he is with me and I am with him—how does it take place? Who is with whom? Greek with barbarian. How do we listen and how talk to each other? By ourselves? But we do not know each other's language. With an interpreter then? A third per-

8   son is added as a witness to things which need to be hidden. But assume that this too has taken place, even though it has not. Next it was necessary to give and receive a pledge. What would the pledge be? An oath? Who was apt to trust me, the traitor? Perhaps there were hostages? Who? For instance, I might have given my brother (for I had no one else),

Source: "A Defense on Behalf of Palamedes" by Gorgias from Rosamond Kent Sprague, *The Older Sophists*, University of South Carolina Press (Columbia: 1972), © 1972, pp. 54–63. Reprinted with permission of the publisher.

[1]   Without the emendation of Stephanus-Blass, the meaning would be "of course not."

and the barbarian might have given one of his sons; in this way the pledge would have been most secure to me from him and to him from me. But these things, if they happened, would have been clear to you all. Someone will say that we made the contract for money, ⁹ he giving it, I taking it. Was it for little? But it is not probable that a man would take a little money for a great service. For much money? Who was the go-between? How could one person bring it? Perhaps there were many? If many brought it, there would have been many witnesses of the plot, but if one brought it, what was brought would not have been anything much. Did they bring it by day or by night? But the guards are many and closely 10 placed and it is not possible to escape their notice. But by day? Certainly the light militates against such things. Well then. Did I go out and get it or did the opponent come bringing it? For both are impossible. If I had in fact taken it, how would I have hidden it both from those in the camp and from those outside it? Where would I have put it? How would I have protected it? If I made use of it, I would have been conspicuous; if I didn't, what advantage would I have gotten from it? Still, assume that what did not happen has happened. 11 We met, we talked, we reached an understanding, I took money from them, I was not detected after taking it, I hid it. It was then necessary to perform that for the sake of which these arrangements were made. Now this is still stranger than what has been discussed. For in doing it, I acted by myself or with others. But the action was not the work of one man. But was it with others? Who? Clearly my associates. Were they free men or slaves? My free associates are you. Who then among you was aware? Let him speak. How is it credible that I would use slaves? For they bring charges <both> in hopes of their freedom and out of necessity when hard pressed. As for the action, how < would> it have taken place? Clearly enemy forces outnumbering you had to be brought in, which was impossible. How could I have brought them in? Through the gates? But it was not my job to shut or open them, but the commanders were in charge of these. But it was over the walls <by> a ladder? Wouldn't <I have been seen?> The whole place was full of guards. But it was through a hole made in the wall? It would then have been clear to all. Life under arms is carried on outdoors (for this is a camp!), in which <everybody> sees everything and everybody is seen by everybody. Altogether then and in every way it was impossible for me to do all these things.

Consider among yourselves the following point as well. What reason was there to wish 13 to do these things, assuming that I had a special capability? For no one wishes to run the greatest dangers without reward nor to be most wicked in the greatest wickedness. But what reason was there? (For again I revert to this point.) For the sake of rul<ing>? Over you or over the barbarians? But over you it would be impossible for me to rule, considering your numbers and nature and the fact that you have all manner of great resources: nobility of family, wealth of money, fame, strength of heart, the thrones of cities. But over the 14 <barbarians>? Who is going to betray them? By means of what power shall I, a Greek, take over the barbarians, when I am one and they are many? Persuading or constraining them? For they would not wish to be persuaded and I would not be able to constrain. But possibly there are those willing to betray them to a willing receiver by giving money in return for the surrender? But both to believe and accept this is very foolish. For who would choose slavery instead of sovereignty, the worst instead of the best? Someone might say 15 that I ventured on this out of a desire for wealth and money. But I have a moderate amount of money, and I have no need for much. Those who spend much money need much, not those who are continent of the pleasures of nature, but those who are slaves to pleasures and seek to acquire honors from wealth and show. None of this applies to me. I shall offer my past life as sure evidence that I am speaking the truth, and you be witnesses to the witness, for you are my companions and thus know these things. Nor, moreover, 16 would a man even moderately prudent put his hand to such work even for honor. Honors come from goodness, not from badness. How would there be honor for a man who is the betrayer of Greece? And in addition, as it happens, I am not without honor. For I am honored for the most honorable reason by the most honorable men, that is, by you for wisdom. Nor, moreover, would anyone do these things for the sake of security. For the traitor 17 is the enemy of all: the law, justice, the gods, the bulk of mankind. For he contravenes the law, negates justice, destroys the masses, and dishonors what is holy, and a man does not have security whose life <is> of this sort among the greatest dangers. But was I anxious to 18 assist friends or harm enemies? For someone might commit injustice for these reasons. But in my case everything was the opposite. I was harming my friends and helping foes. The action therefore involved no acquisition of goods, and there is no one who does wrong out of desire to suffer loss. The remaining possibility is that I did it to escape some fear or 19 labor or danger. But no one could say that these motives applied to me in any way. All men do all things in pursuit of these two goals: either seeking some profit or escaping some punishment, and whatever knavery is done for reasons other than these <is apt to involve the doer in great evils. That I would most>[2] hurt myself in doing these things is not unclear. For in betraying Greece I was betraying myself, my parents, my friends, the dignity of my ancestors, the cults of my native land, the tombs of my family, and my great country of Greece. Those things which are all in all to all men, I would have entrusted to men who had been wronged.[3] But consider the following as well. Would not my life have been 20 unlivable if I had done these things? Where must I have turned for help? To Greece? Shall I make amends to those who have been wronged? Who of those who suffered could keep his hands off me? Or must I remain among the barbarians? Abandoning everything important, deprived of the noblest honor, passing my life in shameful disgrace, throwing away the labors labored for virtue of my past life? And this of my own accord, although to fail through his own doing is most shameful for a man. Moreover, not even among the 21 barbarians would I be trusted. How could I be, if they knew that I had done something most untrustworthy, had betrayed my friends to my enemies? But life is not livable for a man who has lost the confidence of others. The man who loses his money <or> who falls from power or who is exiled from his country might get on his feet again, but he who throws away good faith would not any more acquire it. Therefore, that I would not <if I could, nor could if I would>, betray Greece has been demonstrated by what has been said.

22   I wish next to address the accuser. What in the world do you trust when, being what you are, you accuse such a one as me? It is worth examining the kind of man you are who says the kind of things you do, like the worthless attacking the worthless. Do you accuse me, knowing accurately what you say, or imagining it? If it is with knowledge, you know

<hr>

[2]   The conjecture of Keil, which Diels approves in the *apparatus*.
[3]   Perhaps "had done wrong"(?), Diels.

either from seeing or participating or learning from someone <who was participating>. If then you saw, tell these judges <the manner>, the place, the time, when, where, how you saw. If you participated, you are liable to the same accusations. And if you heard from someone who participated, who is he? Let him come forward; let him appear; let him bear witness. For if it is witnessed in this way, the accusation will be more credible, since as it is, neither of us is furnishing a witness. You will say perhaps that it is equitable for you not to furnish witnesses of what you allege to have happened, but that I should furnish witnesses of what has not happened. But this is not equitable. For it is quite impossible for what has not happened to be testified to by witnesses, but on the subject of what has happened, not only is it not impossible, but it is even easy, and not only is it easy, but <even necessary. But> for you it was not possible, <not> only to find witnesses, but even to find false witnesses, and for me it was possible to find neither of these. Therefore, it is clear that you do not have knowledge of the things about which you make accusation. It follows that since you do <not> have knowledge, you have an opinion. Do you then, O most daring of all men, trusting in opinion, a most untrustworthy thing, not knowing the truth, dare to bring a capital charge against a man? Why do you share knowledge that he has done such a deed? But surely it is open to all men to have opinions on all subjects, and in this you are no wiser than others. But it is not right to trust those with an opinion instead of those who know, nor to think opinion more trustworthy than truth, but rather truth than opinion.

You accused me through spoken words of two directly opposed things, wisdom and madness, which the same man cannot have. Where you say that I am artful and clever and resourceful, you accuse me of wisdom, and where you say that I was betraying Greece, you accuse me of madness. For it is madness to undertake tasks which are impossible, inexpedient, and shameful, which will harm his friends, help his enemies, and make his own life disgraceful and perilous. Yet how can one trust a man of the sort who in a single speech says to the same man the most inconsistent things about the same subjects? I would like to ask you whether you think wise men are witless or intelligent. If witless, your speech is novel, but not true; if intelligent, surely it is not right for intelligent men to make the worst mistakes and to prefer evils to present goods. If therefore I am wise, I have not erred; if I have erred, I am not wise. Thus in both cases you would be wrong.

I do not want to introduce in reply the many enormities, both old and new, which you have committed, though I could. For <I wish> to escape this charge by means of my own virtues, not by means of your vices. So much, therefore, to you.

To you, O judges, I wish to say something invidious, but true about myself, not appropriate to one who has <not> been accused, but fitting to one who has been accused. For I am now undergoing scrutiny and furnishing an account of my past life. I therefore beg of you, if I remind you of some of the fine things done by me, that no one be annoyed at what is said, but think it necessary for one who is dreadfully and falsely accused to say as well some true things among you who know them. This is the most pleasant for me. First, then, and second and greatest, in every respect from beginning to end my past life has been blameless, free from all blame. No one could truthfully speak any imputation of evil to you about me. For not even the accuser himself has provided any evidence of what he has said. Thus his speech has the impact of abuse lacking proof. I might say, and saying it I would not lie nor would I be refuted, that I am not only blameless but also a great benefactor of you and the Greeks and all mankind, not only of those now alive but <also> of those to come. For who else would have made human life well provided instead of destitute and adorned instead of unadorned, by inventing military equipment of the greatest advantage and written laws, the guardians of justice, and letters, the tool of memory, and measures and weights, the convenient standards of commercial exchange, and number, the guardian of items, and very powerful beacons and very swift messengers, and draughts, the

31   harmless game of leisure? Why do I remind you of these? For the purpose of making it clear <on the one hand> that it is to this sort of thing that I apply myself, and on the other giving an indication of the fact that I abstain from shameful and wicked deeds. For it is impossible for one applying himself to the latter to apply himself to this sort of thing. And I

32   think it right not to be harmed myself by you if I myself have done you no harm. Nor am I, because of other activities, deserving of ill treatment at the hands of younger or older men. For I am inoffensive to the older, not unhelpful to the younger, not envious of the fortunate, but merciful to the unfortunate; not heedless of poverty nor valuing wealth ahead of virtue, but virtue ahead of wealth; neither useless in council nor lazy in war, doing what is assigned to me, obeying those in command. To be sure, it is not for me to praise myself, but the present occasion requires me to make my defense in every possible way since I have been accused of these things.

33   For the rest, my speech is to you and about you; when I have said this I shall end my defense. Appeals to pity and entreaties and the intercession of friends are useful when a trial takes place before a mob, but among you, the first of the Greeks and men of repute, it is not right to persuade you with the help of friends or entreaties or appeals to pity, but it is right for me to escape this charge by means of the clearest justice, explaining the truth,

34   not deceiving. And it is necessary for you to avoid paying more attention to words than to actions, and not to prejudge the bases of the defense nor to think a short time affords wiser judgment than a long time nor to believe that slander is more reliable than firsthand knowledge. For in all matters good men must take great care against erring, and more so in matters irremediable than in those remediable. For these lie within the control of those who have exercised foresight, but are uncorrectable by those with hindsight. And it is a matter of this sort whenever men judge a man on a capital charge, which is now the case

35   before you. If then, by means of words, it were possible for the truth of actions to become free of doubt <and> clear to hearers, judgment would now be easy from what has been said. But since this is not the case, protect my body, wait for a longer while, and make your decision with truth. For your danger is great that by seeming unjust you lose one reputation and acquire another. To good men death is preferable to a shameful reputation. For

36   one is the end of life, and the other is disease in life. If you kill me unjustly, it will be evident to many, for I am < not> unknown, and your wickedness will be known and clear to all Greeks. And you, rather than the accuser, will have a responsibility for the injustice which will be clear to all. For the outcome of the trial rests with you. But greater error than this could not exist. If you give an unjust verdict, you will make a mistake, not only in regard to me and my parents, but by your action you will make yourselves responsible for a dreadful, godless, unjust, unlawful deed, having killed a man who is your fellow soldier, useful to you, a benefactor of Greece, Greeks killing Greek, though convicting him of no clear injustice nor credible fault.

My side of the case is spoken and I rest. For to recapitulate briefly what has been spoken at length is logical before bad judges, but it is not appropriate to think that Greeks who are first of the first do not pay attention and do not remember what has been said.

B. FRAGMENTS

THE *HORAI* [SEASONS] OF PRODICUS

And the wise Prodicus also expresses himself in this manner in his composition on Heracles, which he recited to large audiences. As I recall it, the story went this way. "Heracles," he said, "when he was growing from childhood into man's estate, at that time of life when young men are beginning to make their own decisions and thus to show whether they are embarked on the path of virtue or that of vice, went off to ponder in seclusion which path

22 he should choose. And there appeared to approach him two tall female figures. One had a noble address and a bearing untouched by servility, with skin fair and pure, her glance circumspect, her person modest, dressed in white. The other's figure bespoke softness and luxury, her countenance showing the exaggerated whites and reds induced by cosmetics, her carriage unnaturally lofty and stilted, her eyes darting about restlessly, and wearing a costume such as made her physical ripeness easy to estimate. She paid a great deal of attention to herself, and kept watch to see if she was noticed by others, and often even

23 looked back at her own shadow. As they approached Heracles, the former continued at her same pace, but the latter, anxious to reach him first, barged ahead and accosted Heracles thus: 'I see, Heracles, that you are undecided about the course of your life. If you should accept my friendship and follow me, I shall show you the path of greatest enjoyment and ease, and you will not fail to experience every last pleasure, while living quite free from

24 trouble. First of all, you will have no thought for wars or woes, and your only concern will be to decide which delicious food or drink you may look for, what sights and sounds you might enjoy, or what pleasures of smell or touch will please you, what amorous connections will satisfy you most, how you will sleep most contentedly, and—in short—how you

25 will gain all these good things with the least effort. But if you have any suspicion that the supply of my gifts might fail, have no fear that I would ever subject you to the necessity of physical or mental struggle to obtain your desires. Rather, you will enjoy the use of what other men produce, and never know what it is to restrain yourself from exploiting whatever you can. For, truly, I grant to my associates absolute rights to please their fancy from

26 every source whatsoever.' When she had said this, Heracles asked, 'Lady, what is your name?' She replied, 'I am known to my friends as Happiness, although those with a bilious

27 temper hate me and call me Vice.' At that point the second woman approached and addressed Heracles: 'I too propose my suit to you, Heracles, with some knowledge of your parentage as well as your character as it took shape through the course of your upbringing. Whence in fact I anticipate that if you should take the path to me you will achieve honorable and wondrous deeds, and that you will come to think me still more admirable and estimable because of the excellence you attain. But I shall not deceive you with over-

Source: "Heracles on the Crossroad" by Prodicus from Rosamond Kent Sprague, *The Older Sophists,* University of South Carolina Press (Columbia: 1972), © 1972, pp. 79–82. Reprinted by permission of the publisher.

tures promising pleasures, rather I shall truthfully disclose to you the face of reality as the gods themselves have constituted it. The gods give no real benefits or honors to men without struggle and perseverance: to obtain the gods' favor you must serve them; to achieve the love of friends you must do well by them; to win the honors of a community you must become its benefactor; to gain the admiration you might crave from all Greece you must attempt to serve Greece well; to get abundant fruit from the earth one must cultivate it; to earn wealth from livestock one must learn to care for them; to prosper in war, to gain the power to succor friends and best one's enemies, one must study the techniques of warfare from its masters and exercise oneself in their proper employment—and finally, if you should wish to enjoy physical vigor, it is to the mind that the body must learn subjection, and discipline itself with hard work and sweat.' Vice interrupted at this point, as Prodicus tells it: 'Do you realize, Heracles, that this person is promising you a long and arduous journey to reach her satisfactions? I, on the other hand, shall conduct you on the short and easy road to Happiness.' And then Virtue spoke, 'Hussy! What good have you to offer? Or what pleasure, you who will do nothing to gain even *that*? You who do not even wait for the urging of desire, before you rush to stuff yourself with enjoyments? You eat before hunger and drink before thirst. You drench your food in sauces to enjoy it the more; you scour the world for expensive wines and ices in the summertime in order to get some pleasure from what you drink. To sleep more comfortably you contrive all manner of luxurious bedding—indeed, you seek sleep not to refresh yourself from labors but just because you have nothing to do. You try to incite sexual lusts long before nature prompts them, plying every trick and using men as women. This is how you treat your devotees, debauching them by night and making them sleep away the most important part of the day. Though you are immortal you have been denied the company of the gods, and you gain no honor among decent men either. And that which is most pleasant of all—praise of yourself—you *never* experience; nor do you ever contemplate the most beautiful of all sights, a fair work of your own doing. Who would believe your invitation? Who would grant any request of yours, and who in possession of his senses would become a member of your company? Flabby young men and stupid old ones: those who have passed through youth lazy and shiftless, and pass into old age pained and feeble, those ashamed of what they have done and burdened by what they should do, those who scamper after pleasures in youth and thus must fend off woes in old age. I, on the other hand, am a companion of the gods as well as of upright men; no great deeds are done, in heaven or on earth, except through me. I am honored more highly than all else both among gods and those men who have virtue; I am the favorite spirit of the skilled, the faithful guardian of householders, the ready helper of servingmen, the active promoter of the works of peace and a strong ally in the toils of war, and the best possible sharer of friendship. My friends enjoy a pleasant and untroubled diet, because they leave food and drink alone until they really desire them; their sleep is sweeter than that of the lazy, and they do not grumble when they miss it nor neglect their responsibilities to get it. Young men enjoy the praise of their elders and the latter relish the respect of the young. They take pleasure both in the memory of past deeds and the performance of present tasks. On my account they are befriended by the gods, beloved by their friends, and celebrated in their communities. And when their appointed end comes, they do not lie forgotten and unhonored: their glory flourishes forever in the memory of the race and its poetry. All these things are yours to possess, Heracles, son of noble parents, if you undertake to work diligently for the most genuine form of happiness.'" In some such fashion as this, Prodicus related the instruction of Heracles by Virtue. Of course his performance was a masterpiece of stylistic elegance compared with that I managed just now.

34

ISOCRATES • *Panegyricus*

Many times have I wondered at those who first convoked the national assemblies and established the athletic games, amazed that they should have thought the prowess of men's bodies to be deserving of so great bounties, while to those who had toiled in private for the public good and trained their own minds so as to be able to help also their fellow-men they apportioned no reward whatsoever, when, in all reason, they ought rather to have made provision for the latter; for if all the athletes should acquire twice the strength which they now possess, the rest of the world would be no better off; but let a single man attain to wisdom, and all men will reap the benefit who are willing to share his insight.

    Yet I have not on this account lost heart nor chosen to abate my labours; on the contrary, believing that I shall have a sufficient reward in the approbation which my discourse will itself command, I have come before you to give my counsels on the war against the barbarians and on concord among ourselves. I am, in truth, not unaware that many of those who have claimed to be sophists have rushed upon this theme, but I hope to rise so far superior to them that it will seem as if no word had ever been spoken by my rivals upon this subject; and, at the same time, I have singled out as the highest kind of oratory that which deals with the greatest affairs and, while best displaying the ability of those who speak, brings most profit to those who hear; and this oration is of that character. In the next place, the moment for action has not yet gone by, and so made it now futile to bring up this question; for then, and only then, should we cease to speak, when the conditions have come to an end and there is no longer any need to deliberate about them, or when we see that the discussion of them is so complete that there is left to others no room to improve upon what has been said. But so long as conditions go on as before, and what has been said about them is inadequate, is it not our duty to scan and study this question, the right decision of which will deliver us from our mutual warfare, our present confusion, and our greatest ills?

    Furthermore, if it were possible to present the same subject matter in one form and in no other, one might have reason to think it gratuitous to weary one's hearers by speaking again in the same manner as his predecessors; but since oratory is of such a nature that it is possible to discourse on the same subject matter in many different ways—to represent the great as lowly or invest the little with grandeur, to recount the things of old in a new manner or set forth events of recent date in an old fashion—it follows that one must not shun the subjects upon which others have spoken before, but must try to speak better than they. For the deeds of the past are, indeed, an inheritance common to us all; but the ability to make proper use of them at the appropriate time, to conceive the right sentiments about them in each instance, and to set them forth in finished phrase, is the peculiar gift of the wise. And it is my opinion that the study of oratory as well as the other arts would make the greatest advance if we should admire and honour, not those who make the first beginnings in their crafts, but those who are the most finished craftsmen in each, and not

Source: Reprinted by permission of the publishers and the Loeb Classical Library from Isocrates *Panegyricus*, Volume I (pp. 121–149, 171–181, excerpts 1–51, 85–95), translated by George Norlin, Cambridge, Mass.: Harvard University Press, 1980.

those who seek to speak on subjects on which no one has spoken before, but those who know how to speak as no one else could.

11   Yet there are some who carp at discourses which are beyond the powers of ordinary men and have been elaborated with extreme care, and who have gone so far astray that they judge the most ambitious oratory by the standard of the pleas made in the petty actions of the courts; as if both kinds should be alike and should not be distinguished, the one by plainness of style, the other by display; or as if they themselves saw clearly the happy

12 mean, while the man who knows how to speak elegantly could not speak simply and plainly if he chose. Now these people deceive no one; clearly they praise those who are near their own level. I, for my part, am not concerned with such men, but rather with those who will not tolerate, but will resent, any carelessness of phrase, and will seek to find in my speeches a quality which they will not discover in others. Addressing myself to these,

13 I shall proceed with my theme, after first vaunting a little further my own powers. For I observe that the other orators in their introductions seek to conciliate their hearers and make excuses for the speeches which they are about to deliver, sometimes alleging that their preparation has been on the spur of the moment, sometimes urging that it is difficult

14 to find words to match the greatness of their theme. But as for myself, if I do not speak in a manner worthy of my subject and of my reputation and of the time which I have lived— I bid you show me no indulgence but hold me up to ridicule and scorn; for there is nothing of the sort which I do not deserve to suffer, if indeed, being no better than the others, I have promises so great.

15   So much, by way of introduction, as to my personal claims. But as to our public interests, the speakers who no sooner come before us than they inform us that we must compose our enmities against each other and turn against the barbarian, rehearsing the misfortunes which have come upon us from our mutual warfare and the advantages which will result from a campaign against our natural enemy—these men do speak the truth, but

16 they do not start at the point from which they could best bring these things to pass. For the Hellenes are subject, some to us, others to the Lacedaemonians, the polities by which they govern their states having thus divided most of them. If any man, therefore, thinks that before he brings the leading states into friendly relations, the rest will unite in doing

17 any good thing, he is all too simple and out of touch with the actual conditions. No, the man who does not aim merely to make an oratorical display, but desires to accomplish something as well, must seek out such arguments as will persuade these two states to share and share alike with each other, to divide the supremacy between them, and to wrest from the barbarians the advantages which at the present time they desire to seize for themselves at the expense of the Hellenes.

18   Now our own city could easily be induced to adopt this policy, but at present the Lacedaemonians are still hard to persuade; for they have inherited the false doctrine that leadership is theirs by ancestral right. If, however, one should prove to them that this honour belongs to us rather than to them, perhaps they might give up splitting hairs about this question and pursue their true interests.

19   So, then, the other speakers also should have made this their starting-point and should not have given advice on matters about which we agree before instructing us on the points about which we disagree. I, at all events, am justified by a twofold motive in de-

voting most of my attention to these points: first and foremost, in order that some good may come of it, and that we may put an end to our mutual rivalries and unite in a war against the barbarian; and, secondly, if this is impossible, in order that I may show who they are that stand in the way of the happiness of the Hellenes, and that all may be made to see that even in times past Athens justly held the sovereignty of the sea, so now she not unjustly lays claim to hegemony.

For in the first place, if it is the most experienced and the most capable who in any field of action deserve to be honoured, it is without question our right to recover the hegemony which we formerly possessed; for no one can point to another state which so far excels in warfare on land as our city is superior in fighting battles on the sea. But, in the next place, if there are any who do not regard this as a fair basis of judgement, since the reversals of fortune are frequent (for sovereignty never remains in the same hands), and who believe that the hegemony, like any other prize, should be held by those who first won this honour, or else by those who have rendered the most service to the Hellenes, I think that these also are on our side; for the farther back into the past we go in our examination of both these titles to leadership, the farther behind shall we leave those who dispute our claims. For it is admitted that our city is the oldest and the greatest in the world and in the eyes of all men the most renowned. But noble as is the foundation of our claims, the following grounds give us even a clearer title to distinction: for we did not become dwellers in this land by driving others out of it, nor by finding it uninhabited, nor by coming together here a motley horde composed of many races; but we are of a lineage so noble and so pure that throughout our history we have continued in possession of the very land which gave us birth, since we are sprung from its very soil and are able to address our city by the very names which we apply to our nearest kin; for we alone of all the Hellenes have the right to call our city at once nurse and fatherland and mother. And yet, if men are to have good ground for pride and make just claims to leadership and frequently recall their ancestral glories, they must show that their race boasts an origin as noble as that which I have described.

So great, then, are the gifts which were ours from the beginning and which fortune has bestowed upon us. But how many good things we have contributed to the rest of the world we could estimate to best advantage if we should recount the history of our city from the beginning and go through all her achievements in detail; for we should find that not only was she the leader in the hazards of war, but that the social order in general in which we dwell, with which we share the rights of citizenship and through which we are able to live, is almost wholly due to her. It is, however, necessary to single out from the number of her benefactions, not those which because of their slight importance have escaped attention and been passed over in silence, but those which because of their great importance have been and still are on the lips and in the memory of all men everywhere.

Now, first of all, that which was the first necessity of man's nature was provided by our city; for even though the story has taken the form of a myth, yet it deserves to be told again. When Demeter came to our land, in her wandering after the rape of Kore, and, being moved to kindness towards our ancestors by services which may not be told save to her initiates, gave these two gifts, the greatest in the world—the fruits of the earth, which have enabled us to rise above the life of the beasts, and the holy rite which inspires in those who

29 partake of it sweeter hopes regarding both the end of life and all eternity,—our city was not only so beloved of the gods but also so devoted to mankind that, having been endowed with these great blessings, she did not begrudge them to the rest of the world, but shared with all men what she had received. The mystic rite we continue even now, each year, to reveal to the initiates; and as for the fruits of the earth, our city has, in a word, in-

30 structed the world in their uses, their cultivation, and the benefits derived from them. This statement, when I have added a few further proofs, no one could venture to discredit.

In the first place, the very ground on which we might disparage the story, namely that it is ancient, would naturally lead us to believe that the events actually came to pass; for because many have told and all have heard the story which describes them, it is reasonable to regard this not, to be sure, as recent, yet withal as worthy of our faith. In the next place, we are not obliged to take refuge in the mere fact that we have received the account and

31 the report from remote times; on the contrary, we are able to adduce even greater proofs than this regarding what took place. For most of the Hellenic cities, in memory of our ancient services, send us each year the first-fruits of the harvest, and those who neglect to do so have often been admonished by the Pythian priestess to pay us our due portion of their crops and to observe in relation to our city the customs of their fathers. And about what, I should like to know, can we more surely exercise our faith than about matters as to which the oracle of Apollo speaks with authority, many of the Hellenes are agreed, and the words spoken long ago confirm the practice of to-day, while present events tally with the state-

32 ments which have come down from the men of old? But apart from these considerations, if we waive all this and carry our inquiry back to the beginning, we shall find that those who first appeared upon the earth did not at the outset find the kind of life which we enjoy to-day, but that they procured it little by little through their own joint efforts. Whom, then, must we think the most likely either to have received this better life as a gift from the

33 gods or to have hit upon it through their own search? Would it not be those who are admitted by all men to have been the first to exist, to be endowed with the greatest capacity for the arts, and to be the most devoted in the worship of the gods? And surely it is superfluous to attempt to show how high is the honour which the authors of such great blessings deserve; for no one could find a reward great enough to match the magnitude of their achievements.

34 This much, then, I have to say about that service to humanity which is the greatest, the earliest, and the most universal in its benefits. But at about the same time, our city, seeing the barbarians in possession of most of the country, while the Hellenes were confined within a narrow space and, because of the scarcity of the land, were conspiring and making raids against each other, and were perishing, some through want of daily necessities, others through war,—our city, I say, was not content to let these things be as they were,

35 but sent out leaders to the several states, who, enlisting the neediest of the people, and placing themselves at their head, overcame the barbarians in war, founded many cities on either continent, settled colonies in all the islands, and saved both those who followed them and those who remained behind; for to the latter they left the home country—suffi-

36 cient for their needs—and for the former they provided more land than they had owned since they embraced in their conquests all the territory which we Hellenes now possess. And so they smoothed the way for those also who in a later time resolved to send out

colonists and imitate our city; for these did not have to undergo the perils of war in acquiring territory, but could go into the country marked out by us and settle there. And yet 37 who can show a leadership more ancestral than this, which had its origin before most of the cities of Hellas were founded, or more serviceable than this, which drove the barbarians from their homes and advanced the Hellenes to so great prosperity?

Nor did our city, after she had played her part in bringing to pass the most important 38 benefits, neglect what remained to be done; on the contrary she made it but the beginning of her benefactions to find for those who were in want that sustenance which men must have who are to provide well also for their other needs; but considering that an existence limited to this alone was not enough to make men desire to live, she gave such careful thought to their remaining wants as well that of the good things which are now at the service of mankind—in so far as we do not have them from the gods but owe them to each 39 other—there is not one in which our city has had no part, and most of them are due to her alone. For, finding the Hellenes living without laws and in scattered abodes, some oppressed by tyrannies, others perishing through anarchy, she delivered them from these evils by taking some under her protection and by setting to others her own example; for she was 40 the first to lay down laws and establish a polity. This is apparent from the fact that those who in the beginning brought charges of homicide, and desired to settle their mutual differences by reason and not by violence, tried their cases under our laws. Yes, and the arts also, both those which are useful in producing the necessities of life and those which have been devised to give us pleasure, she has either invented or stamped with her approval and has then presented them to the rest of the world to enjoy.

Moreover, she has established her polity in general in such a spirit of welcome to 41 strangers and friendliness to all men, that it adapts itself both to those who lack means and to those who wish to enjoy the means which they possess, and that it fails to be of service neither to those who are prosperous nor to those who are unfortunate in their own cities; nay, both classes find with us what they desire, the former the most delightful pastimes, the 42 latter the securest refuge. Again, since the different populations did not in any case possess a country that was self-sufficing, each lacking in some things and producing others in excess of their needs, and since they were greatly at a loss where they should dispose of their surplus and whence they should import what they lacked, in these difficulties also our city came to the rescue; for she established the Piraeus as a market in the centre of Hellas—a market of such abundance that the articles which it is difficult to get, one here, one there, from the rest of the world, all these it is easy to procure from Athens.

Now the founders of our great festivals are justly praised for handing down to us a 43 custom by which, having proclaimed a truce and resolved our pending quarrels, we come together in one place, where, as we make our prayers and sacrifices in common, we are reminded of the kinship which exists among us and are made to feel more kindly towards each other for the future, reviving our old friendships and establishing new ties. And nei- 44 ther to common men nor to those of superior gifts is the time so spent idle and profitless, but in the concourse of the Hellenes the latter have the opportunity to display their prowess, the former to behold these contending against each other in the games; and no one lacks zest for the festival, but all find in it that which flatters their pride, the spectators when they see the athletes exert themselves for their benefit, the athletes when they reflect

that all the world is come to gaze upon them. Since, then, the benefits which accrue to us from our assembling together are so great, here again our city has not been backward; for
45 she affords the most numerous and the most admirable spectacles, some passing all bounds in outlay of money, some highly reputed for their artistic worth, and others excelling in both these regards; and the multitude of people who visit us is so great that, whatever advantage there is in our associating together, this also has been compassed by our city, Athens. Besides, it is possible to find with us as nowhere else the most faithful friendships and to enjoy the most varied social intercourse; and, furthermore, to see contests not alone of speed and strength, but of eloquence and wisdom and of all the other
46 arts—and for these the greatest prizes; since in addition to those which the city herself sets up, she prevails upon the rest of the world also to offer prizes; for the judgement pronounced by us command such great approbation that all mankind accept them gladly. But apart from these considerations, while the assemblages at the other great festivals are brought together only at long intervals and are soon dispersed, our city throughout all time is a festival for those who visit her.

47   Philosophy, moreover, which has helped to discover and establish all these institutions, which has educated us for public affairs and made us gentle towards each other, which has distinguished between the misfortunes that are due to ignorance and those which spring from necessity, and taught us to guard against the former and to bear
48 the latter nobly—philosophy, I say, was given to the world by our city. And Athens it is that has honoured eloquence, which all men crave and envy in its possessors; for she realized that this is the one endowment of our nature which singles us out from all living creatures, and that by using this advantage we have risen above them in all other respects as well; she saw that in other activities the fortunes of life are so capricious that in them often the wise fail and the foolish succeed, whereas beautiful and artistic speech is never allotted to ordinary men, but is the work of an intelligent mind, and that it is in this re-
49 spect that those who are accounted wise and ignorant present the strongest contrast; and she knew, furthermore, that whether men have been liberally educated from their earliest years is not to be determined by their courage or their wealth or such advantages, but is made manifest most of all by their speech, and that this has proved itself to be the surest sign of culture in every one of us, and that those who are skilled in speech are not only
50 men of power in their own cities but are also held in honour in other states. And so far has our city distanced the rest of mankind in thought and in speech that her pupils have
51 become the teachers of the rest of the world; and she has brought it about that the name "Hellenes" suggests no longer a race but an intelligence, and that the title "Hellenes" is applied rather to those who share our culture than to those who share a common blood. . . .

85   . . . . Now while our forefathers and the Lacedaemonians were always emulous of each other, yet during that time their rivalry was for the noblest ends; they did not look upon each other as enemies but as competitors, nor did they court the favour of the barbarians for the enslavement of the Hellenes; on the contrary, they were of one mind when the common safety was in question, and their rivalry with each other was solely to see which of them should bring this about.

They first displayed their valour when Darius sent his troops; for when the Persians landed in Attica the Athenians did not wait for their allies, but, making the common war their private cause, they marched out with their own forces alone to meet an enemy who looked with contempt upon the whole of Hellas—a mere handful against thousands upon thousands—as if they were about to risk the lives of others, not their own; the Lacedaemonians, on the other hand, no sooner heard of the war in Attica than they put all else aside and came to our rescue, having made as great haste as if it had been their own country that was being laid waste. A proof of the swiftness and of the rivalry of both is that, according to the account, our ancestors on one and the same day learned of the landing of the barbarians, rushed to the defence of the borders of their land, won the battle, and set up a trophy of victory over the enemy; while the Lacedaemonians in three days and as many nights covered twelve hundred stadia in marching order: so strenuously did they both hasten, the Lacedaemonians to share in the dangers, the Athenians to engage the enemy before their helpers should arrive. Then came the later expedition, which was led by Xerxes in person; he had left his royal residence, boldly taken command as general in the field, and collected about him all the hosts of Asia. What orator, however eager to overshoot the mark, has not fallen short of the truth in speaking of this king, who rose to such a pitch of arrogance that, thinking it a small task to subjugate Hellas, and proposing to leave a memorial such as would make a more than human power, did not stop until he had devised and compelled the execution of a plan whose fame is on the lips of all mankind— a plan by which, having bridged the Hellespont and channelled Athos, he sailed his ships across the mainland, and marched his troops across the main.

It was against a king who had grown so proud, who had carried through such mighty tasks, and who had made himself master of so many men, that our ancestors and the Lacedaemonians marched forth, first dividing the danger: the latter going to Thermopylae to oppose the land forces with a thousand picked soldiers of their own, supported by a few of their allies, with the purpose of checking the Persians in the narrow pass from advancing farther; while our ancestors sailed to Artemisium with sixty triremes which they had manned to oppose the whole armada of the enemy. And they dared to do these things, not so much in contempt of their foes as in keen rivalry against each other: the Lacedaemonians envying our city its victory at Marathon, and seeking to even the score, and fearing, furthermore, lest our city should twice in succession be the instrument of saving Hellas; while our ancestors, on the other hand, desired above all to maintain the reputation they had won, and to prove to the world that in their former battle they had conquered through valour and not through fortune, and in the next place to incite the Hellenes to carry on the war with their ships, by showing that in fighting on the sea no less than on the land valour prevails over numbers.

But though they displayed equal courage, they did not meet with similar fortunes. The Lacedaemonians were utterly destroyed Although in spirit they were victorious, in body they were outworn; for it were sacrilege to say that they were defeated, since not one of them deigned to leave his post. Our ancestors, on the other hand, met and conquered the advance squadron of the Persians; and when they heard that the enemy were masters of the pass, they sailed back home and adopted such measures for what remained to be done that, however many and however glorious had been their previous achievements, they outdid themselves still more in the final hazards of that war.

93   For when all the allies were in a state of dejection, and the Peloponnesians were fortifying their Isthmus and selfishly seeking their own safety; when the other states had submitted to the barbarians and were fighting on the Persian side, save only those which were overlooked because of their insignificance; when twelve hundred ships of war were bearing down upon them, and an innumerable army was on the point of invading Attica; when no light of deliverance could be glimpsed in any quarter, but, on the contrary, the Athe-

94 nians had been abandoned by their allies and cheated of their every hope; and when it lay in their power not only to escape from their present dangers but also to enjoy the signal honors which the King held out to them, since he conceived that if he could get the support of the Athenian fleet he could at once become master of the Peloponnesus also, then

95 our ancestors scorned to accept his gifts; nor did they give way to anger against the Hellenes for having betrayed them and rush gladly to make terms with the barbarians; nay, by themselves they made ready to battle for freedom, while they forgave the rest for choosing bondage. For they considered that while it was natural for the weaker states to seek their security by every means, it was not possible for those states which asserted their right to stand at the head of Hellas to avoid the perils of war; on the contrary, they believed that just as it is preferable for men who are honourable to die nobly rather than to live in disgrace, so too it is better for cities which are illustrious to be blotted out from the sight of

96 mankind rather than to be seen in a state of bondage. It is evident that they were of this mind; for when they were not able to marshal themselves against both the land and the sea forces at once, they took with them the entire population, abandoned the city, and sailed to the neighbouring island, in order that they might encounter each force in turn.

And yet how could men be shown to be braver or more devoted to Hellas than our ancestors, who, to avoid bringing slavery upon the rest of the Hellenes, endured to see their city made desolate, their land ravaged, their sanctuaries rifled, their temples burned, and all the forces of the enemy closing in upon their own country? But in truth even this

97 did not satisfy them; they were ready to give battle on the sea—they alone against twelve hundred ships of war. They were not, indeed, allowed to fight alone; for the Peloponnesians, put to shame by our courage, and thinking, moreover, that if the Athenians should first be destroyed, they could not themselves be saved from destruction, and that if the Athenians should succeed, their own cities would be brought into disrepute, they were constrained to share the dangers. Now the clamours that arose during the action, and the

98 shoutings and the cheers—things which are common to all those who fight on ships—I see no reason why I should take time to describe; my task is to speak of those matters which are distinctive and give claim to leadership, and which confirm the arguments which I have already advanced. In short, our city was so far superior while she stood unharmed that even after she had been laid waste she contributed more ships to the battle for the deliverance of Hellas than all the others put together who fought in the engagement; and no one is so prejudiced against us that he would not acknowledge that it was by winning the sea fight that we conquered in the war, and that the credit for this is due to Athens.

99   Who then should have the hegemony, when a campaign against the barbarians is in prospect? Should it not be they who distinguished themselves above all others in the for-

mer war? Should it now be they who many times bore, alone, the brunt of battle, and in the joint struggles of the Hellenes were awarded the prize of valour? Should it not be they who abandoned their own country to save the rest of Hellas, who in ancient times founded most of the Hellenic cities, and who later delivered them from the greatest disasters? Would it not be an outrage upon us, if, having taken the largest share in the evils of war, we should be adjudged worthy of a lesser share in its honour, and if, having at that time been placed in the lead in the cause of all the Hellenes, we should now be compelled to follow the lead of others? . . .

180 In my treatment of the art of discourse, I desire, like the genealogists, to start at the beginning. It is acknowledged that the nature of man is compounded of two parts, the physical and the mental, and no one would deny that of these two the mind comes first and is of greater worth; for it is the function of the mind to decide both on personal and on public questions, and of the body to be servant to the judgements of the mind. Since this is

181 so, certain of our ancestors, long before our time, seeing that many arts had been devised for other things, while none had been prescribed for the body and for the mind, invented and bequeathed to us two disciplines; physical training for the body, of which gymnastics is a part, and, for the mind, philosophy, which I am going to explain. These are twin arts—

182 parallel and complementary—by which their masters prepare the mind to become more intelligent and the body to become more serviceable, not separating sharply the two kinds of education, but using similar methods of instruction, exercise, and other forms of discipline.

183   For when they take their pupils in hand, the physical trainers instruct their followers in the postures which have been devised for bodily contests, while the teachers of philos-

184 ophy impart all the forms of discourse in which the mind expresses itself. Then, when they have made familiar and thoroughly conversant with these lessons, they set them at exercises, habituate them to work, and require them to combine in practice the particular things which they have learned, in order that they may grasp them more firmly and bring their theories into closer touch with the occasions for applying them—I say "theories" for no system of knowledge can possibly cover these occasions, since in all cases they elude our science. Yet those who most apply their minds to them and are able to discern the consequences which for the most part grow out of them, will most often meet these occasions in the right way.

185   Watching over them and training them in this manner, both the teachers of gymnastic and teachers of discourse are able to advance their pupils to a point where they are better men and where they are stronger in their thinking or in the use of their bodies. However, neither class of teachers is in possession of a science by which they can make capable athletes or capable orators out of whomsoever they please. They can contribute in some degree to these results, but these powers are never found in their perfection save in those who excel by virtue both of talent and of training.

186   I have given you now some impression of what philosophy is. But I think that you will get a still clearer idea of its powers if I tell you what professions I make to those who want

187 to become my pupils. I say to them that if they are to excel in oratory or in managing affairs or in any line of work, they must, first of all, have a natural aptitude for that which they have elected to do; secondly, they must submit to training and master the knowledge of their particular subject, whatever it may be in each case; and, finally, they must become versed and practised in the use and application of their art; for only on

Source: Reprinted by permission of the publishers and the Loeb Classical Library from Isocrates: *Antidosis,* Volume I (pp. 289–295, 335–343, excerpts 180–182, 270–285), translated by George Norlin, Cambridge, Mass.: Harvard University Press, 1980.

these conditions can they become fully competent and pre-eminent in any line of endeavour. In this process, master and pupil each has his place; no one but the pupil can furnish   188
the necessary capacity; no one but the master, the ability to impart knowledge; while both
have a part in the exercises of practical application; for the masts must painstakingly direct
his pupil, and the latter must rigidly follow the master's instructions.

Now these observations apply to any and all the arts. If anyone, ignoring the other   189
arts, were to ask me which of these factors has the greatest power in the education of an
orator I should answer that natural ability is paramount and comes before all else. For
given a man with a mind which is capable of finding out and learning the truth and of
working hard and remembering what it learns, and also with a voice and a clarity of utterance which are able to captivate the audience, not only by what he says, but by the music
of his words, and, finally, with an assurance which is not an expression of bravado, but   190
which, tempered by sobriety, so fortifies the spirit that he is no less at ease in addressing all
his fellow-citizens than in reflecting to himself—who does not know that such a man
might, without the advantage of an elaborate education and with only a superficial and
common training, be an orator such as has never, perhaps, been seen among the Hellenes?   191
Again, we know that men who are less generously endowed by nature and excel in experience and practice, not only improve upon themselves, but surpass others who, though
highly gifted, have been too negligent of their talents. It follows, therefore, that either one
of these factors may produce an able speaker or an able man of affairs, but both of them
combined in the same person might produce a man incomparable among his fellows.

These, then, are my views as to the relative importance of native ability and practice.   192
I cannot, however, make a like claim for education; its powers are not equal nor compara-
ble to theirs. For if one should take lessons in all the principles of oratory and master them
with the greatest thoroughness, he might, perhaps become a more pleasing speaker than
most, but let him stand up before the crowd and lack one thing only, namely, assurance,
and he would not be able to utter a word.

• • •

Now I have spoken and advised you enough on these studies for the present. It remains to   270
tell you about "wisdom" and "philosophy." It is true that if one were pleading a case on
any other issue it would be out of place to discuss these words (for they are foreign to all
litigation), but it is appropriate for me, since I am being tried on such an issue, and since
I hold that what some people call philosophy is not entitled to that name, to define and
explain to you what philosophy, properly conceived, really is. My view of this question is,   271
as it happens, very simple. For since it is not in the nature of man to attain a science by the
possession of which we can know positively what we should do or what we should say, in
the next resort I hold that man to be wise who is able by his powers of conjecture to arrive generally at the best course, and I hold that man to be a philosopher who occupies
himself with the studies from which he will most quickly gain that kind of insight.

What the studies are which have this power I can tell you, although I hesitate to do   272
so; they are so contrary to popular belief and so very far removed from the opinions of the
rest of the world, that I am afraid lest when you first hear them you will fill the whole

court-room with your murmurs and your cries. Nevertheless, in spite of my misgivings, I

273   shall attempt to tell you about them; for I blush at the thought that anyone might suspect me of betraying the truth to save my old age and the little of life remaining to me. But, I beg of you, do not, before you have heard me, judge that I could have been so mad as to choose deliberately, when my fate is in your hands, to express to you ideas which are repugnant to your opinions if I had not believed that these ideas follow logically on what I have previously said, and that I could support them with true and convincing proofs.

274   I consider that the kind of art which can implant honesty and justice in depraved natures has never existed and does not now exist, and that people who profess that power will

275   grow weary and cease from their vain pretensions before such an education is ever found. But I do hold that people can become better and worthier if they conceive an ambition to speak well, if they become possessed of the desire to be able to persuade their hearers and, finally, if they set their hearts on, seizing their advantage—I do not mean "advantage" in

276   the sense given to that word by the empty-minded but advantage in the true meaning of that term; and that this is so I think I shall presently make clear.

For, in the first place, when anyone elects to speak or write discourses which are worthy of praise and honour, it is not conceivable that he will support causes which are unjust or petty or devoted to private quarrels, and not rather those which are great and hon-

277   ourable, devoted to the welfare of man and our common good; for if he fails to find causes of this character, he will accomplish nothing to the purpose. In the second place, he will select from all the actions of men which bear upon his subject those examples which are the most illustrious and the most edifying; and habituating himself to contemplate and appraise such examples, he will feel their influence not only in the preparation of a given discourse but in all the actions of his life. It follows, then, that the power to speak well and think right will reward the man who approaches the art of discourse with love of wisdom and love of honour.

278   Furthermore, mark you, the man who wishes to persuade people will not be negligent as to the matter of character; no, on the contrary, he will apply himself above all to establish a most honourable name among his fellow-citizens; for who does not know that words carry greater conviction when spoken by men of good repute than when spoken by men who live under a cloud, and that the argument which is made by a man's life is of more weight than that which is furnished by words? Therefore, the stronger a man's desire to persuade his hearers, the more zealously will he strive to be honourable and to have the esteem of his fellow-citizens.

279   And let no one of you suppose that while all other people realize how much the scales of persuasion incline in favour of one who has the approval of his judges, the devotees of

280   philosophy alone are blind to the power of good will. In fact, they appreciate this even more thoroughly than others, and they know, furthermore, that probabilities and proofs and all forms of persuasion support only the points in a case to which they are severally applied, whereas an honourable reputation not only lends greater persuasiveness to the words of the man who possesses it, but adds greater lustre to his deeds, and is, therefore, more zealously to be sought after by men of intelligence than anything else in the world.

I come now to the question of "advantage"—the most difficult of the points I have 281
raised. If any one is under the impression that people who rob others or falsify accounts or
do any evil thing get the advantage, he is wrong in his thinking; for none are at a greater
disadvantage throughout their lives than such men; none are found in more difficult
straits, none live in greater ignominy; and, in a word, none are more miserable than they. 282
No, you ought to believe rather that those are better off now and will receive the advantage in the future at the hands of the gods who are the most righteous and the most faithful in their devotions, and that those receive the better portion at the hands of men who
are the most conscientious in their dealings with their associates, whether in their homes
or in public life, and are themselves esteemed as the noblest among their fellows.

This is verily the truth, and it is well for us to adopt this way of speaking on the sub- 283
ject, since, as things now are, Athens has in many respects been plunged into such a state
of topsy-turvy and confusion that some of our people no longer use words in their proper
meaning but wrest them from the most honourable associations and apply them to the 284
basest pursuits. On the one hand, they speak of men who play the buffoon and have a talent for mocking and mimicking as "gifted"—an appellation which should be reserved for
men endowed with the highest excellence; while, on the other hand, they think of men
who indulge their depraved and criminal instincts and who for small gains acquire a base
reputation as "getting the advantage," instead of applying this term to the most righteous
and the most upright, that is, to men who take advantage of the good and not the evil 285
things of life. They characterize men who ignore our practical needs and delight in the
mental juggling of the ancient sophists as "students of philosophy," but refuse this name
to those who pursue and practise those studies which will enable us to govern wisely both
our own households and the commonwealth—which should be the objects of our toil, of
our study and of our every act.

PROTAGORAS • *Great Speech* (as rendered by Plato)

320D There was once a time when there were gods, but no mortal creatures. And when to these also came their destined time to be created, the gods moulded their forms within the earth, of a mixture made of earth and fire and all substances that are compounded with fire and earth. When they were about to bring these creatures to light, they charged Prometheus and Epimetheus to deal to each the equipment of his proper faculty. Epimetheus besought

320E Prometheus that he might do the dealing himself; "And when I have dealt," he said, "you shall examine." Having thus persuaded him he dealt; and in dealing he attached strength without speed to some, while the weaker he equipped with speed; and some he armed, while devising for others, along with an unarmed condition, some different faculty for preservation. To those which he invested with smallness he dealt a winged escape or an un-

321A derground habitation; those which he increased in largeness he preserved by this very means; and he dealt all the other properties on this plan of compensation. In contriving all this he was taking precaution that no kind should be extinguished; and when he had equipped them with avoidances of mutual destruction, he devised a provision against the seasons ordained by Heaven, in clothing them about with thick-set hair and solid hides, suf-

321B ficient to ward off winter yet able to shield them also from the heats, and so that on going to their lairs they might find in these same things a bedding of their own that was native to each; and some he shod with hoofs, others with claws and solid, bloodless hides. Then he proceeded to furnish each of them with its proper food, some with pasture of the earth, others with fruits of trees, and others again with roots; and to a certain number for food he gave other creatures to devour: to some he attached a paucity in breeding, and to oth-

321C ers, which were being consumed by these, a plenteous brood, and so procured survival of their kind. Now Epimetheus, being not so wise as he might be, heedlessly squandered his stock of properties on the brutes; he still had left unequipped the race of men, and was at a loss what to do with it. As he was casting about, Prometheus arrived to examine his distribution, and saw that whereas the other creatures were fully and suitably provided, man was naked, unshod, unbedded, unarmed; and already the destined day was come, whereon man like the rest should emerge from earth to light. Then Prometheus, in his perplexity as

321D to what preservation he could devise for man, stole from Hephaestus and Athena wisdom in the arts together with fire—since by no means without fire could it be acquired or help-fully used by any—and he handed it there and then as a gift to man. Now although man acquired in this way the wisdom of daily life, civic wisdom he had not, since this was in the possession of Zeus; Prometheus could not make so free as to enter the citadel which is the

321E dwelling place of Zeus, and moreover the guards of Zeus were terrible: but he entered un-observed the building shared by Athena and Hephaestus for the pursuit of their arts, and stealing Hephaestus's fiery art and all Athena's also he gave them to man, and hence it is that man gets facility for his livelihood, but Prometheus, through Epimetheus' fault, later

322A on (the story goes) stood his trial for theft.

Source: Reprinted by permission of the publishers and the Loeb Classical Library from Protagoras: *Great Speech*, Volume I (pp. 129–151), translated by W.R.M. Lamb, Cambridge, Mass.: Harvard University Press, 1977.

And now that man was partaker of a divine portion, he, in the first place, by his nearness of kin to deity, was the only creature that worshipped gods, and set himself to establish altars and holy images; and secondly, he soon was enabled by his skill to articulate speech and words, and to invent dwellings, clothes, sandals, beds, and the foods that are of the earth. Thus far provided, men dwelt separately in the beginning, and cities there 322B were none; so that they were being destroyed by the wild beasts, since these were in all ways stronger than they; and although their skill in handiwork was a sufficient aid in respect of food, in their warfare with the beasts it was defective; for as yet they had no civic art, which includes the art of war. So they sought to band themselves together and secure their lives by founding cities. Now as often as they were banded together they did wrong to one another through the lack of civic art, and thus they began to be scattered again and 322C to perish. So Zeus, fearing that our race was in danger of utter destruction, sent Hermes to bring respect and right among men, to the end that there should be regulations of cities and friendly ties to draw them together. Then Hermes asked Zeus in what manner then was he to give men right and respect: "Am I to deal them out as the arts have been dealt? That dealing was done in such wise that one man possessing medical art is able to treat many ordinary men, and so with the other craftsmen. Am I to place among men right and respect in this way also, or deal them out to all?" "To all," replied Zeus; "let all have their 322D share; for cities cannot be formed if only a few have a share of these as of other arts. And make thereto a law of my ordaining, that he who cannot partake of respect and right shall die the death as a public pest."

(ARGUMENT FOLLOWING THE 'GREAT SPEECH')

Hence it comes about, Socrates, that people in cities, and especially in Athens, consider it the concern of a few to advise on cases of artistic excellence or good craftsmanship, and if 322E anyone outside the few gives advice they disallow it, as you say, and not without reason, as I think: but when they meet for a consultation on civic art, where they should be guided 323A throughout by justice and good senses, they naturally allow advice from everybody, since it is held that everyone should partake of this excellence, or else that states cannot be. This, Socrates, is the explanation of it. And that you may not think you are mistaken, to show how all men verily believe that everyone partakes of justice and the rest of civic virtue, I can offer yet a further proof. In all other excellences, as you say, when a man professes to be good at flute-playing or any other art in which he has no such skill, they either laugh him to scorn or are annoyed with him, and his people come and reprove him for being so 323B mad: but where justice or any other civic virtue is involved, and they happen to know that a certain person is unjust, if he confesses the truth about his conduct before the public, that truthfulness which in the former arts they would regard as good sense they here call madness. Everyone, they say, should profess to be just, whether he is so or not, and whoever does not make some pretension to justice is made; since it is held that all without exception must needs partake of it in some way or other, or else not be of human kind. 323C

Take my word for it, then, that they have good reason for admitting everybody as adviser on this virtue, owing to their belief that everyone has some of it; and next, that they do not regard it as natural or spontaneous, but as something taught and acquired after careful preparation by those who acquire it,—of this I will now endeavour to convince

323D you. In all cases of evils which men deem to have befallen their neighbours by nature or fortune, nobody is wroth with them or reproves or lectures or punishes them, when so afflicted, with a view to their being other than they are; one merely pities them. Who, for instance, is such a fool as to try to do anything of the sort to the ugly, the puny, or the weak? Because, I presume, men know that it is by nature and fortune that people get these things, the graces of life and their opposites. But as to all good things that people are sup-

323E posed to get by application and practice and teaching, where these are lacking in anyone and only their opposite evils are found, here surely are the occasions for wrath and pun-

324A ishment and reproof. One of them is injustice, and impiety, and in short all that is opposed to civic virtue; in such case anyone will be wroth with his neighbour and reprove him, clearly because the virtue is to be acquired by application and learning. For if you will consider punishment, Socrates, and what control it has over wrong-doers, the facts will inform you that men agree in regarding virtue as procured. No one punishes a wrong-doer from the mere contemplation or on account of his wrong-doing, unless one takes unreasoning

324B vengeance like a wild beast. But he who undertakes to punish with reason does not avenge himself for the past offence, since he cannot make what was done as though it had not come to pass; he looks rather to the future, and aims at preventing that particular person and others who see him punished from doing wrong again. And being so minded he must

324C have in mind that virtue comes by training: for you observe that he punishes to deter. This then is the accepted view of all who seek requital in either private or public life; and while men in general exact requital and punishment from those whom they suppose to have wronged them, this is especially the case with the Athenians, your fellow-citizens, so that by our argument the Athenians also share the view that virtue is procured and taught. Thus I have shown that your fellow-citizens have good reason for admitting a smith's or cobbler's counsel in public affairs, and that they hold virtue to be taught and procured: of

324D this I have given you satisfactory demonstration, Socrates, as it appears to me.

I have yet to deal with your remaining problem about good men, why it is that these good men have their sons taught the subjects in the regular teachers' courses, and so far make them wise, but do not make them excel in that virtue wherein consists their own

324E goodness. On this point, Socrates, I shall give you argument instead of fable. Now consider: is there, or is there not, some one thing whereof all the citizens must needs partake, if there is to be a city? Here, and nowhere if not here, is the solution of this problem of yours. For if there is such a thing, and that one thing, instead of being the joiner's or

325A smith's or potter's art, is rather justice and temperance and holiness—in short, what I may put together and call a man's virtue; and if it is this whereof all should partake and wherewith everyone should proceed to any further knowledge or action, but should not if he lacks it; if we should instruct and punish such as we do not partake of it, whether child or husband or wife, until the punishment of such persons has made them better, and should

325B cast forth from our cities or put to death as uncurable whoever fails to respond to such punishment and instruction;—if it is like this, and yet, its nature being so, good men have their sons instructed in everything else but this, what very surprising folk the good are found to be! For we have proved that they regard this thing as teachable both in private and in public life, and then, though it may be taught and fostered, are we to say that they have their sons taught everything in which the penalty for ignorance is not death, but in a matter where the death-penalty or exile awaits their children if not instructed and culti-vated in virtue—and not merely death, but confiscation of property and practically the en-tire subversion of their house—here they do not have them taught or take the utmost care of them? So at any rate we must conclude, Socrates. 325C

They teach and admonish them from earliest childhood till the last day of their lives. As soon as one of them grasps what is said to him, the nurse, the mother, the tutor, and the father himself strive hard that the child may excel, and as each act and word occurs they teach and impress upon him that this is just, and that unjust, one thing noble, another base, one holy, another unholy, and that he is to do this, and not do that. If he readily obeys,—so; but if not, they treat him as a bent and twisted piece of wood and straighten him with threats and blows. After this they send them to school and charge the master to take far more pains over their children's good behaviour than over their letters and harp-playing. The masters take pains accordingly, and the children, when they have learnt their letters and are getting to understand the written word as before they did only the spoken, are furnished with works of good poets to read as they sit in class, and are made to learn them off by heart: here they meet with many admonitions, many descriptions and praises and eulogies of good men in times past, that the boy in envy may imitate them and yearn to become even as they. Then also the music-masters, in a similar sort, take pains for their self-restraint, and see that their young charges do not go wrong: moreover, when they learn to play the harp, they are taught the works of another set of good poets, the song-makers, while the master accompanies them on the harp; and they insist on familiarizing the boys' souls with the rhythms and scales, that they may gain in gentleness, and by ad-vancing in rhythmic and harmonic grace may be efficient in speech and action; for the whole of man's life requires the graces of rhythm and harmony. Again, over and above all this, people send their sons to a trainer, that having improved their bodies they may per-form the orders of their minds, which are now in fit condition, and that they may not be forced by bodily faults to play the coward in wars and other duties. This is what people do, who are most able; and the most able are the wealthiest. Their sons begin school at the ear-liest age, and are freed from it at the latest. And when they are released from their schooling the city next compels them to learn the laws and to live according to them as after a pattern, that their conduct may not be swayed by their own light fancies, but just as writing-masters first draw letters in faint outline with the pen for their less advanced pupils, and then give them the copy-book and make them write according to the guidance of their lines, so the city sketches out for them the laws devised by good lawgivers of yours, and constrains them to govern and be governed according to these. She punishes anyone who steps out-side these borders, and this punishment among you and in many other cities, from the cor-rective purpose of the prosecution, is called a Correction. Seeing then that so much care is taken in the matter of both private and public virtue, do you wonder, Socrates, and make it a great difficulty, that virtue may be taught? Surely there is no reason to wonder at that: you would have far greater reason, if it were not so. 325D 325E 326A 326B 326C 326D 326E

Then why is it that many sons of good fathers turn out so meanly? Let me explain this also: it is no wonder, granted that I was right in stating just now that no one, if we are to have a city, must be a mere layman in this affair of virtue. For if what I say is the case—and 327A it is supremely true—reflect on the nature of any other pursuit or study that you choose to mention. Suppose that there could be no state unless we were all flute-players, in such sort as each was able, and suppose that everyone were giving his neighbour both private and public lessons in the art, and rebuked him too, if he failed to do it well, without grudging

327B   him the trouble—even as no one now thinks of grudging or reserving his skill in what is just and lawful as he does in other expert knowledge; for our neighbours' justice and virtue, I take it, is to our advantage, and consequently we all tell and teach one another what is just and lawful—well, if we made the same zealous and ungrudging efforts to instruct each other in flute-playing, do you think, Socrates, that the good flute-players would be more likely than the bad to have sons who were good flute-players? I do not

327C   think they would: no, wherever the son had happened to be born with a nature most apt for flute-playing, he would be found to have advanced to distinction, and where unapt, to obscurity. Often the son of a good player would turn out a bad one, and often of a bad, a good. But, at any rate, all would be capable players as compared with ordinary persons who had no inkling of the art. Likewise in the present case you must regard any man who

327D   appears to you the most unjust person ever reared among human laws and society as a just man and a craftsman of justice, if he had to stand comparison with people who lacked education and law courts and laws and any constant compulsion to the pursuit of virtue, but were a kind of wild folk such as Pherecrates the poet brought on the scene at last year's Lenaeum. Sure enough, if you found yourself among such people, as did the misanthropes among his chorus, you would be very glad to meet with Eurybatus and Phrynondas, and

327E   would bewail yourself with longing for the wickedness of the people here. Instead of that you give yourself dainty airs, Socrates, because everyone is a teacher of virtue to the extent of his powers, and you think there is no teacher. Why, you might as well ask who is a

328A   teacher of Greek; you would find none anywhere; and I suppose you might ask, who can teach the sons of our artisans the very crafts which of course they have learnt from their fathers, as far as the father was competent in each case, and his friends who followed the same trade,—I say if you asked who is to give these further instruction, I imagine it would be hard, Socrates, to find them a teacher, but easy enough in the case of those starting with

328B   no skill at all. And so it must be with virtue and everything else; if there is somebody who excels us ever so little in showing the way to virtue, we must be thankful. Such an one I take myself to be, excelling all other men in the gift of assisting people to become good and true, and giving full value for the fee that I charge—nay, so much more than full, that the learner himself admits it. For this reason I have arranged my charges on a particular plan: when anyone has had lessons from me, if he likes he pays the sum that I ask; if not,

328C   he goes to a temple, states an oath the value he sets on what he has learnt, and disburses that amount. So now, Socrates, I have shown you by both fable and argument that virtue is teachable and is so deemed by the Athenians, and that it is no wonder that bad sons are born of good fathers and good of bad, since even the sons of Polycleitus, companions of Paralus and Xanthippus here, are not to be compared with their father, and the same is the

328D   case in other craftsmen's families. As for these two, it is not fair to make this complaint of them yet; there is still hope in their case, for they are young.

LYSIAS' SPEECH ON THE NON-LOVER

You know how I am situated, and I have told you that I think it to our advantage that this should happen. Now I claim that I should not be refused what I ask simply because I am not your lover. Lovers, when their craving is at an end, repent of such benefits as they have conferred, but for the other sort no occasion arises for regretting what has passed. For being free agents under no constraint, they regulate their services by the scale of their means, with an eye to their own personal interest. Again, lovers weigh up profit and loss accruing to their account by reason of their passion, and with the extra item of labor expended decide that they have long since made full payment for favors received, whereas the nonlovers cannot allege any consequential neglect of their personal affairs, nor record any past exertions on the debit side, nor yet complain of having quarreled with their relatives; hence, with all these troubles removed, all they have left to do is to devote their energies to such conduct as they conceive likely to gratify the other party.

Again, it is argued that a lover ought to be highly valued because he professes to be especially kind toward the loved one, and ready to gratify him in words and deeds while arousing the dislike of everyone else. If this is true, however, it is obvious that he will set greater store by the loved one of tomorrow than by that of today, and will doubtless do an injury to the old love if required by the new.

And really, what sense is there in lavishing what is so precious upon one laboring under an affliction which nobody who knew anything of it would even attempt to remove? Why, the man himself admits that he is not sound, but sick, that he is aware of his folly, but cannot control himself. How then, when he comes to his senses, is he likely to approve of the intentions that he formed in his aberration?

And observe this. If you are to choose the best of a number of lovers, your choice will be only among a few, whereas a general choice of the person who most commends himself to you gives you a wide field, so that in that wide field you have a much better prospect of finding someone worthy of your friendship.

Now maybe you respect established conventions, and anticipate odium if people get to hear about you; if so, it may be expected that a lover, conceiving that everyone will admire him as he admires himself, will be proud to talk about it and flatter his vanity by declaring to all and sundry that his enterprise has been successful, whereas the other type, who can control themselves, will prefer to do what is best rather than shine in the eyes of their neighbors.

Again, a lover is bound to be heard about and seen by many people, consorting with his beloved and caring about little else, so that when they are observed talking to one another, the meeting is taken to imply the satisfaction, actual or prospective, of their desires, whereas, with the other sort, no one ever thinks of putting a bad construction on their association, realizing that a man must have someone to talk to by way of friendship or gratification of one sort or another.

Source: Edith Hamilton, ed., *Plato: The Collected Dialogues,* Bollingen Series. Copyright © 1989 by Princeton University Press, pp. 479–482, in *Phaedrus,* 230E–234C. Reprinted by permission of Princeton University Press.

And observe this. Perhaps you feel troubled by the reflection that it is hard for friendship to be preserved, and that whereas a quarrel arising from other sources will be a calamity shared by both parties, one that follows the sacrifice of your all will involve a grievous hurt to yourself; in that case it is doubtless the lover who should cause you the more alarm, for he is very ready to take offense, and thinks the whole affair is to his own hurt. Hence he discourages his beloved from consorting with anyone else, fearing that a wealthy rival may overreach him with his money, or a cultured one outdo him with his intelligence, and he is perpetually on guard against the influence of those who possess other advantages. So by persuading you to become estranged from such rivals he leaves you without a friend in the world; alternatively, if you look to your own interest and show more good sense than your lover, you will find yourself quarreling with him. On the other hand, one who is not a lover, but has achieved what he asked of you by reason of his merit, will not be jealous of others who seek your society, but will rather detest those who avoid it, in the belief that the latter look down on him, whereas the former are serving his turn. Consequently the object of his attentions is far more likely to make friends than enemies out of the affair.

And observe this. A lover more often than not wants to possess you before he has come to know your character or become familiar with your general personality, and that makes it uncertain whether he will still want to be your friend when his desires have waned, whereas in the other case, the fact that the pair were already friends before the affair took place makes it probable that instead of friendship diminishing as the result of favors received, these favors will abide as a memory and promise of more to come.

And observe this. It ought to be for your betterment to listen to me rather than to a lover, for a lover commends anything you say or do even when it is amiss, partly from fear that he may offend you, partly because his passion impairs his own judgment. For the record of Love's achievement is, first, that when things go badly, he makes a man count that an affliction which normally causes no distress; secondly, that when things go well, he compels his subjects to extol things that ought not to gratify them, which makes it fitting that they should be pitied far more than admired by the objects of their passion. On the other hand, if you listen to me, my intercourse with you will be a matter of ministering not to your immediate pleasure but to your future advantage, for I am the master of myself, rather than the victim of love; I do not bring bitter enmity upon myself by resenting trifling offenses. On the contrary, it is only on account of serious wrongs that I am moved, and that but slowly, to mild indignation, pardoning what is done unintentionally, and endeavoring to hinder what is done of intent, for these are the tokens of lasting friendship. If however you are disposed to think that there can be no firm friendship save with a lover, you should reflect that in that case we should not set store by sons, or fathers, or mothers, nor should we possess any trustworthy friends. No, it is not to erotic passion that we owe these, but to conduct of a different order.

Again, if we ought to favor those who press us most strongly, then in other matters too we should give our good offices not to the worthiest people but to the most destitute, for since their distress is the greatest, they will be the most thankful to us for relieving them. And observe this further consequence. When we give private banquets, the right people to invite will be not our friends but beggars and those in need of a good meal, for it is they that will be fond of us and attend upon us and flock to our doors; it is they that will be most delighted and most grateful and call down blessings on our heads. No, the proper course, surely, is to show favor not to the most importunate but to those most able to make us a return—not to mere beggars, but to the deserving; not to those who will regale themselves with your youthful beauty, but to those who will let you share their prosperity when you are older; not to those who, when they have had their will of you, will flatter their vanity by telling the world, but to those who will keep a strict and modest silence; not to those who are devoted to you for a brief period, but to those who will continue to be your friends as long as you live; not to those who, when their passion is spent, will look for an excuse to turn against you, but to those who, when your beauty is past, will make that the time for displaying their own goodness.

Do you therefore be mindful of what I have said and reflect that, while lovers are admonished by their friends and relatives for the wrongness of their conduct, the other sort have never been reproached by one of their family on the score of behaving to the detriment of their own interest.

Perhaps you will ask me whether I recommend you to accord your favors to all and sundry of this sort. Well, I do not suppose that even a lover would bid you to be favorable toward all and sundry lovers; in the first place a recipient would not regard it as meriting so much gratitude, and in the second you would find it more difficult if you wished to keep your affairs concealed, and what is wanted is that the business should involve no harm, but mutual advantage.

And now I think I have said all that is needed; if you think I have neglected anything, and want more, let me know.

SOCRATES • *First Speech on the Non-Lover*

SOCRATES. Come then, O tuneful Muses, whether ye receive this name from the quality of your song or from the musical race of the Ligyans, grant me your aid in the tale this most excellent man compels me to relate, that his friend whom he has hitherto considered wise, may seem to him wiser still.

Now there was once upon a time a boy, or rather a stripling, of great beauty: and he had many lovers. And among these was one of peculiar craftiness, who was as much in love with the boy as anyone, but had made him believe that he was not in love; and once in wooing him, he tried to persuade him of this very thing, that favours ought to be granted rather to the non-lover than to the lover; and his words were as follows:—

There is only one way, dear boy, for those to begin who are to take counsel wisely about anything. One must know what the counsel is about, or it is sure to be utterly futile, but most people are ignorant of the fact that they do not know the nature of things. So, supposing that they do know it, they come to no agreement in the beginning of their enquiry, and as they go on they reach the natural result,—they agree neither with themselves nor with each other. Now you and I must not fall into the error which we condemn in others, but, since we are to discuss the question, whether the lover or the non-lover is to be preferred let us first agree on a definition of love, its nature and its power, and then, keeping this definition in view and making constant reference to it, let us enquire whether love brings advantage or harm. Now everyone sees that love is a desire; and we know too that non-lovers also desire the beautiful. How then are we to distinguish the lover from the non-lover? We must observe that in each one of us there are two ruling and leading principles, which we follow whithersoever they lead; one is the innate desire for pleasures, the other an acquired opinion which strives for the best. These two sometimes agree within us and are sometimes in strife; and sometimes one, and sometimes the other has the greater power. Now when opinion leads through reason toward the best and is more powerful, its power is called self-restraint, but when desire irrationally drags us toward pleasures and rules within us, its rule is called excess. Now excess has many names, for it has many members and many forms; and whichever of these forms is most marked gives its own name, neither beautiful nor honourable, to him who possesses it. For example, if the desire for food prevails over the higher reason and the other desires, it is called gluttony, and he who possesses it will be called by the corresponding name of glutton, and again, if the desire for drink becomes the tyrant and leads him who possesses it toward drink, we know what he is called; and it is quite clear what fitting names of the same sort will be given when any desire akin to these acquires the rule. The reason for what I have said hitherto is pretty clear by this time, but everything is plainer when spoken than when unspoken; so I say that the desire which overcomes the rational opinion that strives toward the right, and which is led away toward the enjoyment of beauty and again is strongly forced by the desires that are kindred to itself toward personal beauty, when it gains the victory, takes its name from that very force, and is called love.

Source: Harold N. Fowler, tr., Plato, *Phaedrus,* 1914, New York: G. P. Putnam's Sons, pp. 443–457.

Well then, my dearest, what the subject is, about which we are to take counsel, has been said and defined, and now let us continue, keeping our attention fixed upon that definition, and tell what advantage or harm will naturally come from the lover or the non-lover to him who grants them his favours.

He who is ruled by desire and is a slave to pleasure will inevitably desire to make his beloved as pleasing to himself as possible. Now to one who is of unsound mind everything is pleasant which does not oppose him, but everything that is better or equal is hateful. So the lover will not, if he can help it, endure a beloved who is better than himself or his equal, but always makes him weaker and inferior; but the ignorant is inferior to the wise, the coward to the brave, the poor speaker to the eloquent, the slow of wit to the clever. Such mental defects, and still greater than these, in the beloved will necessarily please the lover, if they are implanted by Nature, and if they are not, he must implant them or be deprived of his immediate enjoyment. And he is of necessity jealous and will do him great harm by keeping him from many advantageous associations, which would most tend to make a man of him, especially from that which would do most to make him wise. This is divine philosophy, and from it the lover will certainly keep his beloved away, through fear of being despised; and he will contrive to keep him ignorant of everything else and make him look to his lover for everything, so that he will be most agreeable to him and most harmful to himself. In respect to the intellect, then, a man in love is by no means a profitable guardian or associate.

We must next consider how he who is forced to follow pleasure and not good will keep the body of him whose master he is, and what care he will give to it. He will plainly court a beloved who is effeminate, not virile, not brought up in the pure sunshine, but in mingled shade, unused to manly toils and the sweat of exertion, but accustomed to a delicate and unmanly mode of life, adorned with a bright complexion of artificial origin, since he has none by nature, and in general living a life such as all this indicates, which it is certainly not worth while to describe further. We can sum it all up briefly and pass on. A person with such a body, in war and in all important crises, gives courage to his enemies, and fills his friends, and even his lovers themselves, with fear.

This may be passed over as self-evident, but the next question, what advantage or harm the intercourse and guardianship of the lover will bring to his beloved in the matter of his property, must be discussed. Now it is clear to everyone, and especially to the lover, that he would desire above all things to have his beloved bereft of the dearest and kindest and holiest possessions; for he would wish him to be deprived of father, mother, relatives and friends, thinking that they would hinder and censure his most sweet intercourse with him. But he will also think that one who has property in money or other possessions will be less easy to catch and when caught will be less manageable; wherefore the lover must necessarily begrudge his beloved the possession of property and rejoice at its loss. Moreover the lover would wish his beloved to be as long as possible unmarried, childless, and homeless, since he wishes to enjoy as long as possible what is pleasant to himself.

Now there are also other evils, but God has mingled with most of them some temporary pleasure; so, for instance, a flatterer is a horrid creature and does great harm, yet Nature has combined with him a kind of pleasure that is not without charm, and one might find fault with a courtesan as an injurious thing, and there are many other such creatures and practices which are yet for the time being very pleasant; but a lover is not only harmful to his beloved but extremely disagreeable to live with as well. The old proverb says, "birds of a feather flock together"; that is, I suppose, equality of age leads them to similar pleasures and through similarity begets friendship; and yet even they grow tired of each other's society. Now compulsion of every kind is said to be oppressive to every one, and the lover not only is unlike his beloved, but he exercises the strongest compulsion. For he is old while his love is young, and he does not leave him day or night, if he can help it, but is driven by the sting of necessity, which urges him on, always giving him pleasure in seeing, hearing, touching, and by all his senses perceiving his beloved, so that he is glad to serve him constantly. But what consolation or what pleasure can he give the beloved? Must not his protracted intercourse bring him to the uttermost disgust, as he looks at the old, unlovely face, and other things to match, which it is not pleasant even to hear about, to say nothing of being constantly compelled to come into contact with them? And he is suspiciously guarded in all ways against everybody, and has to listen to untimely and exaggerated praises and to reproaches which are unendurable when the man is sober, and when he is in his cups and indulges in wearisome and unrestrained freedom of speech become not only unendurable but disgusting.

And while he is in love he is harmful and disagreeable, but when his love has ceased he is thereafter false to him whom he formerly hardly induced to endure his wearisome companionship through the hope of future benefits by making promises with many prayers and oaths. But now that the time of payment has come he has a new ruler and governor within him, sense and reason in place of love and madness, and has become a different person; but of this his beloved knows nothing. He asks of him a return for former favours, reminding him of past sayings and doings, as if he were speaking to the same man; but the lover is ashamed to say that he has changed, and yet he cannot keep the oaths and promises he made when he was ruled by his former folly, now that he has regained his reason and come to his senses, lest by doing what he formerly did he become again what he was. He runs away from these things, and the former lover is compelled to become a defaulter. The shell has fallen with the other side up; [1] and he changes his part and runs away; and the other is forced to run after him in anger and with imprecations, he who did not know at the start that he ought never to have accepted a lover who was necessarily without reason, but rather a reasonable non-lover; for otherwise he would have to surrender himself to one who was faithless, irritable, jealous, and disagreeable, harmful to his property, harmful to his physical condition, and most harmful by far to the cultivation of his soul, than which there neither is nor ever will be anything of higher importance in truth either in heaven or on earth. These things, dear boy, you must bear in mind, and you must know that the fondness of the lover is not a matter of goodwill, but of appetite which he wishes to satisfy:

Just as the wolf loves the lamb, so the lover adores his beloved.

There it is, Phaedrus! Do not listen to me any longer; let my speech end here.

[1]   This refers to a game played with oyster shells, in which the players ran away or pursued as the shell fell with one or the other side uppermost.

SOCRATES • *Second Speech on Love*

SOCRATES. Understand then, fair youth, that the former discourse was by Phaedrus, the son of Pythocles (Eager for Fame) of Myrrhinus (Myrrhtown); but this which I shall speak is by Stesichorus, son of Euphemus (Man of pious Speech) of Himera (Town of Desire). And I must say that this saying is not true, which teaches that when a lover is at hand the non-lover should be more favoured, because the lover is insane, and the other sane. For if it were a simple fact that insanity is an evil, the saying would be true; but in reality the greatest of blessings come to us through madness, when it is sent as a gift of the gods. For the prophetess at Delphi and the priestesses at Dodona when they have been mad have conferred many splendid benefits upon Greece both in private and in public affairs, but few or none when they have been in their right minds; and if we should speak of the Sibyl and all the others who by prophetic inspiration have foretold many things to many persons and thereby made them fortunate afterwards, anyone can see that we should speak a long time. And it is worth while to adduce also the fact that those men of old who invented names thought that madness was neither shameful nor disgraceful; otherwise they would not have connected the very word mania with the noblest of arts, that which foretells the future, by calling it the manic art. No, they gave this name thinking that mania, when it comes by gift of the gods, is a noble thing, but nowadays people call prophecy the mantic art, tastelessly inserting a T in the word. So also, when they gave a name to the investigation of the future which rational persons conduct through observation of birds and by other signs, since they furnish mind (nous) and information (historia) to human thought (oiesis) from the intellect (dianoia) they called it the oionoïstic (oionoistike) art, which modern folk now call oiōnistic, making it more high-sounding by introducing the long O. The ancients, then testify that in proportion as prophecy (mantike) is superior to augury, both in name and in fact, in the same proportion madness, which comes from god, is superior to sanity, which is of human origin. Moreover, when diseases and the greatest troubles have been visited upon certain families through some ancient guilt, madness has entered in and by oracular power found a way of release for those in need, taking refuge in prayers and the service of the gods, and so, by purifications and sacred rites, he who has this madness is made safe for the present and the after time, and for him who is rightly possessed of madness a release from present ills is found. And a third kind of possession and madness comes from the Muses. This takes hold upon a gentle and pure soul, arouses it and inspires it to songs and other poetry, and thus by adorning countless deeds of the ancients educates later generations. But he who without the divine madness comes to the doors of the Muses, confident that he will be a good poet by art, meets with no success, and the poetry of the sane man vanishes into nothingness before that of the inspired madmen.

All these noble results of inspired madness I can mention, and many more. Therefore let us not be afraid on that point, and let no one disturb and frighten us by saying that the reasonable friend should be preferred to him who is in a frenzy. Let him show in addition that love is not sent from heaven for the advantage of lover and beloved alike, and we will

Source: Harold N. Fowler, tr., Plato, *Phaedrus,* 1914, New York: G. P. Putnam's Sons, pp. 465–505.

grant him the prize of victory. We, on our part, must prove that such madness is given by the gods for our greatest happiness; and our proof will not be believed by the merely clever, but will be accepted by the truly wise. First, then, we must learn the truth about the soul divine and human by observing how it acts and is acted upon. And the beginning of our proof is as follows:

Every soul is immortal. For that which is ever moving is immortal; but that which moves something else or is moved by something else, when it ceases to move, ceases to live. Only that which moves itself, since it does not leave itself, never ceases to move, and this is also the source and beginning of motion for all other things which have motion. But the beginning is ungenerated. For everything that is generated must be generated from a beginning, but the beginning is not generated from anything; for if the beginning were generated from anything, it would not be generated from a beginning. And since it is ungenerated, it must be also indestructible; for if the beginning were destroyed, it could never be generated from anything nor anything else from it, since all things must be generated from a beginning. Thus that which moves itself must be the beginning of motion. And this can be neither destroyed nor generated, otherwise all the heavens and all generation must fall in ruin and stop and never again have any source of motion or origin. But since that which is moved by itself has been seen to be immortal, one who says that this self-motion is the essence and the very idea of the soul, will not be disgraced. For every body which derives motion from without is soulless, but that which has its motion within itself has a soul, since that is the nature of the soul; but if this is true,—that that which moves itself is nothing else than the soul,—then the soul would necessarily be ungenerated and immortal.

Concerning the immortality of the soul this is enough; but about its form we must speak in the following manner. To tell what it really is would be a matter for utterly superhuman and long discourse, but it is within human power to describe it briefly in a figure; let us therefore speak in that way. We will liken the soul to the composite nature of a pair of winged horses and a charioteer. Now the horses and charioteers of the gods are all good and of good descent, but those of other races are mixed; and first the charioteer of the human soul drives a pair, and secondly one of the horses is noble and of noble breed, but the other quite the opposite in breed and character. Therefore in our case the driving is necessarily difficult and troublesome. Now we must try to tell why a living being is called mortal or immortal. Soul, considered collectively, has the care of all that which is soulless, and it traverses the whole heaven, appearing sometimes in one form and sometimes in another; now when it is perfect and fully winged, it mounts upward and governs the whole world; but the soul which has lost its wings is borne along until it gets hold of something solid, when it settles down, taking upon itself an earthly body, which seems to be self-moving, because of the power of the soul within it; and the whole, compounded of soul and body, is called a living being, and is further designated as mortal. It is not immortal by any reasonable supposition, but we, though we have never seen or rightly conceived a god, imagine an immortal being which has both a soul and a body which are united for all time. Let that, however, and our words concerning it, be as is pleasing to God; we will now consider the reason why the soul loses its wings. It is something like this.

The natural function of the wing is to soar upwards and carry that which is heavy up to the place where dwells the race of the gods. More than any other thing that pertains to the body it partakes of the nature of the divine. But the divine is beauty, wisdom, goodness, and all such qualities; by these then the wings of the soul are nourished and grow, but by the opposite qualities, such as vileness and evil, they are wasted away and destroyed. Now the great leader in heaven, Zeus, driving a winged chariot, goes first, arranging all things and caring for all things. He is followed by an army of gods and spirits, arrayed in eleven squadrons; Hestia alone remains in the house of the gods. Of the rest, those who are included among the twelve great gods and are accounted leaders, are assigned each to his place in the army. There are many blessed sights and many ways hither and thither within the heaven, along which the blessed gods go to and fro attending each to his own duties; and whoever wishes, and is able, follows, for jealousy is excluded from the celestial band. But when they go to a feast and a banquet, they proceed steeply upward to the top of the vault of heaven, where the chariots of the gods, whose well matched horses obey the rein, advance easily, but the others with difficulty; for the horse of evil nature weighs the chariot down, making it heavy and pulling toward the earth the charioteer whose horse is not well trained. There the utmost toil and struggle await the soul. For those that are called immortal, when they reach the top, pass outside and take their place on the outer surface of the heaven, and when they have taken their stand, the revolution carries them round and they behold the things outside of the heaven.

But the region above the heaven was never worthily sung by any earthly poet, nor will it ever be. It is, however, as I shall tell; for I must dare to speak the truth, especially as truth is my theme. For the colourless, formless, and intangible truly existing essence, with which all true knowledge is concerned, holds this region and is visible only to the mind, the pilot of the soul. Now the divine intelligence, since it is nurtured on mind and pure knowledge, and the intelligence of every soul which is capable of receiving that which befits it, rejoices in seeing reality for a space of time and by gazing upon truth is nourished and made happy until the revolution brings it again to the same place. In the revolution it beholds absolute justice, temperance, and knowledge, not such knowledge as has a beginning and varies as it is associated with one or another of the things we call realities, but that which abides in the real eternal absolute; and in the same way it beholds and feeds upon the other eternal verities, after which, passing down again within the heaven, it goes home, and there the charioteer puts up the horses at the manger and feeds them with ambrosia and then gives them nectar to drink.

Such is the life of the gods; but of the other souls, that which best follows after God and is most like him, raises the head of the charioteer up into the outer region and is carried round in the revolution, troubled by the horses and hardly beholding the realities; and another sometimes rises and sometimes sinks, and, because its horses are unruly, it sees some things and fails to see others. The other souls follow after, all yearning for the upper region but unable to reach it, and are carried round beneath, trampling upon and colliding with one another, each striving to pass its neighbour. So there is the greatest confusion and sweat of rivalry, wherein many are lamed, and many wings are broken through the incompetence of the drivers; and after much toil they all go away without gaining a view of reality, and when they have gone away they feed upon opinion. But the reason of the great eagerness to see where the plain truth is, lies in the fact that the fitting pasturage for the best part of the soul is in the meadow there, and the wing on which the soul is raised up is nourished by this. And this is a law of Destiny, that the soul which follows after God and obtains a view of any of the truths is free from harm until the next period, and if it can always attain this, is always unharmed; but when, through inability to follow, it fails to see, and through some mischance is filled with forgetfulness and evil and grows heavy, and when it has grown heavy, loses its wings and falls to the earth, then it is the law that this soul shall never pass into any beast at its first birth, but the soul that has seen the most shall enter into the birth of a man who is to be a philosopher or a lover of beauty, or one of a musical or loving nature, and the second soul into that of a lawful king or a warlike ruler, and the third into that of a politician or a man of business or a financier, the fourth into that of a hard-working gymnast or one who will be concerned with the cure of the body, and the fifth will lead the life of a prophet or someone who conducts mystic rites; to the sixth, a poet or some other imitative artist will be united, to the seventh, a craftsman or a husbandman, to the eighth, a sophist or a demagogue, to the ninth, a tyrant.

Now in all these states, whoever lives justly obtains a better lot, and whoever lives unjustly, a worse. For each soul returns to the place whence it came in ten thousand years; for it does not regain its wings before that time has elapsed, except the soul of him who has been a guileless philosopher or a philosophical lover; these, when for three successive periods of a thousand years they have chosen such a life, after the third period of a thousand years become winged in the three thousandth year and go their way; but the rest, when they have finished their first life, receive judgment, and after the judgment some go to the places of correction under the earth and pay their penalty, while the others, made light and raised up into a heavenly place by justice, live in a manner worthy of the life they led in human form. But in the thousandth year both come to draw lots and choose their second life, each choosing whatever it wishes. Then a human soul may pass into the life of a beast, and a soul which was once human, may pass again from a beast into a man. For the soul which has never seen the truth can never pass into human form. For a human being must understand a general conception formed by collecting into a unity by means of reason the many perceptions of the senses; and this is a recollection of those things which our soul once beheld, when it journeyed with God and, lifting its vision above the things which we now say exist, rose up into real being. And therefore it is just that the mind of the philosopher only has wings, for he is always, so far as he is able, in communion through memory with those things the communion with which causes God to be divine. Now a man who employs such memories rightly is always being initiated into perfect mysteries and he alone becomes truly perfect; but since he separates himself from human interests and turns his attention toward the divine, he is rebuked by the vulgar, who consider him mad and do not know that he is inspired.

All my discourse so far has been about the fourth kind of madness, which causes him to be regarded as mad, who, when he sees the beauty on earth, remembering the true beauty, feels his wings growing and longs to stretch them for an upward flight, but cannot do so, and, like a bird, gazes upward and neglects the things below. My discourse has shown that this is, of all inspirations, the best and of the highest origin to him who has it or who shares in it, and that he who loves the beautiful, partaking in this madness, is called a lover. For, as has been said, every soul of man has by the law of nature beheld the realities, otherwise it would not have entered into a human being, but it is not easy for all souls to gain from earthly things a recollection of those realities, either for those which had but a brief view of them at that earlier time, or for those which, after falling to earth, were so unfortunate as to be turned toward unrighteousness through some evil communications and to have forgotten the holy sights they once saw. Few then are left which retain an adequate recollection of them; but these when they see here any likeness of the things of that other world, are stricken with amazement and can no longer control themselves; but they do not understand their condition, because they do not clearly perceive. Now in the earthly copies of justice and temperance and the other ideas which are precious to souls there is no light, but only a few, approaching the images through the darkling organs of sense, behold in them the nature of that which they imitate, and these few do this with difficulty. But at that former time they saw beauty shining in brightness, when, with a blessed company—we following in the train of Zeus, and others in that of some other god—they saw the blessed sight and vision and were initiated into that which is rightly called the most blessed of mysteries, which we celebrated in a state of perfection, when we were without experience of the evils which awaited us in the time to come, being permitted as initiates to the sight of perfect and simple and calm and happy apparitions, which we saw in the pure light, being ourselves pure and not entombed in this which we carry about with us and call the body, in which we are imprisoned like an oyster in its shell.

So much, then, in honour of memory, on account of which I have now spoken at some length, through yearning for the joys of that other time. But beauty, as I said before, shone in brilliance among those visions; and since we came to earth we have found it shining most clearly through the clearest of our senses; for sight is the sharpest of the physical senses, though wisdom is not seen by it, for wisdom would arouse terrible love, if such a clear image of it were granted as would come through sight, and the same is true of the other lovely realities; but beauty alone has this privilege, and therefore it is most clearly seen and loveliest. Now he who is not newly initiated, or has been corrupted, does not quickly rise from this world to that other world and to absolute beauty when he sees its namesake here, and so he does not revere it when he looks upon it, but gives himself up to pleasure and like a beast proceeds to lust and begetting; he makes licence his companion and is not afraid or ashamed to pursue pleasure in violation of nature. But he who is newly initiated, who beheld many of those realities, when he sees a god-like face or form which is a good image of beauty, shudders at first, and something of the old awe comes over him, then, as he gazes, he reveres the beautiful one as a god, and if he did not fear to be thought stark mad, he would offer sacrifice to his beloved as to an idol or a god. And as he looks upon him, a reaction from his shuddering comes over him, with sweat and unwonted heat; for as the effluence of beauty enters him through the eyes, he is warmed; the effluence moistens the germ of the feathers, and as he grows warm, the parts from which the feathers grow, which were before hard and choked, and prevented the feathers from sprouting, become soft, and as the nourishment streams upon him, the quills of the feathers swell and begin to grow from the roots over all the form of the soul; for it was once all feathered.

Now in this process the whole soul throbs and palpitates, and as in those who are cutting teeth there is an irritation and discomfort in the gums, when the teeth begin to grow, just so the soul suffers when the growth of the feathers begins; it is feverish and is uncomfortable and itches when they begin to grow. Then when it gazes upon the beauty of the boy and receives the particles which flow thence to it (for which reason they are called yearning), it is moistened and warmed, ceases from its pain and is filled with joy; but when it is alone and grows dry, the mouths of the passages in which the feathers begin to grow become dry and close up, shutting in the sprouting feathers, and the sprouts within, shut in with the yearning, throb like pulsing arteries, and each sprout pricks the passage in which it is, so that the whole soul, stung in every part, rages with pain; and then again, remembering the beautiful one, it rejoices. So, because of these two mingled sensations, it is greatly troubled by its strange condition; it is perplexed and maddened, and in its madness it cannot sleep at night or stay in any one place by day, but it is filled with longing and hastens wherever it hopes to see the beautiful one. And when it sees him and is bathed with the waters of yearning, the passages that were sealed are opened, the soul has respite from the stings and is eased of its pain, and this pleasure which it enjoys is the sweetest of pleasures at the time. Therefore the soul will not, if it can help it, be left alone by the beautiful one, but esteems him above all others, forgets for him mother and brothers and all friends, neglects property and cares not for its loss, and despising all the customs and proprieties in which it formerly took pride, it is ready to be a slave and to sleep wherever it is allowed, as near as possible to the beloved; for it not only reveres him who possesses beauty, but finds in him the only healer of its greatest woes. Now this condition, fair boy, about which I am speaking, is called Love by men, but when you hear what the gods call it, perhaps because of your youth you will laugh. But some of the Homeridae, I believe, repeat two verses on Love from the spurious poems of Homer, one of which is very outrageous and not perfectly metrical. They sing them as follows:

"Mortals call him winged Love, but the immortals call him The Winged One, because he must needs grow wings."

You may believe this, or not; but the condition of lovers and the cause of it are just as I have said.

Now he who is a follower of Zeus, when seized by Love can bear a heavier burden of the winged god; but those who are servants of Ares and followed in his train, when they have been seized by Love and think they have been wronged in any way by the beloved, become murderous and are ready to sacrifice themselves and the beloved. And so it is with the follower of each of the other gods; he lives, so far as he is able, honouring and imitating that god, so long as he is uncorrupted, and is living his first life on earth, and in that way he behaves and conducts himself toward his beloved and toward all others. Now each one chooses his love from the ranks of the beautiful according to his character, and he fashions him and adorns him like a statue, as though he were his god, to honour and worship him. The followers of Zeus desire that the soul of him whom they love be like Zeus; so they seek for one of philosophical and lordly nature, and when they find him and love him, they do all they can to give him such a character. If they have not previously had experience, they learn then from all who can teach them anything; they seek after information themselves, and when they search eagerly within themselves to find the nature of their god, they are successful, because they have been compelled to keep their eyes fixed upon the god, and as they reach and grasp him by memory they are inspired and receive from him character and habits, so far as it is possible for a man to have part in God. Now they consider the beloved the cause of all this, so they love him more than before, and if they draw the waters of their inspiration from Zeus, like the bacchantes, they pour it out upon the beloved and make him, so far as possible, like their god. And those who followed after Hera seek a kingly nature, and when they have found such an one, they act in a corresponding manner toward him in all respects; and likewise the followers of Apollo, and of each of the gods, go out and seek for their beloved a youth whose nature accords with that of the god, and when they have gained his affection, by imitating the god themselves and by persuasion and education they lead the beloved to the conduct and nature of the god, so far as each of them can do so; they exhibit no jealousy or meanness toward the loved one, but endeavour by every means in their power to lead him to the likeness of the god whom they honour. Thus the desire of the true lovers, and the initiation into the mysteries of love, which they teach, if the accomplish what they desire in the way I describe, is beautiful and brings happiness from the inspired lover to the loved one, if he be captured; and the fair one who is captured is caught in the following manner:—

In the beginning of this tale I divided each soul into three parts, two of which had the form of horses, the third that of a charioteer. Let us retain this division. Now of the horses we say one is good and the other bad; but we did not define what the goodness of the one and the badness of the other was. That we must now do. The horse that stands at the right hand is upright and has clean limbs; he carries his neck high, has an aquiline nose, is white in colour, and has dark eyes; he is a friend of honour joined with temperance and modesty, and a follower of true glory; he needs no whip, but is guided only by the word of command and by reason. The other, however, is crooked, heavy, ill put together, his neck is short and thick, his nose flat, his colour dark, his eyes grey and bloodshot; he is the friend of insolence and pride, is shaggy-eared and deaf, hardly obedient to whip and spurs. Now when the charioteer beholds the love-inspiring vision, and his whole soul is warmed by the sight, and is full of the tickling and prickings of yearning, the horse that is obedient to the charioteer, constrained then as always by modesty, controls himself and does not leap upon the beloved; but the other no longer heeds the pricks or the whip of the charioteer, but springs wildly forward, causing all possible trouble to his mate and to the charioteer, and forcing them to approach the beloved and propose the joys of love. And they at first pull back indignantly and will not be forced to do terrible and unlawful deeds; but finally, as the trouble has no end, they go forward with him, yielding and agreeing to do his bidding. And they come to the beloved and behold his radiant face.

And as the charioteer looks upon him, his memory is borne back to the true nature of beauty, and he sees it standing with modesty upon a pedestal of chastity, and when he sees this he is afraid and falls backward in reverence, and in falling he is forced to pull the reins so violently backward as to bring both horses upon their haunches, the one quite willing, since he does not oppose him, but the unruly beast very unwilling. And as they go away, one horse in his shame and wonder wets all the soul with sweat, but the other, as soon as he is recovered from the pain of the bit and the fall, before he has fairly taken breath, breaks forth into angry reproaches, bitterly reviling his mate and the charioteer for their cowardice and lack of manhood in deserting their post and breaking their agreement; and again, in spite of their unwillingness, he urges them forward and hardly yields to their prayer that he postpone the matter to another time. Then when the time comes which they have agreed upon, they pretend that they have forgotten it, but he reminds them; struggling, and neighing, and pulling he forces them again with the same purpose to approach the beloved one, and when they are near him, he lowers his head, raises his tail, takes the bit in his teeth, and pulls shamelessly. The effect upon the charioteer is the same as before, but more pronounced; he falls back like a racer from the starting-rope, pulls the bit backward even more violently than before from the teeth of the unruly horse, covers his scurrilous tongue and jaws with blood, and forces his legs and haunches to the ground, causing him much pain. Now when the bad horse has gone through the same experience many times and has ceased from his unruliness, he is humbled and follows henceforth the wisdom of the charioteer, and when he sees the beautiful one, he is overwhelmed with fear; and so from that time on the soul of the lover follows the beloved in reverence and awe.

Now the beloved, since he receives all service from his lover, as if he were a god, and since the lover is not feigning, but is really in love, and since the beloved himself is by nature friendly to him who serves him, although he may at some earlier time have been prejudiced by his schoolfellows or others, who said that it was a disgrace to yield to a lover, and may for that reason have repulsed his lover, yet, as time goes on, his youth and destiny cause him to admit him to his society. For it is the law of fate that evil can never be a friend to evil and that good must always be friend to good. And when the lover is thus admitted, and the privilege of conversation and intimacy has been granted him, his good will, as it shows itself in close intimacy, astonishes the beloved, who discovers that the friendship of all his other friends and relatives is as nothing when compared with that of his inspired lover. And as this intimacy continues and the lover comes near and touches the beloved in the gymnasia and in their general intercourse, then the fountain of that stream which Zeus, when he was in love with Ganymede, called "desire" flows copiously upon the lover; and some of it flows into him, and some, when he is filled, overflows outside; and just as the wind or an echo rebounds from smooth, hard surfaces and returns whence it came, so the stream of beauty passes back into the beautiful one through the eyes, the natural inlet to the soul, where it reanimates the passages of the feathers, waters them and makes the feathers begin to grow, filling the soul of the loved one with love. So he is in love, but he knows not with whom; he does not understand his own condition and cannot explain it; like one who has caught a disease of the eyes from another, he can give no reason for it; he sees himself in his lover as in a mirror, but is not conscious of the fact. And in the lover's presence, like him he ceases from his pain, and in his absence, like him he is filled with yearning such as he inspires, and love's image, requited love, dwells within him; but he calls it, and believes it to be, not love, but friendship. Like the lover, though less strongly, he desires to see his friend, to touch him, kiss him, and lie down by him; and naturally these things are soon brought about. Now as they lie together, the unruly horse of the lover has something to say to the charioteer, and demands a little enjoyment in return for his many troubles; and the unruly horse of the beloved says nothing, but teeming with passion and confused emotions he embraces and kisses his lover, caressing him as his best friend; and when they lie together, he would not refuse his lover any favour, if he asked it; but the other horse and the charioteer oppose all this with modesty and reason.

If now the better elements of the mind, which lead to a well ordered life and to philosophy, prevail, they live a life of happiness and harmony here on earth, self controlled and orderly, holding in subjection that which causes evil in the soul and giving freedom to that which makes for virtue; and when this life is ended they are light and winged, for they have conquered in one of the three truly Olympic contests. Neither human wisdom nor divine inspiration can confer upon man any greater blessing than this. If however they live a life less noble and without philosophy, but yet ruled by the love of honour, probably, when they have been drinking, or in some other moment of carelessness, the two unruly horses, taking the souls off their guard, will bring them together and seize upon and accomplish that which is by the many accounted blissful; and when this has once been done, they continue the practice, but infrequently, since what they are doing is not approved by the whole mind. So these two pass through life as friends, though not such friends as the others, both at the time of their love and afterwards, believing that they have exchanged the most binding pledges of love, and that they can never break them and fall into enmity. And at last, when they depart from the body, they are not winged, to be sure, but their wings have begun to grow, so that the madness of love brings them no small reward; for it is the law that those who have once begun their upward progress shall never again pass into darkness and the journey under the earth, but shall live a happy life in the light as they journey together, and because of their love shall be alike in their plumage when they receive their wings.

These blessings, so great and so divine, the friendship of a lover will confer upon you, dear boy; but the affection of the non-lover, which is alloyed with mortal prudence and follows mortal and parsimonious rules of conduct, will beget in the beloved soul the narrowness which the common folk praise as virtue; it will cause the soul to be a wanderer upon the earth for nine thousand years and a fool below the earth at last. There, dear Love, thou hast my recantation, which I have offered and paid as beautifully and as well as I could, especially in the poetical expressions which I was forced to employ on account of Phaedrus. Pardon, I pray, my former words and accept these words with favour; be kind and gracious to me; do not in anger take from me the art of love which thou didst give me, and deprive me not of sight, but grant unto me to be even more than now esteemed by the beautiful. And if in our former discourse Phaedrus and I said anything harsh against thee, blame Lysias, the father of that discourse, make him to cease from such speeches, and turn him, as his brother Polemarchus is turned, toward philosophy, that his lover Phaedrus may no longer hesitate, as he does now, between two ways, but may direct his life with all singleness of purpose toward love and philosophical discourses.

CICERO • *The Catilinarian Orations*

THE FIRST SPEECH AGAINST LUCIUS SERGIUS CATILINA

DELIVERED IN THE SENATE

1 In heaven's name, Catiline, how long will you take advantage of our forebearance? How much longer yet will that madness of yours make playthings of us? When will your unbridled effrontery stop vaunting itself? Are you impressed not at all that the Palatine has a garrison at night, that the city is patrolled, that the populace is panic-stricken, that all loyal citizens have rallied to the standard, that the Senate is meeting here behind stout defences, and that you can see the expression on the faces of the senators? Do you not appreciate that your plans are laid bare? Do you not see that your conspiracy is held fast by the knowledge of all these men? Do you think that there is a man among us who does not know what you did last night or the night before last, where you were, whom you sum-

2 moned to your meeting, what decision you reached? What an age we live in! The Senate knows it all, the consul sees it, and yet—this man is still alive. Alive did I say? Not only is he alive, but he attends the Senate, takes part in our debates, picks us all out one by one and with his gaze marks us down for death. We, however, brave fellows that we are, think that we are doing our duty to the Republic if only we avoid his frenzy and his cold steel. You, Catiline, should have been led to your death long ago and on a consul's orders. It is

3 upon yourself that the fate which you have long been planning for all of us ought to be visited. Publius Scipio,[1] a man of distinction and the chief pontiff, was a private citizen when he killed Tiberius Gracchus even though he was not seriously undermining the constitution of the Republic. Shall we, the consuls, then tolerate Catiline whose aim it is to carry fire and the sword throughout the whole world? I pass over precedents that are too old, the fact that Gaius Servilius Ahala killed Spurius Maelius with his own hand when Maelius was planning revolution.[2] Gone, gone for ever is that valour that used to be found in this Republic and caused brave men to suppress a citizen traitor with keener punishment than the most bitter foe. We have a decree of the Senate against you, Catiline, a decree of power and authority.[3] It is not the deliberations and decisions of this body that the Republic

4 lacks. It is we,—I say it openly—we consuls, who are lacking. Once the Senate passed a decree[4] that the consul Lucius Opimius should see that the Republic came to no harm: not

Source: Reprinted by permission of the publishers and the Loeb Classical Library from *Cicero, Volume X*, translated by C. MacDonald, Cambridge, Mass.: Harvard University Press, 1976.

1 Publius Cornelius Scipio Nasica Serapio, head of the college of pontiffs from 141? to 132, led the attack by senators and their clients in which Tiberius Gracchus, tribune in 133, was killed. He could legitimately be called a private citizen—in contrast with the consuls of the following sentence—because his religious office was not a magistracy.

2 Ahala was Master of the Horse *(magister equitum)* to the dictator Cincinnatus and with his own hand killed Maelius, a wealthy plebeian, who had been accused of aiming at illegal power after selling corn to the populace at a low price during a famine in 440. This is one of the stories often introduced by Cicero to provide him with precedents for wishing to destroy political opponents.

3 See p. xxxii and Appendix B, pp. 567–574 [of Harvard University Press edition, here and following].

4 Lucius Opimius, consul in 121, with the backing of the *senatus consultum ultimum*, attacked the Aventine where Tiberius Gracchus' younger brother Gaius, tribune in 123 and 122, had assembled his support-

a single night intervened: Gaius Gracchus, for all the distinction of his father, grandfather and ancestors, was killed on vague suspicions of treason; Marcus Fulvius, an ex-consul, was killed together with his children. A similar decree of the Senate entrusted the Republic to the consuls, Gaius Marius and Lucius Valerius[5]: did the tribune of the commons, Lucius Saturninus, and the praetor, Gaius Servilius, have to wait a single day for the death penalty imposed by the Senate?[6] For twenty days now[7] we have been allowing the edge of the Senate's authority to grow blunt. We have a decree of the Senate like theirs, but it is locked up with the records like a sword buried in its sheath; yet it is a decree under which you, Catiline, ought to have been executed immediately.[8] You still live and, as long as you live, you do not cease your acts of recklessness but add to their number. It is my wish, gentlemen, to be a man of compassion,[9] it is my wish not to seem easygoing at a time of serious danger for the Republic, but now I condemn myself for my inaction and my negligence.

There is in Italy a camp of enemies of the Roman people situated in the passes of Etruria[10] and the number of those enemies is increasing daily. The commander of that camp and the leader of those enemies you see within the walls and even, indeed, in the Senate, plotting daily in our midst the destruction of the Republic. If I give orders, Catiline, for your instant arrest and execution, what I shall have to fear, I suppose, is not that all loyal citizens will say that I have acted too late but that some individual will say that I have acted too harshly. In fact there is one particular reason why I, for my part, cannot bring myself to do what I ought to have done long ago. You will only be executed when there can no longer be found a single individual so evil, so abandoned, so like yourself, as to say that it was an act of injustice. So long as there remains a single man bold enough to defend you, you will live, and live as you live now, hemmed in by all my stout guards to prevent your making a move against the Republic. Furthermore, although you will not be aware of them, there will be, as there have been in the past, many eyes and ears observing you and keeping watch upon you.

What point is there, Catiline, in your waiting any longer, if night cannot conceal your criminal assemblies in its shadows nor a private house contain the voices of your conspirators within its walls, if they are all in a blaze of light and exposed to view? Take my advice; abandon your scheme and forget your murder and arson. You are trapped on every side; all your plans are as clear as daylight to us. Let us go through them together. Do you remember that I said in the Senate on the 21st of October that Gaius Manlius, your tool and

ers. Gaius and his supporter, Marcus Fulvius Flaccus, consul in 125, were killed in the attack. For the constitutional implications of this affair, see p. 571.
5   In 100.
6   They had proposed revolutionary measures and the Senate, after passing the *senatus consultum ultimum,* called upon Marius for protection. In the subsequent disorders Saturninus and Servilius Glaucia were confined in the Senate-house and there stoned to death by their opponents. For the bizarre resurrection of this incident earlier this year, see p. xxviii.
7   See E. G. Hardy, "A Catilinarian Date," *Journal of Roman Studies* 6 (1916), 56–58.
8   *Cf. in Catilinam* 4. 10, p. 144.
9   It must remain doubtful whether this emphasis upon his natural clemency in the speeches against Catiline and in others delivered this year or shortly afterwards appeared in the original versions. It would not be appropriate at the time and would be inserted in editing *post eventum* when Cicero was seeking to defend himself against political attack for his execution of the conspirators.
10   At Faesulae.

lackey in your wild scheme, would take up arms on a certain day and that the day would be the 27th of October? Was I not right, Catiline, both in the seriousness of the plot, beyond belief in its ferocity though it was, and—a much more remarkable feat—in the date? I also said in the Senate that you had postponed the massacre of leading citizens until the 28th of October even though by that date many of the leading figures in the State had left Rome, not so much to save themselves as to thwart your plans. You cannot deny, can you, that, on that very day after the others had departed, my guards and my elaborate precautions had hemmed you in and you could not move against the Republic? And that you said

8   that you were quite content with the slaughter of those of us who had remained behind? You confidently expected to take Praeneste[11] in a night assault on the 1st of November, but were you aware that the defences of that colony[12] had been set on my orders with my garrison, my guard-posts, and my sentinels? Nothing you do, no attempt you make, no plan you form, but I hear of it, see it, and know it all.

Go over with me, please, the events of the night before last. You will appreciate now that my concern for the safety of the Republic is much deeper than is yours for its destruction. I say that on the night before last you came to the street of the scythe-makers— I shall be precise—to the house of Marcus Laeca. There you were joined by many of your accomplices in your criminal folly. You do not have the effrontery to deny it, do you? Why are you silent then? If you deny it, I shall prove it. In fact, I see some of those who were

9   with you here in the Senate. In heaven's name! Where in the world are we? What State is ours? What city are we living in? Here, gentlemen, here in our very midst, in this, the most sacred and important council in the world, there are men whose plans extend beyond the death of us all and the destruction of this city to that of the whole world. As consul, I see these men and call for their views upon affairs of state, and as yet I am not even wounding with my tongue men who ought to be butchered with the sword. You were, then, at the house of Laeca on that night, Catiline; you allocated the regions of Italy, you decided where you wanted each man to go, you chose those whom you were leaving at Rome and those whom you were taking with you, you assigned the parts of the city to be burnt, and you confirmed that you were on the point of departure yourself, but said that you still had to wait a little longer because I was alive. Two Roman knights[13] were found to free you from that particular anxiety and to promise that they would kill me in my bed that very

10   night, shortly before dawn. Your meeting had scarcely broken up when I learned all this. I strengthened the guards, made my house more secure, and barred the door against the men whom you had sent to call upon me early in the morning; and there duly arrived the

[11]   A stronghold in the Hernican mountains, some twenty miles S.E. of Rome.
[12]   One of the colonies founded by Sulla. Its previous inhabitants had been put to death for their support of the Marians.
[13]   Gaius Cornelius and Lucius Vargunteius. Sallust, *Bellum Catilinae* 28. 1, says that Vargunteius was a senator. This conflict about his status, as was first suggested by Halm, probably arises from the fact that Vargunteius, in all likelihood in 66, was indicted and eventually condemned on a charge of electoral corruption under the *lex Calpurnia de ambitu* (*cf. pro Sulla* 6, p. 318). One of the penalties under this law was exclusion from the Senate for ever. This explanation has been rejected by, among others, R. F. Robinson, "*Duo Equites Romani,*" *Classical Weekly* 40 (1947) 138–143, who argues that the second knight was Marcus Ceparius. But Cicero is right to call Vargunteius a knight in 63 and he had been a senator. J. Linderski, "Cicero and Sallust on Vargunteius," *Historia* 12 (1963), 511–512.

very individuals whom, as I had already told many prominent citizens, I expected to come at that time.

In these circumstances, Catiline, finish the journey you have begun: at long last leave the city; the gates are open: be on your way. Manlius and that camp of yours have all too long been waiting for their general. Take all your men with you or, if you cannot take them all, take as many as you can. Cleanse the city. You will free me from my great fear, once there is a wall between us. You cannot remain among us any longer; I cannot, I will not, I must not permit it.

We owe a heavy debt of gratitude to the immortal gods and not least to Jupiter Stator, the most venerable guardian of this city, in whose temple we are today, because so often in the past have we escaped this pestilence, so foul, so loathsome, so deadly to the Republic. Never again must one man have the power to imperil the very existence of the State. As long as you, Catiline, plotted against me when I was consul-designate, I protected myself not with a public guard but by my own alertness. At the last consular elections when I was consul you wanted to kill me and your fellow candidates in the Campus Martius[14]; I sounded no public call to arms but foiled your wicked efforts with a guard provided by a force of friends; whenever you went for me, I thwarted you in person, although I saw that my death would be a major disaster to the Republic. Now you are openly attacking the whole commonwealth; you are hailing to their destruction and devastation the temples of the immortal gods, the buildings of this city, the lives of all the citizens and the whole of Italy. I do not yet, however, presume to take the most obvious course, the course appropriate to the authority of my position and the stern tradition of our ancestors, and I shall therefore act in a way that is more lenient in degree of severity but more conducive to the common safety. If I give an order for you to be killed, there will remain in the State the rest of the conspirators; but if, as I have long been urging, you leave the city, there will then be drained from it that flood of the State's deadly sewage[15]—your accomplices. Well, Catiline? Surely you are not hesitating to do at my bidding what you were minded to do of your own free will?[16] The consul orders a public enemy to leave the city. You ask me, "You don't mean exile?" I do not command that but, if you ask my opinion, that is my advice.

What is there, Catiline, that can give you any pleasure in this city now? There is not here outside that conspiracy of ruined men a single person who does not fear you, not one who does not hate you. What mark of family scandal is there not branded upon your life? What deplorable episode in your personal affairs does not help form your reputation? What lust has never shone in your eyes, what crime has never stained your hands, what shameful deed has never fouled your entire body? What young man that you had ensnared with the allurements of your seduction have you not provided with a weapon for his crime

11

12

13

14

[14]   See Appendix A, p. 562.
[15]   This word is a regular term for the urban proletariat and need not mean down-and-out unemployables. The epithet here, however, makes it opprobrious.
[16]   Our oldest scrap of Cicero preserves part of this and the next two sections. It is a papyrus fragment from Upper Egypt (?) of the 3rd/4th centuries and contains parts or traces of nine lines of this section and nine of sections 14 and 15. W. H. Willis, "A Papyrus Fragment of Cicero," *Transactions of the American Philological Association* 94 (1963), 321–327.

or a torch for his passion? Or again, shortly after you had made room for a new bride by murdering your former wife, did you not compound this deed with yet another crime that defies belief? I do not dwell on this and readily allow it to be glossed over in silence lest it be thought that this State has allowed so heinous a crime to have been committed or to have gone unpunished. I pass over the total ruin of your fortune which you will feel hanging over you on the coming Ides[17]; I come to the events which are not concerned with the disgrace brought upon you by the scandals of your private life or with the poverty and shame of your family, but with the supreme interests of the State and the life and safety of

15   us all. Can the light of this sun, Catiline, or can the breath of this air give you any pleasure when you know that there is not one man present who does not know that on the last day of December, in the consulship of Lepidus and Tullus,[18] you were standing in the comitium[19] armed with a weapon, that you were organizing a band to kill the consuls and leading men in the State, and that it was not any reflection on your part or fear that foiled your mad crime but the Fortune\[20] of the Roman people? I omit these crimes too—they are no secret and you have committed many crimes since then; think of all the occasions on which you tried to kill me when I was consul-designate and even when I was consul! Think of all your thrusts which seemed bound to find their mark but which I dodged with a slight swerve and, as they say, by a body-movement! You achieve nothing, you accomplish noth-

16   ing, but that does not stop you still trying and still hoping. Think of all the times when your dagger has been wrenched from your grasp and when it has slipped out by some chance and fallen to the ground! With what rites you have consecrated and dedicated it I do not know, that you must plunge it into the body of a consul.

      At the end of it all what sort of a life are you living? I shall speak to you now so as to show that I feel not the hatred that I ought to feel but the pity that you do not at all deserve. A short time ago you came into the Senate. Who out of all that crowd, out of all your many friends and intimates greeted you? If no one else has received such treatment within the memory of man, are you waiting for condemnation to be voiced aloud, although you have been convicted by the hostile verdict of their silence? What of the fact that at your arrival the seats near you emptied, that the moment you sat down all the ex-consuls whom you had repeatedly marked out for death left the seats around you bare and

17   empty—how do you think you ought to feel about that? Heavens above! If my slaves feared me as much as all your countrymen fear you, I would think that I should get out of my house. Do you not consider that *you* should leave the city? And if I saw that—even undeservedly—I was so deeply suspected and loathed by my fellow-citizens, I should wish not to see a single one of them rather than meet the hostile gaze of them all. Yet you, recognizing as you do in your guilty knowledge of your crimes that the universal hatred you attract is justified and has long been your due, do you hesitate to avoid the sight and presence of those whose hearts and minds you are wounding? If your own parents feared and hated you, and nohow could you be reconciled to them, you would, I imagine, retire

17   When interest upon loans fell due for payment.
18   See pp. xx–xxii.
19   The chief place of political assembly in Republican Rome, it was situated to the north of the Forum. See E. Nash, *Pictorial Dictionary of Ancient Rome* 1, 287–289.
20   If printed, as by Clark, with a capital letter, the goddess of good-fortune.

somewhere out of their sight. As it is, your native land which is the mother of us all hates you and dreads you and has long since decided that you have been planning nothing but her destruction. Will you not respect her authority, bow to her judgement, or fear her power? She addresses you, Catiline, and though silent somehow makes this appeal to you: "For some years now you have been behind every crime, involved in every scandal. No one but you has killed a host of citizens[21] and oppressed and plundered the allies unpunished and scot-free. Not only have you been able to ignore the laws and law-courts but you have been able to overturn and shatter them.[22] I tolerated as well as I could those earlier crimes, insupportable as they were, but that I should now be in a state of total terror on your account, that Catiline should be feared at every sound, that no scheme can be hatched against me without assuming your criminal complicity, truly this is intolerable. Depart, then, and free me from this dread; if it is well founded, that I may not be destroyed: if groundless, that I may at long last cease to feel afraid." If our country were to appeal to you with these words, should not her request be granted, even if she cannot force you?

What of the fact that you gave yourself into custody, that in order to avoid suspicion you said that you were willing to live at the house of Manius Lepidus?[23] And when he would not have you, you even had the effrontery to come to me and ask me to guard you at my home. I gave you the same answer and said that if I was in great danger because we lived together in the same city, I certainly would not be safe with you in the same house. You then came to the praetor, Quintus Metellus.[24] Rebuffed by him, you went off to your boon-companion, Marcus Marcellus,[25] clearly because you thought that he would be very careful guarding you, very astute at suspecting you and very active in punishing you. How far off do you think detention in prison ought to be for a man who already thinks that he should be kept in custody?

If in this situation, Catiline, you cannot face death calmly, do you hesitate to leave for some other land and consign to exile and solitude a life that you have rescued from the numerous penalties that it so richly deserves? "Put the proposal," you say, "to the Senate." Yes, this is what you demand; and you say that, if they vote for you to go into exile, you will obey. I shall not put it to the Senate, for that is contrary to my practice,[26] but I shall see to it that you are left in no doubt about what the Senate feels about you. Leave the city, Catiline, free the commonwealth from fear and, if these are the words that you are waiting

18

19

20

---

21 A reference to the part he was alleged to have played in the Sullan proscriptions. See p. 6.
22 Propraetor of Africa in 67, he was in 65 tried for extortion and acquitted. See p. 3.
23 In answer to the charges of *vis* (see p. 17). A Roman citizen was not held in prison pending a criminal trial. He either gave surety or, as here, was placed in the charge of a fellow-citizen who became responsible for his appearance in court.
24 Quintus Caecilius Metellus Celer, praetor this year and consul in 60.
25 The identity of this man is uncertain. W. E. Gwatkin, Jr., "Cicero *in Catilinam* 1. 19," *Transactions of the American Philological Association* 65 (1934), 271–281, suggests that the correct reading is that of *a*, "Metellum without any initial, and that this refers to Quintus Caecilius Metellus Nepos. In pursuit of an opportunist policy he accepted Catiline and the heavy irony of the sentence is the result of Cicero's collision with Nepos at the turn of the year after which this passage was written. *Cf.* Quintilian 9. 2. 45. This identification is implausible. We know of two Marcelli, father and son, who were supporters of Catiline, and this passage may well refer to one of them.
26 His real reason was that the Senate was not a judicial body and had no power to pass sentence upon an individual. See Appendix B, p. 569 f.

for, go into exile. Well, Catiline? What are you waiting for? Do you not notice the Senate's silence? They accept it, they are silent. Why are you waiting for them to voice their deci-

21 sion, when you see clearly their wish expressed by their silence? If I had spoken these same words to this distinguished young man, Publius Sestius, or to the gallant Marcus Marcellus,[27] the Senate would have been fully justified in laying violent hands upon me this instant, consul though I am, and in the precincts of this temple. In your case, however, Catiline, their inaction signifies approval, their acquiescence a decision and their silence applause. And I am not only referring to these men whose decision presumably means a lot to you although you value their lives so lightly. I also mean those Roman knights, the most honourable and excellent of men, and the other citizens who are standing around the Senate, whose crowds you could see, whose support you could observe and whose voices you could hear just now. For a long time now only with difficulty have I kept their hands and weapons away from you, and I shall easily persuade them to accompany you as far as the city gates, when you leave all that you have for so long been longing to lay waste.

22 And yet, why do I bother to say this? Would anything break your resolve? Would you ever take yourself in hand? Consider flight? Or ever think of exile? If only the immortal gods would put *that* idea into your head! Yet I see what a storm of unpopularity would break over my head if you are frightened by what I say and decide upon exile. It may not come immediately, while the memory of your crimes is still fresh, but in the future. But it is worth it, provided that your ruin remains the ruin of one man and is kept clear of peril to the Republic. But that you should be shifted from your evil ways, that you should fear the penalties of the law, that you should yield to exigences of state, that is too much to ask. No, Catiline, you are not the man to be turned back from infamy by a sense of shame,

23 from danger by fear, or from an act of madness by rational thought. Be on your way then!—I have said it often enough—and, if you wish to fan men's hatred of me, your enemy as you call me, go straight into exile. It will be hard for me to bear men's criticism, if you do that; hard to sustain the burden of that hostility, if you go into exile at the consul's command. If, however, you prefer to do my good name and my reputation a service, depart with that reckless gang of criminals and take yourself off to Manlius, gather to your cause the citizens who have abandoned all hope, separate yourself from loyal men, wage war upon your native land, revel in the banditry of traitors; for then men will think not

24 that I drove you into the arms of men unlike yourself, but that I invited you to join your own kind. And yet why should I be pressing you? I know that you have already sent men on ahead to await you under arms at Forum Aurelium][28]; I know that you have agreed and fixed a day with Manlius; I know that you have also sent on ahead that silver eagle[29] which will, I trust, bring death and destruction to you and all your followers and for which an evil shrine has been set up at your house. Could you be parted any longer from that eagle which you used to worship on your way to commit murder and from whose altar your sacrilegious hand often passed to the slaughter of citizens?

---

[27] Publius Sestius was quaestor this year; Marcus Marcellus became consul in 51.
[28] A small town about fifty miles from Rome, situated on the Aurelian Way en route to Faesulae.
[29] This silver eagle, one of the legionary standards introduced by Marius, had been carried in his army during the war against the Cimbri.

You will, then, at last be going where your ungovernable and crazed greed was long   25
taking you; and your path causes you no grief but a kind of pleasure that is incomprehensible to others. It was for madness such as this that Nature bore you, that your will has trained you, and that fortune has preserved you. Never have you wanted—I will not mention peace—even a war that was not a criminal enterprise. You have got a band of evil men,   26
swept together from the refuse of society and from those who have been abandoned by all fortune and all hope. What a wonderful time you will have with them, what pleasures will delight you and what evils will thrill you in your debauchery, for among all those friends of yours you will not see or hear a single decent man! These exertions of yours that men are always talking about have been good training for the pursuit of a life such as this; lying on the bare ground to attempt an act of indecency—for committing a crime; spending nights of wakefulness to trick husbands while they sleep—for seizing the possessions of peaceful citizens. You have an opportunity to show your famous ability to endure hunger, cold and deprivation of every necessity; an ability which you will shortly realize has de-   27
stroyed you. I achieved this much when I kept you from the consulship, that you would only be able to attack the State as an exile and not harry it as a consul, and that this criminal attack upon which you have embarked would go under the name of banditry not war.

At this point, gentlemen, in order most firmly to reject a complaint by our fatherland that might be thought justified, listen carefully, I beg of you, to what I say, and memorize it deep down in your hearts and minds. If my country, which means much more to me than my own life, if all Italy, if the whole commonwealth were to say this to me: "What are you doing, Marcus Tullius? Are you going to let this man who is, as you have discovered, a public enemy; who will, as you see, be the leader in war; who, as you know, is awaited in the enemy's camp as their general, who is the instigator of crime, the leader of the conspiracy, the recruiter of slaves[30] and society's outcasts; are you going to let him leave, not apparently despatched by you from the city but let into it? Are you not going to order him to be put in chains, taken off to execution and suffer the supreme penalty? What on earth is stopping you? The practice of our ancestors? In this Republic even private individuals   28
have frequently punished dangerous citizens with death.[31] Is it the laws that have been passed concerning the punishment of Roman citizens?[32] Never in this city have those who have rebelled against the State kept the rights of citizens.[33] Or do you fear the hatred of posterity? Fine thanks indeed you are giving to the Roman people who have raised you so quickly through all the steps of office to the supreme power,[34] when you were a man

---

[30] This was not true of Catiline. Although urged by some of his supporters to call upon the slaves to rise, he refused to do this. A slave-revolt, particularly after the war against Spartacus in 73–71, was a perpetual nightmare to Romans and a useful bogey with which to frighten people away from Catiline. See p. 13.

[31] See p. 249, n.1.

[32] See Appendix B, p. 571.

[33] Possibly not part of the speech as delivered. One of Cicero's arguments justifying his execution of the conspirators was that by their behaviour they had forfeited their rights as citizens and that his action was therefore no contravention of the laws protecting these rights. This argument is untenable because the crucial point of these laws was that only the people could make such a decision.

[34] Cicero held all his magistracies *suo anno, i.e.* in the first year in which he was eligible under the provisions of the various *leges annales* regulating the age at which a magistracy might be held. Before a man could become consul he had successively to be quaestor and praetor.

known only through your own efforts and without any backing from ancestors![35] Fine
thanks if you neglect the safety of your fellow citizens because you are afraid of unpopularity or any danger to yourself! If you are afraid of unpopularity, surely the unpopularity
caused by severity and resoluteness is not to be feared any more than that caused by sloth
and negligence. Or when Italy is laid waste by war, when her cities are destroyed, her
dwellings in flames, do you not think that then you will be consumed by a blaze of unpopularity?"

To these most solemn words of the Republic and of those who share her feelings I
shall give a brief reply. If I judged it best, gentlemen, to punish Catiline with death, I
would not have given that cut-throat another hour to live. If our leading men and most
distinguished citizens have been honoured rather than besmirched by the blood of Saturninus, the Gracchi, Flaccus,[36] and of many before them, I certainly had no call to fear
that any wave of unpopularity would flood over me because I had executed this murderer
of citizens. If, however, it did seriously threaten me, I have always been of the opinion that
unpopularity derived from doing what is right is not unpopularity but honour. Yet there
are some in this body who either cannot see what threatens us or pretend that they cannot, who have fed Catiline's hopes by their feeble decisions[37] and put heart into the growing conspiracy by refusing to believe that it existed; who would have influenced many, the
merely naïve as well as those of ill will, into saying that my action was cruel and tyrannical,
if I had punished Catiline. As it is, I am sure that, if he arrives at Manlius' camp to which
he is on his way, no one will be such a fool as not to see that a conspiracy has been formed
and no one such a traitor as to deny it. Yet I believe that, if Catiline alone is killed, this cancer in the State can be held in check for a short time, but not eliminated for ever. If, however, he banishes himself and marches off his followers with him, and rounds up in one
place the other castaways whom he has collected from every corner, then there will be
wiped out and destroyed not only this cancer now grown so large in the State but with it
the root and seed of all our ills.

We have lived among these dangers and plots of conspiracy for a long time, gentlemen, but it has turned out that all these crimes and the reckless frenzy of such long standing have come to a head in my consulship. If he alone is removed out of all this band of
brigands, we shall appear perhaps to have gained a short respite from anxiety and fear, but
the danger will remain and be set deep in the veins and vitals of the Republic. Men who
are seriously ill often toss to and fro with the heat of their fever and, if they drink cold water, seem to get relief at first, but then are much more seriously and acutely distressed. In
the same way this disease from which the Republic is suffering will be temporarily relieved
by his punishment, but so long as the others remain alive will grow more serious. Let the
traitors, then, depart; let them separate themselves from the loyal citizens, let them gather
in one place and lastly, as I have now said so often, let them be separated from us by the
city wall. Let them stop attacking the consul in his own home, surrounding the tribunal of

[35] See p. 178, n. *e* and p. 204, n. *b*.
[36] See p. 414, n. *a*.
[37] *Cf. pro Murena* 51, p. 252.

the urban praetor,[38] besieging the Senate-house with swords, and preparing burning arrows and torches to set fire to the city; finally, let there be written upon the brow of every man what he feels about the Republic. I make this promise to you, gentlemen, that we consuls will take such pains, that you senators will display such authority, the Roman knights such valour, all loyal citizens such close agreement that with Catiline's departure you will see everything not only revealed and illumined but crushed and punished.

With omens such as these, Catiline, go forth to your impious and wicked war, and 33 bring sure salvation to the Republic, disaster and ruin upon yourself, and destruction upon those who have joined you in every crime and act of treason. You, Jupiter, whom Romulus established with the same auspices as this city, whom we justly call the Supporter of this city and empire, will keep him and his confederates from your temple and those of the other gods, from the houses and the walls of the city, from the lives and fortunes of all her citizens. And these men, the foes of loyal citizens, public enemies of their native land, plunderers of Italy, men who are joined together in an evil alliance and companionship of crime, these men alive or dead you will visit with eternal punishment.

THE SECOND SPEECH AGAINST LUCIUS SERGIUS CATILINA

DELIVERED BEFORE THE PEOPLE

At long last, citizens, we have expelled Lucius Catilina, or, if you prefer, sent him off, or 1 followed him on his way with our farewells as he left Rome of his own accord, roused to a frenzy of audacity, breathing crime, foully plotting the destruction of his country, and ceaselessly threatening you and this city with fire and the sword. He has gone, left us, got away, broken out. No longer will that misbegotten monster plan the destruction of our very walls within these walls; no longer is our victory over the one true leader of this civil war in doubt; no longer will that dagger be twisted in our sides; no longer shall we tremble in the Campus Martius, in the Forum, in the Senate-house,—yes, even in our own homes. He was shifted from his vantage-point when he was driven from the city. We shall now wage open war without hindrance upon a public enemy. There is no doubt that we destroyed the man and won a glorious victory when we drove him from secret plots to open banditry. Because he did not bear off a dagger stained with blood as he wished, be- 2 cause he left us still alive, because we wrenched his weapon from his hands, because he left the city still standing and its citizens safe and sound—just think of the sense of desolation that weighed him down! He lies helpless now, citizens, and realizes that he has been struck down and laid low. Again and again, I know, he gazes back at this city in his anguish that his prey has been snatched from his jaws. And the city? I think that it is thankful that it has vomited forth that deadly pestilence and rid itself of it.

One of you, however, may react with feelings that all should share and make a violent 3 attack upon me for the very decision that is the triumphant boast of my speech, that I did

---

[38]   The senior of the eight praetors. Their business was largely judicial and they tried their cases at a tribunal in the Forum

not arrest so fatal an enemy but let him go. That fault is not mine, citizens, but lies in the circumstances. Lucius Catilina ought to have suffered the supreme penalty and been put to death long ago, a course required of me by the practice of our ancestors, the stern tradition of my office, and by interests of state. But how many do you think there were who did not believe my charges, who were too stupid to have any views at all, who went so far as to defend him, or who were criminal enough to support him? If I thought that by removing him I could free you from all danger, I would long ago have risked not merely unpopularity but my very life and got rid of Lucius Catilina. At a time, however, when some even of you still remained unconvinced of the facts, I saw that, if I had inflicted the death penalty that he deserved, the unpopularity of that action would have prevented me from tackling his confederates. I therefore created a situation in which you could see your enemy clearly and fight him in the open. You may judge too, citizens, how formidable an enemy I consider him to be, now that he has left the city, from my concern that he left Rome with so few companions. If only he had left at the head of all his forces! I see that he did take with him Tongilius with whom he had started a liaison when he was still a lad.[1] He also took Publicius and Minucius whose debts run up in taverns could not cause the least disturbance in the State, but the men he has left behind! What debts they have![2] What power! What distinguished birth!

If I compare that army of his with the Gallic legions[3] and the levy which Quintus Metellus has held in Picenum and Umbria[4] and with these forces which we are building up every day, I treat it with deep contempt—that collection of old men without hope, of spendthrift peasants,[5] of bankrupts from the country, of men who would rather jump their bail than desert their ranks. They will collapse if I show them the praetor's edict,[6] let alone our army's battle-line. As for these men whom I see flitting about in the Forum, standing in front of the Senate-house, even coming into the Senate, who glisten with unguents, who are resplendent in purple, these I would prefer him to have taken with him as his soldiers. Remember that, if they remain here, it is not so much his army that we ought to fear as those who have deserted it. They are all the more frightening because they are unmoved in spite of their realization that I know their plans. I see to whom Apulia has been assigned, who has Etruria, who Picenum, who Umbria, and who has demanded as his task the plans for murder and arson in Rome itself. They know that all their plans laid the other night have been reported to me. I revealed them in the Senate yesterday; Catiline himself was terrified and fled. What are *these* men waiting for? I can assure them that they are very much mistaken if they expect the clemency that I have shown in the past to last for ever.

---

[1]   The phrase means that he was still wearing the purple-edged *toga praetexta,* the dress for boys up to the age of sixteen (as well as for curule magistrates).
[2]   Catiline took only the small fry with him. The debts of the men left behind were large enough to be politically and economically important. On *nobilis,* see p. 178, n. *e.*
[3]   *i.e.,* composed of the inhabitants of Cisalpine Gaul; the regular forces there.
[4]   Metellus Celer, see p. 17. As praetor he had been ordered by the Senate to levy troops in Picenum and the *ager Gallicus,* the coastal district of Umbria between Ariminum and Ancona, so called because it had been the land of the Senones, the last Gauls to settle in Italy.
[5]   Particularly Sulla's veterans who had been settled in his colonies.
[6]   Presumably the praetorian edict dealing with the seizure of persons.

I have now achieved what I have been waiting for—you all see that a conspiracy has been openly formed against the Republic; unless, of course, anyone thinks that men like Catiline are not in agreement with him. There is no longer any place for clemency; the situation demands severity but I shall even at this late hour make one concession; let them leave, let them depart, so that they do not allow poor Catiline to pine away in longing for them. I will show them the road; he left by the Aurelian Way,[7] and if they are prepared to hurry, they will catch him up by evening. What a relief for the Republic to have baled out   7 of it this bilge-water! I feel that the disposal of Catiline alone has lightened the Republic and restored it. Can you rack your brain for a single misdeed or crime that has not already occurred to him? What poisoner in the whole of Italy, what gladiator, what bandit, what assassin, what parricide, what forger of wills, what cheat, what glutton, what spendthrift, what adulterer, what whore, what corrupter of youth, what rogue, what scoundrel can be found who does not admit to having lived on the most intimate terms with Catiline? What murder over all these years in which he has not had a hand? What criminal debauchery for which he has not been responsible? Who ever proved so active a seducer of the young as   8 he? Upon some he satisfied his own foul passion, for others he pandered to their filthy desires. To some he offered the satisfaction of their lust and to others the murder of their parents, offering encouragement and even assistance. How quickly, too, he had collected a huge crowd of desperate men from the countryside as well as from the city! There was not a single man overwhelmed by debt, whether in Rome or in the furthest corner of Italy, whom he did not enrol in this incredible alliance of crime.

Let me now help you to note his varied aptitudes of a different sort. There is no one   9 in a gladiatorial school, rather more criminally inclined than the others, who does not claim Catiline as a bosom friend; no actor, more frivolous and vicious than his fellows, who does not claim to have been his almost constant companion. Catiline, moreover, trained by his life of debauchery and crime to endure cold, hunger, thirst and lack of sleep, won in the eyes of these men a reputation for endurance, although by his sexual excesses and his violence he was exhausting those faculties which foster long toil and provide the outlets for a man's natural ability. If his companions follow him, if the criminal bands of desperate men leave Rome, how happy we shall be! What good fortune for the Republic!   10 What a glorious reward for my consulship! The depravity of these men is no longer any ordinary depravity, their violence is no longer the violence of men and we cannot endure it; they think of nothing but murder, arson and pillage. They have squandered their inheritances; they have mortgaged their estates; money began to fail them long ago and their credit has now started to run out; but the expensive tastes that they had in their days of plenty still remain. If in their drinking and gambling they only looked for wild revelry and whores, they would admittedly be beyond hope, but we could still tolerate them; but who could stand by and watch wastrels hatch plots against men of action, fools against the wise, sots against the sober, sluggards against the wakeful? Reclining at their banquets, embracing their whores, stupefied by wine, stuffed with food, crowned with garlands, reeking with scent, enfeebled by debauchery, they belch out in their conversation the murder of loyal citizens and the firing of Rome. I am confident that some doom hangs over these   11

7   The road to Faesulae and to Marseilles where according to Cicero Catiline pretended that he was going.

men and that the punishment long due for their dishonesty, their wickedness, their crimes, and their depravity is—if not upon them this very instant—at least on its way. My consulship cannot cure these men but, if it removes them, then it will have prolonged the life of the Republic, not for a few fleeting seconds, but for many centuries. There is no foreign people left for us to fear, no king able to make war on the Roman people. Peace reigns abroad by land and sea thanks to the valour of one man.[8] The sole remaining war is on our own soil; the plots, the danger, the enemy are in our own midst. The battles we have to fight are against luxury, folly, and crime. That is the war for which I offer myself as your leader, citizens. I accept the enmity of scoundrels. I shall find a way to cure what can be cured; what needs excising, I shall not allow to remain to destroy the State. Let them either go, then, or keep the peace; if they remain in Rome without a change of heart, they can expect their deserts.

12   There are others, however, who say that I have driven out Catiline. If I could achieve this merely by saying the word, I would drive out the men who are saying this. The fellow was so timid or even sensitive, of course, that he could not bear to hear what the consul said; the minute he was ordered to go into exile, he obeyed. In fact, when I had come within an ace of death in my own home, I summoned the Senate yesterday to the temple of Jupiter Stator and brought the whole matter up before the House. When Catiline arrived, what senator spoke to him? Who greeted him? Who treated him as a citizen, though a scoundrel, and not as the most dangerous of outlaws? They went further; the most senior members of the House left empty and bare the benches around that upon which he had 13 seated himself. Your stern consul who drives citizens into exile with a mere word then asked Catiline whether or not he had been at the meeting the previous night at the house of Marcus Laeca. When the man for all his effrontery was overcome by the knowledge of his guilt and did not at first reply, I disclosed the rest of the story. I described what he had done that night, where he had been, what he had planned for the following night, and how he had mapped out the plan for the whole war. Since he was at a loss and was trapped, I asked him why he was hesitating to go where he had long been preparing to go, for I knew that the arms, the axes, the fasces, the trumpets, the military standards, that silver ea- 14 gle for which he had even built a shrine in his own home had been sent on ahead. Was I driving him into exile when I had seen that he had already begun operations? Manlius, that mere centurion, was acting on his own account, I suppose, when he set up camp in the territory of Faesulae and declared war upon the Roman people, and that camp is not at this moment waiting for its commander, Catiline; and Catiline himself, driven out into exile, is making for Marseilles—that's what they say—and not for this camp.

The preservation of the Republic no less than governing it—what a thankless task it is! If all the measures that I have taken and the efforts that I have made at such danger to myself have trapped Lucius Catilina and reduced him to impotence and if, as a result, he is now suddenly seized with panic, changes his mind, deserts his confederates, abandons his plan to make war, and turns from his path of war and crime to flight and exile, there are men who will claim, not that a violent criminal was stripped of his arms, baffled and terri-

---

[8]   Pompey had crushed the pirates in 67 and in the following years had defeated Mithridates, king of Pontus.

fied by my energy, frustrated of his hopes and thwarted in his enterprises, but that a man, untried and innocent, was driven into exile by the violent threats of the consul; and, if he does take this course, there will be others who will want to make him an object of pity rather than a criminal, and myself the cruellest of tyrants rather than the most vigilant of consuls. Citizens, it is worth my enduring the storm of this ill-deserved and unfounded hatred, provided only that you are spared the horror and danger of civil war. By all means let men say that I drove him out, provided that he does go into exile. But he has no intention of going, take my word for it. I shall never pray to the immortal gods, citizens, to be cleared of this hatred at the cost of your hearing that Lucius Catilina is marching to and fro under arms at the head of an army of enemies; but that is what you will be hearing in three days' time. I am afraid of being attacked in the future much more for letting him go than for driving him out. And if there are men who say that he was driven into exile when in fact he went voluntarily, what would they be saying, if he had been killed? Yet those who keep on saying that Catiline is going to Marseilles are more afraid than sorry. None of them is tender-hearted enough to wish him to go there rather than join Manlius. If he had never before even dreamt of doing what he is doing now, he would still rather die a bandit than live an exile. As it is, everything has so far gone for him according to plan and just as he wished—except that I was still alive when he left Rome—let us hope, then, that he is going into exile, and not complain about it.

Why, though, am I talking so long about one enemy, an enemy at that who now admits that he is an enemy and one of whom I am not afraid because—and this is what I have always wanted—the city wall lies between us, and yet do not mention those who pretend that they are not enemies, who remain in Rome, and are still among us? I do not wish so much to take revenge upon these men as to bring them to their senses in any way that I can, and to reconcile them to the Republic, a task that should not prove impossible if only they are now willing to listen to me. I shall list for you, citizens, the types of men from which the revolutionary forces are recruited and I shall then offer to each of them in my speech the remedy of any advice that I can give.

One group consists of those who have heavy debts and possess estates more than large enough to pay them, but are so attached to their estates that they cannot be parted from them.[9] These men have the most respectable outward appearance—for they are wealthy—but their intentions and attitudes are quite unscrupulous. Could *you* be richly and abundantly supplied with lands, houses, silver plate, slaves and possessions of every sort and yet hesitate to give up part of your estate in order to improve your credit? What are you waiting for? War? All right; but would you think that your estates will be regarded as sacred in the general devastation? Or are you waiting for new books?[10] You need not expect them from Catiline; but my good offices are indeed providing new books—auctioneers' catalogues.[11] This the only way in which men who possess estates can be solvent. If they had been willing to do this earlier and had not been so stupid as to try to meet the in-

15

16

17

18

---

[9] Politics at Rome required large sums of ready cash, but the capital of most of those involved was tied up in land. They therefore borrowed the money they required and ran up huge debts. *Cf. pro Sulla 56,* p. 370.
[10] *i.e.,* account books—the cancellation of their debts.
[11] At the auction sale of their estates to pay their debts.

terest on their debts from the income of their estates, we should find them both richer and better citizens. I think, however, that these men need cause us little concern because they can be induced to change their attitude or, if they persist, are in my view more likely to attack the Republic with vows than with arms.

19   The second group consists of those who are overwhelmed by debt but still expect to enjoy absolute power. They want to gain control of the government and think that revolution can bring them the offices of which they have no hope in times of peace. This is my best advice to them—as it is, needless to say, to all the others—to give up all hope of attaining their goal. First of all, I personally am on the alert, I am right at hand, I am guarding the Republic; in the second place, the body of loyal citizens has rare courage, complete harmony, and strength in their large numbers, and there is too a strong force of soldiers; and finally, the immortal gods will bring help in person to this unconquered people, this most renowned of empires and fairest of cities. Let us suppose, however, that they were to attain the goal to which their utter madness directs them, do they then hope—for this is the heart's desire of these wicked criminals—to be consuls, dictators or even kings amid the ashes of their city and in the blood of their fellow-countrymen? Do they not see that, if they get what they want, they will be bound to lose it to some runaway slave or gladiator?

20   The third group comprises men who are now getting on in years but whose active life has kept them physically fit. The Manlius from whom Catiline has taken over is in this class. They are men from those colonies which Sulla founded and which, I appreciate, are as a whole composed of men of complete loyalty and outstanding bravery.[12] Nevertheless there are some colonists who have used their sudden and unexpected wealth to give a display of luxury to which they were quite unaccustomed and which was beyond their means. Putting up buildings as men of wealth and enjoying their choice of farms, their large establishments, and their sumptuous banquets, they have run so deeply into debt that they would have to raise Sulla from the dead if they wanted to be in the clear. They have also induced some poor small-holders to share their hopes that earlier confiscations will be repeated. I include both these groups in the one class of thieves and robbers; but I give them this advice: let them give up their wild thoughts of proscriptions and dictatorships. The horror of that period is so deeply branded upon the State that not even the dumb animals, let alone men, will tolerate its return.

21   The fourth group is a motley assortment of troublemakers; those who have been in financial straits for years, who never get their heads above water, who are staggering under age-old debts which result partly from laziness, partly from failures in business, partly too from extravagance. Many of them have been worn down by summonses on bail, judgements given against them and enforced sales of property, and are said to be making off from town and country alike to Catiline's camp. These men, I would say, are not so much eager soldiers as reluctant defaulters. If these men cannot stand on their own feet,[13] let them crash as soon as possible, but don't let the State or even the neighbours next door hear the thud. I do not understand why men who cannot live an honourable life should

---

[12]   Cicero speaks so approvingly in deference to the Sullan affiliations of some of those to whom he looked for support against the conspirators.

[13]   *i.e.,* are bankrupt.

want to die in disgrace or why they think that it will be less painful to perish in a crowd than to die alone.

The fifth group is composed of parricides, assassins and every sort of criminal. These men I have no wish to redeem from Catiline; indeed, they cannot be torn from him. Let them perish in the course of their crime, for there are too many of them for the prison[14] to hold them all.   22

The last group is not only last in order but also in character and way of life. It is Catiline's very own; his special choice—let me say—or rather his most intimate and bosom friends. These are the men you see with their carefully combed hair, dripping with oil, some smooth as girls, others with shaggy beards, with tunics down to their ankles and wrists, and wearing frocks not togas. All the activity of their lives and all the efforts of their waking hours are devoted to banquets that last till dawn. In this herd you find all the gamblers, all the adulterers, all the filthy minded lechers. These boys, so dainty and effeminate, have learnt not only to love and be loved, not only to dance and sing, but also to brandish daggers and sow poison. Unless they leave Rome, unless they perish, even if Catiline has perished, rest assured that there will remain in the Republic this spawning-ground of Catilines. Yet what do those wretches want for themselves? They are not going to take their mistresses to the camp with them, are they? How can they be parted from them, and on nights like these? How will they stand the frosts and snows of the Apennines? Perhaps they think that they will withstand the winter more easily because they have learned to dance naked at banquets.   23

What a truly terrifying war if Catiline is going to have this élite force of ponces! Now, citizens, marshal your garrisons and your field forces against these brilliant troops of Catiline! First, pit your consuls and your generals against that part-worn gladiator; then lead out against that castaway band of shipwrecked men at their last gasp the flower and the pick of the whole of Italy. Why, the colonies and boroughs of Italy[15] will prove strongholds to match Catiline's wooded hills.[16] I do not need to compare all your other resources, your equipment, your garrisons, with that bandit's down-and-out and impoverished band. If, however, we were to ignore all these resources with which we are supplied and which Catiline lacks, the Senate, the equestrian order, the capital itself, the treasury, the revenue, all Italy, all the provinces, the foreign nations; if, leaving all these on one side, we were willing to make a comparison of the causes which are opposed to each other, we could tell from that alone how utterly abject is the position of our enemies. On our side fights decency, on theirs viciousness; on our side morality, on theirs debauchery; on ours good faith, on theirs deceit; on ours respect for right, on theirs crime; on ours firmness of purpose, on theirs wild irresponsibility; on ours honour, on theirs disgrace; on ours self-control, on theirs a surrender to passion; in short, justice, moderation, bravery, wisdom,   24

                                                                                                    25

---

14   Imprisonment was not a punishment for which Roman citizens were liable; the Tullianum under the Capitol, the place of execution, was the sole prison in Rome. See E. Nash, *Pictorial Dictionary of Ancient Rome* 1. 206–207.
15   Strictly speaking, a *municipium* was a self-governing community that had become part of the Roman State, while a *colonia* was in origin a settlement planted by Rome. The phrase *municipia et coloniae* means in effect "the towns of Italy." A. N. Sherwin-White, *The Roman Citizenship* 143 f.
16   The haunt of bandits like Catiline and suitable for the guerrilla warfare of which alone he is capable.

all the virtues, contend with injustice, intemperateness, cowardice, folly, all the vices. In a word, plenty fights against poverty, incorrupt principles against corrupt, sanity against insanity, well-founded hope against general desperation. In a contest and battle of this sort, even if men's ardour fail them, would not the immortal gods by themselves force such a sink of iniquity to yield to these sterling virtues?

26   In such a situation as this, citizens, I urge you, as I did before, to defend your homes with patrols and guards. For my part, I have made full provision for the protection of the city without alarming you or declaring a state of emergency. All your fellow-citizens in the colonies and boroughs of Italy have been informed by me of this night attack planned by Catiline and they will defend their cities and territories with ease. The gladiators who, he thought, would be his most valuable adherents, although they are better disposed towards us than some patricians, will be kept under control by our forces. I foresaw this and sent Quintus Metellus ahead to Umbria and Picenum. He will either crush Catiline or prevent any movement or attempt on his part. I shall refer to the Senate, whom, as you see, I am convening, the decision upon all other measures, their despatch and their execution.

27   To those who have remained in Rome, or rather to those who have been left in Rome by Catiline to destroy both the city and all of you, I now wish to reiterate my warning; for although they are enemies, still they were born citizens. My former clemency may have been thought too lax, but it was only waiting for what lay hidden to be revealed. For the future, no longer can I forget that this is my fatherland, that I am consul of these men, and that I must either live with them or die for them. The city gates are not guarded, the road is not watched. If they want to leave, I can connive at it; but if anyone makes a move in the city, if I detect any plan or attempt upon our fatherland, let alone any act, he will find that there are vigilant consuls in this city, incomparable magistrates, a vigorous Senate, that there are arms and a place of execution[17] where following the ordinances of our ancestors we exact the penalty for heinous crimes when they have been exposed.

28   In all these measures I shall ensure that a major crisis is resolved with the least disturbance, that acute dangers are averted without a state of emergency, and that the most bitter and widespread civil war within the memory of man is suppressed with a single civil magistrate as your general to lead you.[18] I shall handle the situation in such a way, citizens, that if it can possibly be avoided, not even a common criminal will suffer in this city the penalty for his crime. If, however, the extent of the conspiracy now revealed, if the danger that threatens our fatherland compels me to abandon my policy of clemency, then I shall certainly see to it—an aim that might be thought virtually hopeless in so extensive and treacherous a war—that no patriot perishes and that by the punishment of only a few you can all be saved.

[17]   The Tullianum.
[18]   The word *togatus* makes its first appearance in these speeches in this passage. The toga is the dress of the civilian, of peace (*cf.* Cicero's famous line *Cedant arma togae, concedat laurea laudi* quoted in his speech *in Pisonem* 73–74) and Cicero develops his theme in his speeches *in Catilinam* 3. 15 and 23, pp. 116 and 126, and *pro Sulla* 85, p. 398, a speech in which he had to defend himself against charges of acting tyrannically. His civilian status and his suppression of the conspiracy in Rome without having resort to arms is contrasted with the constant menace of intervention by the *imperatores*. They are men of war with violent solutions to Rome's political problems. C. Nicolet, *"Consul togatus,"* Revue des Études latines 38 (1960), 240–245. Also, with particular reference to Pompey, p. 130, n. *a*.

When I make this promise, citizens, I do not rely upon my own good sense or upon   29
any human wisdom, but upon the many clear omens from the immortal gods under whose
guidance I entertained these hopes and embarked upon this policy.[19] No longer, as was once
their practice, do they guard us from afar against a foreign and distant enemy, but here at
our side they defend their temples and the city's buildings with the protection of their divine power. These gods, citizens, have ordained that this city be the most beautiful, the
most prosperous, the most powerful in the world, and now that all the forces of her foreign foes have been defeated on land and sea, you ought to pray to them, to worship them,
to implore them to defend her from criminal attack by traitors among her own citizens.

[19]   In a number of passages (*cf. in Catilinam* 3. 1 and 18–22, pp. 100 and 120–124; *pro Sulla* 40, p. 352)
Cicero attributes the suppression of the conspiracy in part to the *virtus* of the Senate or the *providentia* of
the gods. See Quintilian 11. 1. 23. Quintilian seems to think that Cicero only did this out of a sense of what
was right and proper, but he surely had sound political reasons for making the Senate a partner in his actions, and *ad Atticum* 1. 16. 6 suggests that his belief in divine assistance was to some extent genuine. See
W. Allen, Jr., "Cicero's Conceit," *Transactions of the American Philological Association* 85 (1954), 142 f.

ISOCRATES • *Hymn to Logos*

But the fact is that since they have not taken the trouble to make distinctions after this manner in each instance, they are ill-disposed to all eloquence; and they have gone so far astray as not to perceive that they are hostile to that power which of all the faculties that belong to the nature of man is the source of most of our blessings. For in the other powers which we possess we are in no respect superior to other living creatures; nay, we are inferior to many in swiftness and in strength and in other resources; but, because there has been implanted in us the power to persuade each other and to make clear to each other whatever we desire, not only have we escaped the life of wild beasts, but we have come together and founded cities and made laws and invented arts; and, generally speaking, there is no institution devised by man which the power of speech has not helped us to establish. For this it is which has laid down laws concerning things just and unjust, and things base and honourable; and if it were not for these ordinances we should not be able to live with one another. It is by this also that we confute the bad and extol the good. Through this we educate the ignorant and appraise the wise; for the power to speak well is taken as the surest index of a sound understanding, and discourse which is true and lawful and just is the outward image of a good and faithful soul. With this faculty we both contend against others on matters which are open to dispute and seek light for ourselves on things which are unknown; for the same arguments which we use in persuading others when we speak in public, we employ also when we deliberate in our own thoughts; and, while we call eloquent those who are able to speak before a crowd, we regard as sage those who most skilfully debate their problems in their own minds. And, if there is need to speak in brief summary of this power, we shall find that none of the things which are done with intelligence take place without the help of speech, but that in all our actions as well as in all our thoughts speech is our guide, and is most employed by those who have the most wisdom. Therefore, those who dare to speak with disrespect of educators and teachers of philosophy deserve our opprobrium no less than those who profane the sanctuaries of the gods.

Source: Reprinted by permission of the publishers and the Loeb Classical Library from *Isocrates,* Volume I, translated by George Norlin, Cambridge, Mass.: Harvard University Press, 1928, from *Nicocles,* 5–9.

INDEX